INTERNATIONAL RESPONSIBILITY FOR HOSTILE ACTS OF PRIVATE PERSONS AGAINST FOREIGN STATES

INTERNATIONAL RESPONSIBILITY FOR HOSTILE ACTS OF PRIVATE PERSONS AGAINST FOREIGN STATES

by

MANUEL R. GARCÍA-MORA
Professor of Law, Fordham University

THE HAGUE
MARTINUS NIJHOFF
1962

ISBN 978-94-015-0218-4 ISBN 978-94-015-0722-6 (eBook)
DOI 10.1007/978-94-015-0722-6

TO MARILYN

IN GRATEFUL AND LOVING TRIBUTE TO

HER FAITH, ENTHUSIASM AND DEDICATION

PREFACE

Mankind's preoccupation with survival in this age has given renewed impetus to the idea of a world community deeply concerned with the prevention of friction between nations. The achievement to date has been largely in terms of efforts to control acts of aggression committed by governments. Most people have assumed that the military rivalry between the great powers is the only threat confronting the world today. While readily conceding that this threat has placed mankind in a highly precarious situation, this book, on the other hand, reflects my conviction that any program designed to attain world peace will be significantly incomplete without the control of hostile actions which private persons have been known to commit against foreign nations. Experience shows that these actions not only endanger the good relations between states, but are also likely to plunge the world community into wars, thus spreading destruction and human suffering everywhere.

The relation between hostile acts of private individuals and international peace was briefly discussed by Judge Philip C. Jessup in his book *A MODERN LAW OF NATIONS*. Speaking of the use of force by individuals, which is clearly the business of a new law of nations, he says on page 178 that "The problem of international law would be to catalogue those acts of individuals which have sufficient international significance to warrant placing their punishment under international auspices. Some of these would involve the illegal use of force and others would not. They might include terroristic activities, assassination of heads of state, counterfeiting of foreign currencies, the slave trade, traffic in narcotics, and unauthorized manufacture of atomic or other weapons."

Undoubtedly, there are many hostile actions which private persons may commit against foreign states. Judge Jessup has given us a partial catalogue of them. Another scholar may well mention others. It is probably hard to get a consensus on the actions that should be included in a book of this kind. Bearing this in mind, I have limited the scope of this study by treating those acts which are likely to have a more immediate significance in the contemporary world, without losing sight of the knowledge given to us by experience. I am well aware that there may be objections to my arrangement, but in my decision I feel supported by the Draft Code of Offenses Against the Peace and Security of Mankind, proposed by the United Nations International Law Commission in 1951, which includes many of the offenses treated in these pages. The conclusions of the International Law Commission are thus close to those which have led me to reinterpret much of the law of international responsibility of private persons in the context of world peace. This may largely explain why I have also attempted to assess the methods by which states usually obtain jurisdiction to punish offenders. The appraisal of these methods has led me to believe that the establishment of an international criminal jurisdiction is the most desirable alternative, and perhaps the only one that may adequately satisfy the demands of justice.

It is a great pleasure to express my deep appreciation to those who, in a general way, have assisted me in the research and writing of this book. I should like to single out the following: the members of the Staff of the University of Detroit Library, especially Mrs. Alice E. Courtis, for their help in locating books and documents, and their promptness in processing material through inter-library loans; the libraries of Harvard, Yale and Michigan Law Schools for their courtesy in lending me all the material I requested; the editors of the *Fordham Law Review*, *Indiana Law Journal* and the *University of Pittsburgh Law Review* for graciously allowing me to reproduce material previously published in those journals; my good friends, Betty and Edward Stevens, who as a husband and wife team showed great skill and patience in deciphering and typing a rather unattractive and difficult manuscript; to the publisher of this work for its courtesy, consideration and understanding shown me in connection with publication; to my boy, Jay, for his patience and understanding in quietly accepting restrictions upon his freedom of movement while I was engaged in research and writing at home; and above all, I owe a profound debt of gratitude to my wife, to whom this book is dedicated, not only for her invaluable suggestions and patient assistance in many ways, but also for her unfailing faith, encouragement and dedication.

Manuel R. García-Mora

Detroit, Michigan
March, 1961

TABLE OF CONTENTS

TABLE OF CASES

LIST OF ABBREVIATIONS

A.C.	Law Reports, Appeal Cases, House of Lords (Great Britain)
Am. J. Comp. L.	American Journal of Comparative Law
Am. J. Int. L.	American Journal of International Law
Am. J. Int. L. Supp.	Supplement to the American Journal of International Law
Am. Pol. Sci. Rev.	American Political Science Review
Annual Digest	Annual Digest and Reports of Public International Law Cases. Beginning in 1950, they appear as International Law Reports.
Brit. Y.B. Int. L.	British Year Book of International Law
Calif. L. R.	California Law Review
Can. Rev. Stat.	Revised Statutes of Canada
Colum. L. R.	Columbia Law Review
Cong.	Congress of the United States
Co. Rep.	Coke's Law Reports (Great Britain)
Dept. State Bull.	Department of State Bulletin (United States)
Edw. III, Stat.	Statutes at Large of the United Kingdom
Fed.	Federal Reporter (United States)
F. 2d	Federal Reporter, Second Series (United States)
Fordham L. R.	Fordham Law Review
Geo.	Statutes at Large of the United Kingdom
Hague Recueil	Recueil des Cours, Académie de Droit International de la Haye

Harvard L. R.	Harvard Law Review
H. R.	House of Representatives (United States)
How.	Howard's United States Supreme Court Reports
Ind. L. J.	Indiana Law Journal
Inter-Amer. J. Y. B.	Inter-American Juridical Year Book
Int. & Comp. L. Q.	International and Comparative Law Quarterly
I. C. J., Reports	Reports of the International Court of Justice
Int. L. Q.	International Law Quarterly
J. Crim. L. & Criminology	Journal of Criminal Law and Criminology
L. Q. R.	Law Quarterly Review
L. T. R.	Law Times Reports (Great Britain)
Mich. L. R.	Michigan Law Review
N. Y. Times	New York Times
P. C. I. J.	Publications of the Permanent Court of International Justice
Proc. Am. Soc. Int. L.	Proceedings of the American Society of International Law
Q. B.	Law Reports, Queen's Bench Division (Great Britain)
Rev. Gén. de Droit Int. Public	Revue Général de Droit International Public
Rev. Stat.	Revised Statutes (United States)
South Dakota L. R.	South Dakota Law Review
Stat.	Statutes at Large of the United States
T. S.	United States Treaty Series
U.N.	United Nations
U.N. Treaty Ser.	United Nations Treaty Series
U. Pa. L. R.	University of Pennsylvania Law Review
U. of Toronto L. J.	University of Toronto Law Journal
U.S.	United States Supreme Court Reports

U.S.C.	United States Code
U.S.C.A.	United States Code Annotated
U.S. Const.	United States Constitution
U.S. Const. Amend.	United States Constitution, Amendment
U.S. Foreign Rel.	Papers Relating to the Foreign Relations of the United States
Vic.	Statutes at Large of the United Kingdom
Virginia L. R.	Virginia Law Review
W. Va. L. Q.	West Virginia Law Quaterly
Wheat.	Wheaton's United States Supreme Court Reports
Yale L. J.	Yale Law Journal

CHAPTER I

THE INDIVIDUAL AND WORLD ORDER

The shortcomings of the international legal order are all too obvious to any casual observer of the world scene. The need to eliminate friction between states in an atomic age is painfully clear. Past efforts to establish an effective international law have ended in disheartening failures. Witness the breakdown of the League of Nations and its attempts to establish a collective security system carrying with it the high hopes of peoples everywhere. More recently, when mankind emerged from the "social cataclysm" of 1939–1945, the rebuilding of the international order was viewed as the only available alternative to save "succeeding generations from the scourge of war."[1] A new world order was not only conceived under a sense of deep frustration for the failure of the old, but also under the full realization that the survival of mankind depends on its effective operation.[2] The reorganization of the international order was thus posed in terms of a desperate necessity, simply because mankind was compelled to choose between such antithetical alternatives as survival or destruction.[3] Yet almost two decades after the termination of World War II, the community of mankind is still without any effective means of controlling international conflicts.

The search for the causes that have contributed to this disheartening international picture is a task that has engaged the attention of scholars for the last twenty years. Many worthwhile and cogent proposals have emerged from their labor. Thus, some have called attention to the fact that an international law founded on *laissez-faire* juridical conceptions according to which each state is free to act as it sees fit is clearly obso-

[1] Borrowed from the Preamble of the United Nations Charter.

[2] Thus, Professor Filmer S. C. Northrop says: "World survival and progress in an atomic epoch depend on an effective international law," F. S. C. Northrop, "Contemporary Jurisprudence and International Law," *Yale L. J.*, Vol. 61, p. 623 (1952). See also his *Philosophical Anthropology and Practical Politics*, ch. 1, (1960).

[3] J. Stone, *Legal Controls of International Conflict*, pp. xxxvi–xxxviii (1954). Also G. W. Keeton and G. Schwarzenberger, *Making International Law Work* (1946), whose choice is between destruction or world federation. In the same vein, C. Meyer, *Peace or Anarchy* (1947). Professor Myres S. McDougal takes a dim view of such thinking. See M. S. McDougal, "The Impact of International Law upon National Law: A Policy-Oriented Perspective," *South Dakota L. R.*, Vol. 4, pp. 25, 92 (1959).

lete today.[4] Others have imperatively called for the abolition of the state system as presently known and its substitution for some kind of world government[5] or a federation of states.[6] Still others have proposed that since the state is likely to continue as the medium through which nations deal with one another across national frontiers, no reform of international law can successfully be approached unless the role of the state within the world community is critically appraised.[7] That these approaches render a great service in calling attention to future objectives can hardly be denied. But, more significantly, they show that no consensus is attainable either as to the exact causes underlying the collapse of the international legal order or as to the bases on which an effective international law must rest. The problem is really much more complex than most publicists have assumed.

Many factors have undoubtedly contributed to the present discouraging international situation. No attempt is made here to discuss them. Nevertheless, it may be suggested that the failure of governments to control adequately the unlawful actions of private persons against foreign nations must be counted among them. More specifically, it is believed that international lawyers have not paid enough attention to the legal problems which arise when private persons engage in actions which are offensive to the peace and security of foreign nations.[8] And they have accordingly underestimated the possibility that these actions may often be irritants in the relations between states, thus constituting a serious danger to world peace. But, to avoid misconceptions, it should immediately be added that this is by no means the only problem plaguing mankind. It will be considered in this book as a part of a larger problem and one which, in conjunction with the

[4] A. Alvarez, "The Reconstruction and Codification of International Law," *Int. L. Q.*, Vol. I, pp. 469, 471 (1947). See also his dissenting opinion in the Advisory Opinion of the International Court of Justice on the International Status of South-West Africa, I.C.J., *Reports*, 1950, p. 174 (1950).

[5] See in this connection, R. M. Hutchins and others, *Preliminary Draft of a World Constitution* (1948), assuming that a world government will be established on a democratic basis, an assumption which is highly questionable.

[6] See G. W. Keeton and Schwarzenberger, *op. cit.*

[7] See W. Friedmann, "Some Impacts of Social Organization on International Law," *Am. J. Int. L.*, Vol. 50, pp. 475, 477 (1956).

[8] It will be seen in subsequent chapters that international lawyers usually dismiss this point by simply saying that the state is not responsible for the action of private persons. Thus, after an exhaustive study of the case law of international tribunals, Dr. Bin Cheng concluded that "Acts of private individuals are not acts of the state, whether individuals are acting singly or in groups, such as mobs, rioters, or bandits. In international law, states are not held responsible for acts committed by them." See B. Cheng, *General Principles of Law as Applied by International Courts and Tribunals*, p. 208 (1953).

views of many scholars, must be taken into account in the rebuilding of international law.

THE WORLD COMMUNITY AND ITS VALUES

The program presented in these pages is decisively based upon the premise that the future of world peace is intimately bound up with international law, but the future of the latter is indissolubly linked with the frank recognition and promotion of the values of the world community.[9] Precisely because law is "the regulation of the life of the community,"[10] the legal order must of necessity reflect the values which it is trying to preserve. Deeply embedded in this proposition is the sociological axiom that any community must maintain an agreement upon certain fundamentals if it is to survive.[11] This is similarly true of the international community. Thus, the problem to be explored is the extent of consensus existing on this level. In this connection, it is a matter of common observation that the world community, instead of representing a cohesive and integrated whole, is divided into a multiplicity of particular societies with diverse loyalties and conflicting sentiments, shattering the conception of a community of interests and solidarity.[12] Simple as it may sound, it nevertheless remains true that anarchy exists in the international community in proportion to the extent to which governments allow considerations of power to occupy the center of the scene. Such a situation is indeed cause for dismay, but it is not conclusive upon individuals and governments trying to formulate a conception of the world community where human beings can live in peace and security.

The reality of the world community may accurately be described in terms of three intimately related postulates, which usefully provide the basis for the reorganization of international law. The first is simple enough, namely, that the peoples of the world have been united in particular communities with their individual aspirations, and these societies are each independent of the other;[13] the second rests upon

[9] E. H. Carr, *The Twenty Years' Crisis 1919–1939*, p. 170 (1946).

[10] H. Triepel, *Droit International et Droit Interne*, p. 27 (French transl. from the German by R. Brunet, 1920).

[11] A. Hacker, "Liberal Democracy and Social Control," *Am. Pol. Sci. Rev.* Vol. 51, p. 1009 (1957).

[12] P. E. Corbett, *Law and Society in the Relations of States*, p. 12 (1951).

[13] "An international society requires the coexistence of two or more groups each independent of the rest." G. Schwarzenberger, *Power Politics: A Study in International Relations*, p. 25 (2nd ed., 1951).

the observable fact that these particular communities are so mutually related that each finds satisfaction by means of the others, thus forming a system of complete interdependence;[14] and the third is really a synthesis of the preceding two, namely, that all the national communities are held together by common interests in the preservation of peace and security, and these interests are superior to their particular interests, thus forming the basis of social cooperation.[15] These three postulates constitute the contemporary structure of the world community,[16] and they clearly correspond to the idea that mankind is a moral and political unit kept together by interests which are common to all peoples irrespective of the political divisions of the world. This idea provides a most useful *point de départ* for the creation of an effective international law. As an irreducible minimum, the latter must have sufficient authority both to define the rights of the states and to subordinate these rights to values existing on the international level. Surely, if the function of international law were exclusively confined to the preservation of the rights of the states, the resulting situation would undoubtedly be a Hobbesian type of international society where the most powerful may ultimately dominate all, thus leading to a complete denial of international law itself. It was precisely because a heavy emphasis was formerly placed on this conception that no organic, political or moral integration of the world community was ever attained. And it is perhaps with this kind of consideration in mind that an able commentator has recently noted that "An international order founded, not on the solid and overmastering community of interests which bind mankind, but on the shifting interests of the state which divide it, cannot endure."[17] However, since the function of international law is the preservation of the values of the world community, which reflect human values everywhere, international law has thus become "the medium for systematizing the relations and coordinating the

[14] F. Hegel, *Philosophy of Right*, pp. 122–123 (Transl. by T. M. Knox, 1942).

[15] It should be recalled that the Spanish Jesuit Francisco Suárez formulated a conception of the world society where the states of the world are held together by the natural necessity of communion and mutual aid. He further implied that as long as they are not united, they remain imperfect societies. See F. Suárez, *De Legibus ac Deo Legislatore*, bk. II, c. 19, sec. 9 (Transl. by G. L. Williams, 1944). For a discussion of the Suarezian conception in a contemporary context, see M. R. García-Mora, *International Law and Asylum as a Human Right*, pp. 23–25 (1956).

[16] Dr. Wallace McClure has said in this connection that "The existence of the world community is concrete and real." W. McClure, *World Legal Order: Possible Contributions by the People of the United States*, p. 176 (1960).

[17] M. Moskewitz, *Human Rights and World Order: The Struggle for Human Rights in the United Nations*, p. 19 (1958).

activities of independent entities in that sphere of action over which each has a vital measure of control."[18] Conceived in these terms, international law is profoundly transformed into the law of social cooperation without which the interests of the international community cannot be attained. Put in its simplest terms, the present values of the world community require the states to work together toward common goals and it is left to international law to work out the rules of cooperation accordingly.[19]

INTERNATIONAL LAW AND HOSTILE ACTIONS OF PRIVATE PERSONS

International law has long recognized that certain actions of private persons are likely to have decisive international effects. This is particularly true when the action is harmful to the peace and well-being of a foreign nation. An assertion of this nature immediately raises the preliminary and vital question as to the relation of international law to the actions of private individuals. In dealing with this question two possible approaches quite naturally emerge. One approach suggests the possibility of treating this matter from the standpoint of the relation of the state to international law, while the other is more closely concerned with the position of private persons under the law of nations. Thus, to ask whether international law regulates hostile actions of private individuals is really to ask two separate questions, namely, first, whether international law imposes some kind of liability upon the state in whose jurisdiction the offenses were committed and, secondly, whether legal obligations are directly imposed upon private individuals. These questions can best be discussed separately.

Obligation Of The State

It is common learning among international lawyers that the right of jurisdiction which a government exercises within its territory carries with it the obligation to prevent the commission of injurious actions against other states.[20] This has been said to be an obligation inherent in territorial sovereignty. Judge Max Huber aptly summarized this obligation in the following terms:

[18] W. L. Gould, *An Introduction to International Law*, p. 290 (1957).
[19] See the remarks of D. A. Avram in *Proc. Am. Soc. Int. L.*, pp. 122–124 (1954).
[20] C. G. Fenwick, *International Law*, p. 301 (3d ed., 1948).

> Territorial sovereignty... involves the exclusive right to display the activities of the state. This right has as a corollary a duty: the obligation to protect within the territory the rights of other states, in particular their right to integrity and inviolability in peace and in war, together with the rights which each state may claim for its nationals in foreign territory.[21]

As a proposition of classic international law, the foregoing passage is not open to doubt. It is an accurate expression of nineteenth century conceptions based on the individualistic nature of international law. It essentially reflects the dominant anarchical patterns of the international community, in which international law is mainly concerned with the rights of sovereignty and the jurisdiction of the states.[22] The technical legal doctrine by which these patterns are expressed is that of absolute sovereignty singularly free from any regulation and only admitting such limitations as originate from the sovereignty of others. Particularly significant in its bearing upon the existence of a world community is Judge Huber's failure to recognize that over and above the states there is a world community with such values of peace and solidarity that states must promote and cultivate. This classic view of international law has been so well characterized by Judge Alejandro Alvarez that his words may be quoted here in full. He says:

> According to the classic international law, the sovereignty of states and the rights which flowed therefrom, were absolute. Consequently, any state could exercise its rights without limit, or rather, the sole limits were the rights of other states (coalition of rights), and only rarely the general interests. In addition, each state was perfectly free to exercise its rights, and even to abuse them, without having to justify its conduct to anybody.[23]

It can readily be seen, therefore, that the key concept in the structure of classical doctrine is that of juristic individualism under which states do not consider themselves bound by any legal obligation, nor are they required to regard the interests of the world community. In all the many varying contexts, these conceptions are, in the view of Professor Percy E. Corbett, "a denial of international society and law,"[24]

[21] Island of Palmas (United States v. The Netherlands), *U.N. Reports of International Arbitral Awards*, Vol. 2, p. 829 (1949). Also Judge John B. Moore, in his dissenting opinion in the celebrated *Lotus Case* said: "It is well settled that a State is bound to use due diligence to prevent the commission within its dominions of criminal acts against another nation or its people." Case of the S.S. "Lotus," P.C.I.J. Ser. A, No. 10, at p. 88 (1927).

[22] C. W. Jenks, "The Scope of International Law," *Brit. Y.B. Int. L.* 1954, Vol. 31, pp. 1, 3 (1956).

[23] Dissenting Opinion of Judge A. Alvarez in the Advisory Opinion of the International Court of Justice regarding the Competence of the General Assembly for the Admission of a State to the United Nations, I.C.J. *Reports*, 1950, p. 14 (1950).

[24] P. E. Corbett, *op. cit.*, p. 76 (1951).

and, it may be added, they rob international law of much of its *raison d'être*. Contrasting this legal individualism with what he considers to be the new international law, Judge Alvarez goes on to say that "The general interest, the interests of international society, must constitute the limits of the rights of states and make it possible to determine whether there has been an *abuse* of these rights."[25] So far as the issue of preventing hostile private acts against foreign states is concerned, Judge Alvarez' approach may offer a useful avenue of escape from the overriding demands of sovereignty, for it sets up the general interest as the criterion by which the international obligations of the state can most effectively be met. On this view, a superior common interest imposes upon the states the obligation not to permit within their jurisdiction the commission of acts which are injurious to the peace and security of another nation.[26] Certainly, this is an absolute obligation which stems from a world community deeply concerned with peace and cooperation between governments.[27] Because international law is designed for the benefit of peoples and not merely to justify the action of certain states, this most basic policy must underlie the obligation of governments in preventing any action which may unnecessarily destroy the values of another nation.

Obligation of Private Persons

In the matter of private persons' obligations, most discussions have long been dominated by the traditional principle that international law only governs relations between states, and not between individuals, not even between individuals and states.[28] Though the Nürnberg Judgment has been generally regarded as a landmark in making the individual human person criminally liable for the commission of international crimes, it must nevertheless be observed that the liability there involved is confined to persons acting as agents of the state. Thus, the liability of private persons acting on their own cannot reasonably be deduced from the Nürnberg Trial and Judgment. International law, therefore, still remains largely unconcerned with the possibility of

[25] Dissenting Opinion of Judge A. Alvarez in the Advisory Opinion of the International Court of Justice regarding the Competence of the General Assembly for the Admission of a State to the United Nations. I.C.J., *Reports*, 1950, p. 14 (1950). Italics are those of Judge Alvarez.

[26] C. C. Hyde, *International Law Chiefly as Interpreted and Applied by the United States*, Vol. I, p. 33 (2d ed., 1945).

[27] For an exhaustive discussion of world community values, see M. S. McDougal, *op. cit.*, pp. 25–27, 32–34.

[28] P. C. Jessup, *A Modern Law of Nations*, pp. 8–9 (1947).

imposing obligations upon private persons for actions which clearly affect the peace and security of mankind. The learned literature upon this subject has mostly proceeded upon the assumption that the unlawful actions of private persons are adequately controlled by the state in whose jurisdiction the acts are committed. But a position based on such an assumption might be expected to yield unsatisfactory results, for it will shortly be seen that the responsibility of the state in this area is legally tested by conceptions laid down by Hugo Grotius some three centuries ago,[29] which not only make the international responsibility somewhat tentative and inconclusive, but also fail to satisfy adequately the requirements of the world community. At this point, it is highly relevant to recall that private persons have increasingly been used by governments as instruments of their international policies. Witness such supposedly private actions as the influx of foreign volunteers into the Spanish Civil Strife in 1936 and into the Korean situation in 1950;[30] also frontier raids of armed bands in Central America and the Middle East,[31] only to mention a few instances where private persons have become vitally involved in international situations. It can scarcely be denied that in these situations the peace and security of the world hung on a precarious balance. Moreover, experience in previous major wars irresistibly suggests that wars often have their roots in local conflicts between minor powers, and often are conducted by proxy through the actions of private persons, as the Chinese volunteers have clearly shown. Confronted with these painful realities, a rational theory must frankly recognize the doubtful validity of the doctrine that private persons have no liability under international law. Even in times of war the ability of belligerents to produce the implements of war is wholly dependent upon the civilian population, a fact that casts even graver doubts upon the doctrine.[32] As the subsequent treatment of these matters will indicate, the doctrine which denies international liability to private persons is untenable today,

[29] One such doctrine is the requirement of fault, which is fully discussed in Chapter II, *infra*. See H. Grotius, *De Jure Belli ac Pacis Libri Tres*, bk. II, c. XXI, sec. 2 (Transl. by F. W. Kelsey, 1925).

[30] This matter is discussed in Chapter V, *infra*.

[31] I. Brownlie, "International Law and the Activities of Armed Bands," *Int. & Comp. L. Q.*, Vol. 7, p. 712 (1958). See also Chapter VII, *infra*.

[32] Cf. J. Stone, *op. cit.*, p. 317. The United Nations International Law Commission said in Article 2, paragraph (12) of the Draft Code of Offenses against the Peace and Security of Mankind that "there can be no question of punishing as accomplices in such an offence [complicity to commit aggression] all the members of the armed forces of a state or the workers in war industries." See Report of the International Law Commission, Covering The Work of its Third Session, 16 May – 27 July, 1951. *U.N. General Assembly, Official Records, Sixth Session, Supplement No. 9* (A/1858), p. 13 (1951).

because it is essentially grounded on the artificial distinction between the state and the individual, thus giving rise to the conclusion that the individual can freely engage in actions which are prohibited to the state. This distinction is really the product of nineteenth century *laissez-faire* conceptions, and they have largely provided the framework of the law in this area. The role which private persons have been known to play in the international policies of their governments forcibly dictates a radical modification of this classical doctrine.

THE INDIVIDUAL AND THE PEACE AND SECURITY OF MANKIND

It is in recognition of the foregoing considerations that the International Law Commission of the United Nations has formulated a Draft Code of Offenses Against the Peace and Security of Mankind, in which certain private actions of individuals are clearly included.[33] A later discussion of this code will show that it is built upon the assumption that certain actions of private persons have international repercussions largely because they lend themselves to the furtherance of aggressive designs without openly engaging the responsibility of the state. Thus, revolutionary propaganda against foreign governments clearly undermine the social and political order of the state without actual intervention.[34] Similarly, allowing volunteers to depart from the territory as well as the toleration of hostile military expeditions permit a state to participate covertly in a conflict without in any way affecting its position as a neutral in an international war or violating its duty of non-intervention in a civil strife. In like vein, the invasion of foreign territory by armed bands is nothing more than an indirect and concealed technique of aggression aimed at the conquest of foreign territory without resort to open hostilities. An objective student of the world situation has observed in this connection, that "the military threat is not necessarily the gravest issue confronting the world today," but rather all kinds of perils which manifest themselves in a variety of ways, "including that of 'concealed aggression' through which forces that are ostensibly domestic in nature seize power, as in China."[35]

[33] For text, see Report of the International Law Commission Covering the Work of its Third Session, 16 May – 27 July, 1951, *U.N. General Assembly, Official Records, Sixth Session, Supplement No. 9* (A/1858), pp. 10–14 (1951).

[34] J. Stone, *op. cit.*, p. 318.

[35] K. W. Thompson, *Political Realism and the Crisis of World Politics: An American Approach to Foreign Policy*, p. 197 (1960).

Many more illustrations could be given where the actions of private persons seriously affect the peace and security of mankind.[36] But since specific actions will be discussed in Part II of this book, it is believed that the few instances given here are enough to emphasize the importance and urgency of the problem.

It may of course be argued that neither the state nor its citizens have the obligation to protect governments whose political ideology is particularly distasteful. If this argument be correct, it would seem inexorably to follow that international law does not impose upon the state the obligation to prevent its citizens from engaging in revolutionary activities or any other hostile act against a totalitarian regime.[37] Admittedly, this argument may have a special appeal to democratic societies, for it can persuasively be argued that no democratic government can safely extend protection to political systems at variance with its ideology. But this argument is intimately tied up with the origin of international law which until recently was essentially European, and since the European countries largely subscribed to the democratic ideology, it was relatively simple to conclude that international law imposed no obligation whatsoever to protect foreign governments whose political ideology was contrary to their beliefs. This argument has lost its useful meaning in the contemporary world where over a hundred states of diverse political systems have come to play a vital role in world community processes, thus transforming the exclusive European nature of international law into a world wide system.[38] Echoing this change, Sir Pierson Dixon of the United Kingdom has said that "The birth of new nations and the contraction of the world through development of communication and economic links between countries have inevitably led to a new conception of international responsibility and interdependence between nations."[39] Therefore, there can be no doubt that the peaceful coexistence of the states in the world community requires that their governments be protected against hostile acts committed by private persons in other jurisdictions.

It might further be suggested that to accept the above analysis would amount to asserting that the international community has become a system of mutual assistance, thus helping to perpetuate ty-

[36] J. Paoli, "Contribution à l'Etude des Crimes de Guerre et des Crimes Contre l'Humanité en Droit Pénal International," *Rev. Gén. de Droit Int. Public*, Vol. 39, pp. 129, 146 (France, 1941–1945).

[37] H. Lauterpacht, "Revolutionary Activities by Private Persons Against Foreign States," *Am. J. Int. L.*, Vol. 22, p. 105 (1928).

[38] C. W. Jenks, *The Common Law of Mankind*, ch. 2 (1958).

[39] Quoted in M. Moskewitz, *op. cit.*, pp. 97–98.

rannical governments.[40] Though there may be substance in this view, it should be recalled that because of the heavy concentration of power in the modern state, popular revolutions are generally doomed to failure,[41] and that, consequently, the interest of the world community in the maintenance of peace is greater than the well intentioned attempts of sporadic groups of individuals to overthrow an existing totalitarian regime. It certainly runs counter to justice to plunge the world community into a conflagration because of the toleration of private activities designed to undermine the government of another nation.[42] In understanding this, it may be quite helpful to remember that the world community reflects the fervent hopes for peace and security of millions of human beings and, most certainly, these legitimate values cannot successfully be overridden by invoking the questionable right of a group of people to overthrow an existing government. It is clearly a matter of weighing competing interests, where the values of the world community occupy a prominent place. This, of course, does not imply that people suffering from persecution and oppression are to be left to the unmitigated violence of tyrannical governments. The respect for human rights and the recognition of the dignity of the individual are also values of the world community, and when these values are the object of aggression by totalitarian regimes, the orderly process of the world community requires that resort be had to organized community action through either the United Nations or a regional organization established under the United Nations Charter. What is decisively rejected is the toleration of actions of private persons which, though perhaps well intentioned and in good faith, are nevertheless likely to bring war in the world community, thus spreading human suffering everywhere. Peace is the first value of the world community that every government must promote and cultivate. This is an overriding moral obligation, and it is in this sense that all states have the additional duty – indeed, a vital interest – to romove the causes which within their jurisdiction are likely to produce disharmony in their mutual relations. To implant successfully the rule of law in the world community, it is necessary to ensure that people live in peace, security, and well-being within their national communities.

If the above observations be correct, it will at once be seen that the problem of hostile actions of private persons against foreign states is

[40] P. C. Jessup, *op. cit.*, pp. 184–187.
[41] H. J. Morgenthau, *In Defense of the National Interest*, p. 59 (1951).
[42] H. Lauterpacht, *op. cit.*, p. 117.

not exclusively confined to the relations between nations. It is a matter in which the world community also has interests vitally at stake. Moreover, the disturbing problems created by these actions cannot be isolated and treated as though the state alone is to be held liable. A more balanced view requires constant efforts to ensure that the individuals committing these offenses do not escape punishment. To do otherwise may undermine respect for international law and may further depress the legitimate aspirations of the peoples of the world. Hence, this book will focus attention on the responsibility of the state and of the individual for the commission by private persons of hostile actions against foreign states. Underlying this inquiry is the firm conviction that certain unlawful actions of private individuals seriously affect the peace and security of mankind. It is therefore hoped that the modest proposal presented in the ensuing pages may help to attain, even in a small measure, a just and peaceful world order.

PART ONE

STATE AND INDIVIDUAL RESPONSIBILITY

CHAPTER II

THE TRADITIONAL LAW CONCERNING THE RESPONSIBILITY OF THE STATE FOR ACTIONS OF PRIVATE PERSONS

The international responsibility of the state for wrongful acts of private persons against foreign nations is a phase of the general law of international responsibility under international law. While the rules concerning certain areas of state responsibility are well established,[1] its liability for hostile actions of individuals remains to be defined.[2] It is perhaps for this reason that most discussions of state responsibility deal with fairly well accepted doctrines, such as responsibility for unauthorized acts of governmental officials or for acts of individuals resulting in injury to aliens. In discussing state liability involving actions of private persons against other nations, authoritative guidance will therefore be sought in more settled branches of the law. Inadvertence to these preliminary matters may explain the inconclusiveness of attempted solutions to the problem, and the almost insuperable difficulties which it raises.

NATURE OF STATE RESPONSIBILITY

In international, as in municipal, society, the law requires that liability result from certain actions of individuals deemed to be unlawful. Certain acts may be so injurious to the welfare of the world community and so detrimental to international order that international law imperatively demands their suppression.[3] The fact that these actions are those of private persons ought not to be a limitation upon

[1] H. W. Briggs, *The Law of Nations: Cases, Documents and Notes*, pp. 680–697 (2d ed., 1952).

[2] In this connection, some authors speak of original and vicarious responsibility, the former describing the responsibility of the state for acts of its government, while the latter includes responsibility for private acts. See L. Oppenheim, *International Law* Vol. I. p. 337 (8th ed. by H. Lauterpacht, 1955). Others speak of direct and indirect responsibility of the state. See M. Miele, *Principi di Diritto Internazionale*, p. 236 (1953); J. Dumas, *De La Responsabilité Internationale des Etats*, pp. 57–64 (1930). Still others speak of primary and secondary liability. See A. D. McNair, *International Law Opinions*, Vol. 2, p. 288 (1956).

[3] C. C. Hyde, *International Law Chiefly as Interpreted and Applied by the United States*, Vol. 1, p. 33 (2d ed., 1945).

this principle, but only upon the process of enforcement. For while in the domestic society municipal law operates directly upon individuals through an organized system of courts and law enforcement, in the world community international law has reached private persons only through the medium of the state. Despite the broad generalizations of the Nürnberg Judgment,[4] traditional international law has been primarily, if not exclusively, concerned with state action or omission, and not at all with a private person's action. In terms of orthodox doctrine, if there is to be any responsibility for an injurious act of a private person against a foreign government, liability will be imposed upon the state and not upon the offender, though in so far as the individual is concerned, international law leaves his fate to the menaced community's discretion should he ever fall into its jurisdiction. The true explanation for this doctrine lies in the old principle of refusing private persons a *locus standi* before international law, thus leaving this branch of the law exclusively concerned with the relations between states. Deplorable as this doctrine has proved to be, it still largely dominates the international legal order significantly affecting situations in which individuals are involved.

The preceding observations are not to imply that the states are held automatically responsible for actions of private persons committed within their jurisdiction, for even in this area the international law position has long been dominated by the well established doctrine that the liability of the state may arise under certain conditions involving its failure to take "such measures as in the circumstances should normally have been taken to prevent, redress or inflict punishment for the acts causing the damage."[5] The orthodox view is therefore that the state is liable for acts of private persons only if it has neglected to take all reasonable measures for the prevention and punishment of the offense. In terms of the traditional doctrine, it is clearly a responsibility based on fault.[6] The somewhat vague formulation of this rule represents what clearly is a compromise between the world community requirement of holding the state responsible for hostile actions which stem from its jurisdiction and the necessity of securing certain measure of respect for state sovereignty. The flexible nature of the rule reveals

[4] For text, see *Am. J. Int'l. L. Supp.* Vol. 41, p. 172 (1947).

[5] This was the rule adopted by the Third Committee of the Hague Codification Conference of 1930, Art. 10. For text, see H. W. Briggs, *op. cit.*, p. 711.

[6] In technical language, this responsibility is referred to as culpability while absolute responsibility is known as liability. See H. Kelsen, *Principles of International Law*, pp. 122–124 (1952).

two conceptions whose validity seems unquestioned in broad terms and in terms of theory. First, a hostile action of an individual against a foreign government does not *per se* engage the responsibility of the state. And, secondly, state responsibility may nevertheless arise if a degree of connection between the person's act and the state can be established by showing a failure of the latter to discharge its duty of prevention. Within this doctrinal structure, the responsibility of the state becomes engaged under a supposed doctrine of implied governmental complicity. Governmental complicity is a well-recognized ground of international liability,[7] and is essentially based on the fictitious assumption that by not using means of prevention, the state has in fact become a party to the private person's act. As this doctrine underlies much of the law of state responsibility for injurious acts of private individuals, it may be profitable to discuss it in detail.

THE NOTION OF IMPLIED STATE COMPLICITY

The various streams of thought which have postulated the responsibility of the state in the manner indicated are historically traceable to the writings of Hugo Grotius, the generally acknowledged father of international law. In so far as this responsibility is concerned, two aspects of his treatment deserve a special mention. One is his general doctrine that "civil authorities are liable for losses caused by their subjects." The other is more specific, for he said that "kings and public officials are liable for neglect if they do not employ the remedies which they can and ought to employ for the prevention of robbery and piracy..."[8] Clearly, this is the doctrine of no liability without fault. Drawing from ancient source, specially from the Roman Law doctrine of *culpa*, Grotius expressed this doctrine in the following terms:

> ... A Civil community, just as any other community, is not bound by the acts of individuals, apart from some act or neglect of its own... But, as we have said, to participate in a crime a person must not only have knowledge of it but also have the opportunity to prevent it. This is what the laws mean when they say that knowledge, when its punishment is ordained, is taken in the sense of toleration, so that he may be held responsible who was able to prevent a crime but did not do so; and that the knowledge to be considered here is that associated with the will, that is, knowledge is to be taken in connection with intent.[9]

[7] E. M. Borchard, *The Diplomatic Protection of Citizens Abroad or The Law of International Claims*, p. 217 (1915).

[8] H. Grotius, *De Jure Belli ac Pacis Libri Tres*, bk. II, ch. XVII, sec. 20 (Transl. by F. W. Kelsey, 1925).

[9] *Ibid.*, bk. II, ch. XXI, sec. 2.

The principle outlined in the preceding paragraph is intended to be applied to the state, for it is contained in the chapter entitled "A community, or its rulers, may be held responsible for the crime of a subject if they know of it and do not prevent it when they could and should prevent it." It, moreover, represented an attempt to apply the standard of civil law to the relations between states and, as has been observed, was a reaction against the medieval custom of imposing responsibility upon a city or political community for the unlawful acts of its inhabitants.[10] The subsequent history of the law of responsibility for acts of individuals revolves around this principle, and it is indeed unfortunate, though quite understandable, that such a doctrine should gain acceptance by states. In the Grotian system, largely founded upon natural law conceptions,[11] the idea that state responsibility depends upon fault (*culpa*) is palpably self-contradictory, since it contributes to the denial of the very sense of community that his natural law doctrines were intended to postulate. For in a society of states based on a community of shared values and social solidarity, the responsibility of the state for injurious actions of private persons against other nations would seem to rest on moral and legal grounds. Morally, it stems from the overriding obligation of all states to contribute to the maintenance of peace and order in the world community, while legally, it proceeds from obligations resulting from the exercise of territorial sovereignty. According to the latter, the use of a state's territory for the commission of acts injurious to a foreign nation is not legally permissible.[12] Though it will shortly be seen that the element of fault is the accepted standard by which the legal obligation is met, exclusive reliance upon it robs the world society of the ethical convictions which alone give the states a sense of community and, thus, of cooperation and solidarity.[13] However, when it is remembered that in the Grotian system of international law, natural law and positivist conceptions

[10] L. A. Podestá Costa, *Derecho Internacional Público*, Vol. I, p. 441 (3d ed., 1955).

[11] W. Schiffer, *The Legal Community of Mankind*, c.2 (1954). It is paradoxical, however, that the theory of responsibility based on fault should be adopted largely by the followers of the natural law school, while the theory of absolute responsibility is usually followed by the so-called positivists. This is even more surprising in view of the fact that the theory of absolute responsibility is not based either on the practice of states or on treaties. It is the doctrine of culpability (liability based on fault), which is based on practice and treaties. See L. A. Podestá Costa, *op. cit.*, Vol. I, pp. 453, 454.

[12] U.N. Secretariat, *Survey of International Law*, U.N. Doc. no. A/CN.4/1 Rev. 1, pp. 34–35 (1949).

[13] Cf. P. E. Corbett, *Law and Society in the Relations of States*, (1951). Professor Josef L. Kunz has said in this connection that "Religious and ethical rules embody higher values and are sometimes more effective than legal rules." J. L. Kunz, "Sanctions in International Law," *Am. J. Int. L.*, Vol. 54, p. 324 (1960).

curiously mixed,[14] his resort to the *culpa* formula becomes more understandable and, even less objectionable.

These Grotian notions were further elaborated by Emerich de Vattel, whose theories on the subject so closely resembled those of his illustrious predecessor as to constitute a substantially similar position. The starting point of the Vattelian doctrine was the recognition of a general duty of the state not to permit its subjects to offend other nations. He thus said:

> ...The Nation, or the sovereign, must not allow its citizens to injure the subjects of another state, much less to offend that state itself; and this not only because no sovereign should permit those under his rule to violate the precepts of the natural law, which forbids such acts, but also because Nations should mutually respect one another and avoid any offense, injury, or wrong; in a word, anything which might be hurtful to others. If a sovereign who has the power to see that his subjects act in a just manner permits them to injure a foreign nation, either the state itself or its citizens, he does no less a wrong to that nation than if he injured it himself. Finally, the very safety of the state and of society at large demands this care on the part of every sovereign.[15]

Underlying the duty embedded in this passage is the necessity of coexistence of the states in the world community, for only then can the fundamental rights of all states be adequately assured. It is precisely because Vattel laid a heavy stress on the fundamental rights of the states that his law of nations had to postulate the precepts which would assure the exercise of these rights by all nations.[16] To permit citizens to injure a foreign state, in the Vattelian conception, would clearly violate the fundamental right of independence, thus seriously impairing the harmonious relations that nations must maintain at all times. Like Grotius, however, Vattel rejected the conception of absolute responsibility, and instead declared quite explicitly that because "it is impossible for the best governed state or for the most watchful and strict sovereign to regulate at will all the acts of their subjects and to hold them on every occasion to the most exact obedience; it would be unjust to impute to the nation, or to the sovereign, all the faults of their citizens..."[17] The only instance in which a state may be held liable is "if the nation or its ruler, approve and ratify the acts of its citizen, [for] it takes upon itself the act, and may then be regarded by

[14] For a comprehensive discussion of Grotius' theories see J. Basdevant in *Les Fondateurs du Droit International*, pp. 125–267 (1904).

[15] E. de Vattel, *Le Droit des Gens*, bk. II, ch. VI, sec. 72 (Transl. by C. G. Fenwick, 1916).

[16] J. Stone, *Legal Controls of International Conflict*, pp. 15–16 (1954).

[17] E. de Vattel, *op. cit.*, bk. II, ch. VI, sec. 73.

the injured party as the real author of the affront of which the citizen was perhaps only the instrument."[18]

This last aspect of the Vattelian position has remained unchallenged, for many modern writers as well as much state practice proceed upon that view. Reduced to its simplest terms, an implied complicity of the state in the injurious act of the individual is postulated on the basis of fault. To put the matter in different terms, when the state is negligent in preventing a harmful act, it becomes implicated in the act, thus giving rise to international responsibility. The contemporary implications of this theory may be most clearly seen in Professor Edwin M. Borchard's writing on the subject. He apparently considers the doctrine of implied governmental complicity as an exception to the rule of non-liability of the state for the wrongful acts of private persons. He says:

> A long line of cases has established certain qualifications upon the non-liability of the government for the wrongful acts of private individuals. These consist in certain manifestations of the actual or implied complicity of the government in the act, before or after it, either by directly ratifying or approving it, or by an implied, tacit or constructive approval in the negligent failure to prevent the injury, or to investigate the case, or to punish the individual, or to enable the victim to pursue his civil remedies against the offender...[19]

Indeed, Professor Borchard rejects every assumption that generally international law does not impose any liability on states for wrongful acts of private individuals. His theory of implied complicity clearly bridges the gap existing between the doctrine of non-liability and absolute liability of the state by carefully prescribing the conditions under which responsibility legally arises. This formula will be seen to crystallize in the now venerable principle that the failure of a government to use due diligence to prevent an injurious act of a private person against a foreign state constitutes an international delinquency.[20]

The ideas implicit in the above analysis have been stoutly followed by most modern writers on international law. The doctrine has been most emphatically endorsed by Professor Hans Kelsen, the contemporary master of international law. Sharply distinguishing between direct responsibility by which he means liability for acts which are imputable to the state, such as an illicit act of a governmental official, and indirect liability, which includes acts of private persons imputable to the state,[21] Professor Kelsen maintains that the latter type of lia-

[18] *Ibid.*, bk. II, ch. VI, sec. 74.
[19] E. M. Borchard, *op. cit.*, p. 217.
[20] C. G. Fenwick, *International Law*, p. 301 (3d ed., 1948).
[21] H. Kelsen, "Théorie du Droit International Public," *Hague Recueil*, Vol. 84, III, 1953, p. 90 (1955).

bility arises in situations where the state has clearly been negligent either in preventing the commission of the act or in punishing the guilty party after the offense has been committed.[22] It seems quite evident that, like the classical theories, Professor Kelsen regards the responsibility of the state for acts of individuals as being wholly dependent upon the element of fault. Apart from the difficulties already encountered with this theory, it may be highly pertinent to add that since only upon proving fault can state responsibility be predicated, in concrete situations there may conceivably be a no-man's-land should such fault be found nonexistent, thus leaving the wronged community without any means of redress under international law.[23] But totally unconcerned with these painful possibilities, the doctrine of international law in this area, as seen in the writings of other contemporary jurists, proceeds largely upon the same premise. Thus Professor Paul Guggenheim has reached similar results apparently through a different reasoning. His doctrine of responsibility can be summarized in three propositions. First, he believes that the state has the double duty to prevent and punish acts of individuals which constitute a violation of an international obligation. Second, the duty thus stated is for the violation of a corresponding obligation which is directly imputable to the individual. And, finally, these two preceding propositions are carefully qualified by his assertion that the responsibility of the state is not absolute, but is one dependent upon negligence. In an effort to illustrate this last proposition he differentiates between a general and an absolute obligation making the former the standard of responsibility. This is most clearly seen in his contention that the state has a general obligation to prevent boycotts, but not an absolute obligation to do so.[24] He is therefore clearly implying that only under certain conditions a duty of prevention becomes operative. This is nothing more than the doctrine of governmental complicity expressed in different terms. Similar statements, with diverse elaborations, could be offered from many other contemporary jurists.[25] It has perhaps al-

[22] *Ibid.*, p. 92. See also his *Principles of International Law*, pp. 119–122 (1952).

[23] Some writers would say, however, that the state still has the right of self-defense, but it will be seen later that this so-called right only brings about anarchy in international relations and contributes to divide rather than unite the states in the world community. Cf. J. L. Kunz, *op. cit.*, pp. 324, 332 (1960).

[24] P. Guggenheim, "Les Principes de Droit International Public," *Hague Recueil*, Vol. 80, I, 1952, p. 138 (1953).

[25] To the authors cited in footnote 2, *supra*, the following may be added: C. Eagleton, *International Government*, p. 89 (3d ed., 1957); A. Ross, *A Textbook of International Law*, pp. 254, 256–259 (1947); D. Antokoletz, *Tratado de Derecho Internacional Público*, Vol. 3, p. 25 (3d ed., 1938).

ready been sufficiently suggested that all these various theories reflect a lack of awareness concerning the values seeking recognition in the world community and, especially, the obligations of the state to contribute to the maintenance of international order. But even more emphatic illustrations of the contemporary attitude may be adduced from the case law of International Tribunals, for the doctrine of state complicity is equally well established in their jurisprudence. Thus, in the *Cotesworth & Powell Case* between the United States and Colombia regarding an alleged denial of justice by the Colombian courts, an arbitration tribunal said:

> One nation is not responsible to another for the acts of its individual citizens, except when it approves or ratifies them. It then becomes a public concern, and the injured party may consider the nation itself as the real author of the injury[26]

Most recently, the International Court of Justice gave expression to this doctrine in the most absolute terms in the *Corfu Channel Case* between Great Britain and Albania, involving the international responsibility of Albania for mines found within its territorial waters. Though this case deals with the responsibility of the state for the acts of its officials, the incorporation of the doctrine of no responsibility without fault is highly pertinent as applied to the matter under consideration. The Court said:

> It is clear that knowledge of the mine-laying cannot be imputed to the Albanian Government by reason merely of the fact that a minefield discovered in Albanian territorial waters caused the explosions of which the British warships were the victims... It cannot be concluded from the mere fact of the control exercised by a state over its territory and waters that that state necessarily knew, or ought to have known, of any unlawful act perpetrated therein, nor yet that it necessarily knew, or should have known, the authors. This fact, by itself and apart from other circumstances, neither involves prima facie responsibility nor shifts the burden of proof...[27]

It requires little effort to perceive that the foregoing holdings merely reaffirm the proposition that the international responsibility of a state for a person's act is inextricably linked to the requirement of negligence or fault. In its doctrinal significance, this principle represents a calculated attempt to maintain the traditional state-individual dichotomy which thus far has underlain much of international law. Starting with the assumption that international law is exclusively concerned with the state, it is logically concluded that the sphere of the state is separate

[26] Cited in B. Cheng, *General Principles of Law as Applied by International Courts and Tribunals*, p. 209 (1953).

[27] Corfu Channel Case, I.C.J. *Reports*, p. 18 (1949).

from that of the individual, and that certain activities in which the state can not engage, the individual can carry on with impunity.[28] This glaring paradox instructively illustrates the fallacy involved in attempting to treat the state independently of the individuals who compose it, for this notion is really partially responsible for the state's virtual freedom from liability for private hostile acts against foreign nations.

Despite the almost universal acceptance of the doctrine of implied state complicity, difficulties may still be anticipated in principle, for the doctrine has been subjected to a well documented attack. Starting with the theory that the state "is not liable for the acts of a private individual, who is not an 'authority' of the state," Professor James L. Brierly has advanced the controversial thesis that even in cases in which the state would appear to be liable for certain acts of private persons, such a responsibility is not really for the acts of the individuals as such, but only for the state's own delinquency.[29] Thus he says:

> Professor Borchard supports this statement of the law [implied state complicity] with ample references to authorities. It will be observed that these 'qualifications' of the non-liability of the state for the acts of individuals are not, in strict theory, exceptions to the general rule. Even in these cases the state is still not liable for the acts of an individual *as such*, but only for its own delinquency; but the theory of the law has been that wrongful failure either to prevent or to punish the individual's act justifies us in inferring the state's complicity in the act, and consequently in regarding the act as the act of the state.[30]

It can be readily seen, therefore, that while Professor Borchard believes that in cases of governmental complicity the state is actually responsible for the acts of private persons, Professor Brierly, on the other hand, forcibly maintains that even in such cases there is not such responsibility. In Professor Brierly's view the various forms of state responsibility are governed by a single legal principle, whether the responsibility concerned be for the act of a person acting for the state or that of a mere private individual. Consequently, such activities

[28] This is particularly true in respect to the law of neutrality. For elaboration, see J. Stone, *op. cit.*, pp. 383–384.

[29] J. L. Brierly, "The Theory of Implied State Complicity in International Claims," *Brit. Y.B. Int. L.*, 1928. Vol. 9, p. 42 (1928). This article was reprinted in J. L. Brierly, *The Basis of Obligation in International Law*, p. 152 (Selected and edited by Sir H. Lauterpacht and C. H. M. Waldock, 1958). References will be made to the latter.

[30] *Ibid.*, pp. 152–153. Italics are those of Professor Brierly. Professor Alf Ross appears to adhere to the same view, for he says in dealing with instances where the state is responsible for acts of individuals, "... the responsibility is then a responsibility for the state's own organs, not for the actions of private individuals." A. Ross, *op. cit.*, p. 254.

as the organization of hostile military expeditions, incursion of armed bands into foreign territory and the dissemination of hostile propaganda against foreign governments carried on by private individuals would be imputed to the state, thus giving rise to international liability only if the state itself becomes guilty of its own delinquency, namely, by its failure to exercise a duty of prevention when confronted with the knowledge of the activities in question. Indeed, the learned writer dismisses the possibility that unlawful activities of persons import activities of which the state is liable unless the state itself forfeits a supposed immunity by not having measured up to its duty of prevention or of punishing the offender.[31] In his view, the responsibility of the state is not for the specific unlawful act of the individual but rather for not having fulfilled an international obligation.

The narrow position which Professor Brierly has suggested is fatally impaired by four doubts. First, in thus divorcing the responsibility of the state from that of the individual it helps to perpetuate the formlessness of much of the traditional international law.[32] It should be observed, however, that this conclusion is quite consistent with Professor Brierly's position, for he regards the state as an "abstraction" and, thus, only responsible for its delinquency.[33] Secondly, the central difficulty it raises lies in that it considers the source of the activity rather than its character, thus clearly avoiding the effort to perceive that if the delinquency of the state is predicated on a negligence of its own, still it is the unlawful act of the individual which makes the international duty of the state practically operative.[34] Thirdly, it similarly avoids setting upon individuals a brand of international criminality, which is highly contrary to the sentiments of most of the peoples of the world. And, fourthly, by removing the possibility of imputing international criminality on individuals, it leaves the menaced state quite free to protect itself by whatever measures it sees fit, a conception which allows resort to measures contrary to international law.[35]

But to disagree with Professor Brierly's strictures is not necessarily to accept the adequacy of the doctrine of implied state complicity, for

[31] Cf. A. D. McNair, *op. cit.*, Vol. 2, pp. 288–289 (1956).

[32] See in this connection, H. Lauterpacht, *International Law and Human Rights*, pp. 40–45 (1950).

[33] J. L. Brierly, *op. cit.*, p. 152.

[34] Cf. C. Rousseau, *Droit International Public*, pp. 376–377 (1953).

[35] Thus, as will be seen, in punishing individuals for hostile acts the state is allowed to exercise jurisdiction extraterritorially on the basis of what is loosely called protection. See, Chapter IX, *infra*. In other respects, the state may resort to the use of force allegedly in the exercise of the right of self-defense, which is also restricted by the United Nations Charter. See, particularly, U.N. Charter, art. 2, sec. 4.

functionally and practically it may be quite deceptive. Its most significant weakness lies in the failure to perceive that a state in whose jurisdiction a harmful act is committed against a foreign nation has in reality violated an international obligation in the preservation of world order. This alone would seem to give rise to state responsibility. The basis of this responsibility clearly proceeds from the nature of the unlawful act and not at all from the source of the violation. This conception is reinforced by the unquestioned fact that the state has full control over its territorial domain and, predicated on this control, a presumption arises that whatever acts take place within its borders are carried out under its acquiescence, if not its outright approval and encouragement. It does not meet the problem to suggest that the government was not aware of the hostile acts in which private persons were engaged, for the realities of the present century would seem to indicate that since these hostile acts have international repercussions, their execution could not possibly be successfully concealed. In addition to these facts, it will subsequently be seen that certain specific acts of private persons are used by the states as concealed means of attack, thus opening up vast opportunities for novel kinds of aggression. Modern developments have therefore expanded the scope of state responsibility and made the requirement of fault too narrow to meet the changes in contemporary world politics. The necessity of a more critical approach to the doctrine of state responsibility for injurious acts of private persons becomes more urgent in the light of these changes. With these insights, the discussion may now turn to the doctrine of absolute or objective liability which may prove to do much towards regulating an otherwise unsatisfactory situation.

THE DOCTRINE OF ABSOLUTE OR STRICT LIABILITY

The Grotian theory of *culpa* as a standard of responsibility was early impaired by Samuel Pufendorf, whose theory seemed to be grounded strictly upon natural law conceptions.[36] He expressed his dissatisfaction with Grotius' theories in the following terms:

> Now of those ways by which the heads of states become exposed to war because of injuries done by their citizens, two come in for special consideration, namely, sufferance and reception. As for sufferance it must be held that he who

[36] For a discussion of Pufendorf's theories, see P. Avril in *Les Fondateurs du Droit International*, pp. 331–383 (1904).

knows a wrong is being done, and is able and obligated to prevent it, when that does not involve the probable danger of a greater evil, is held to have been guilty himself of the wrong. That is, what is required is a union of knowledge of the fact and of the power to prevent it, neither one of these alone being sufficient to implicate one on the crime of another. *Now it is presumed that the heads of a state know what is openly and frequently done by their subjects, and the power to prevent is always presumed, unless its lack be clearly established.*[37]

There is perhaps no more lucid statement of the doctrine of objective responsibility grounded upon the requirements of the world community than that which is found in the above passage. Completely departing from the Grotian tradition, Pufendorf postulated the conception of fault as the general rule by presuming its existence.[38] It is in this sense that Pufendorf was one of the first writers to establish that the responsibility of the state is not subjective but absolute, that it is ultimately based upon justice and the demands of humanity,[39] and that the prevention of harmful acts by individuals against other peoples is a moral obligation. That these propositions underlay his whole treatment of the matter cannot be reasonably doubted, for Pufendorf viewed his doctrine against the background of actions which give rise to the just punishment of a nation.[40] He made it remarkably clear that the responsibility thus postulated is stricter; that the state has certain obligations towards the world community, so that generally it becomes liable if in fact persons within its jurisdiction commit offenses against foreign state thereby prejudicing the cause of world peace. It will be seen throughout this book that this conception has not lost its validity for the contemporary world.

Building upon different foundations, but reaching substantially similar results, are Judge Dionisio Anzilotti's theories on the subject. Totally departing from the theory of responsibility based on fault, Judge Anzilotti postulates a conception of responsibility wholly based upon an objective violation of an international obligation.[41] To him the rule of fault represents an unwarranted and unfortunate application

[37] S. Pufendorf, *De Jure Naturae et Gentium Libri Octo*, bk. VIII, ch. VI, sec. 12 (Transl. by C. H. and W. A. Oldfather, 1934). Italics supplied.

[38] L. Podestá Costa, *op. cit.*, Vol. I, p. 441.

[39] At the beginning of book VI, Pufendorf says that "... it is one of the first principles of natural law that no one unjustly do another hurt or damage..." S. Pufendorf, *op. cit.*, bk. VIII, ch. VI, sec. 2.

[40] It should be mentioned that clearly his theory modifies that of Grotius, for it is prefaced by saying that "... a community, whether civil or of any other kind, is not responsible for the actions of individual members, except by some culpable act of commission or omission on its part..." Here he quotes Grotius. See S. Pufendorf, *op. cit.*, bk. VIII, ch. VI, sec. 12.

[41] For development, see A. Anzilotti, *Cours de Droit International*, Vol. I, pp. 496 *et seq.* (French transl. by G. Gidel, 1920).

to the international legal order of principles governing responsibility in the relations of private individuals.[42] Specifically, Judge Anzilotti demands a violation of international law with respect to a foreign nation, as for instance, a wrongful act against that nation regardless of whether or not fault is present. To him it is apparently sufficient that there has been a violation of the rights of another state for international responsibility to ensue.[43] On this view, when individuals engage in hostile acts against foreign states, the state in whose jurisdiction the act takes place commits an international delinquency regardless of whether it ratifies or approves them directly or tacitly by the negligent failure to prevent them. It can thus be seen that such responsibility is not predicated on any theory of government complicity in the individual's act. It is simply based upon the theory that a violation of an international obligation has taken place for which the state cannot escape responsibility.[44] The international responsibility thus postulated clearly arises from the obligation which the states have undertaken to protect each other's independence and well-being as a guarantee of good international relations.[45]

The foregoing exposition unmistakably reveals that underlying Judge Anzilotti's theories runs the well established principle that, though international law guarantees respect for territorial sovereignty, this respect is predicated upon the assumption that such sovereignty will not be used to harbor a danger to the security of neighboring states.[46] This principle is so generally accepted that the toleration of activities harmful to a foreign nation is regarded as an abuse of right which under customary international law opens the way to compulsive measures of defense otherwise considered as unlawful.[47] Though the use of force to redress wrongs is forbidden under present conventional law,[48] this feature of the traditional law is mentioned only to emphasize the responsibility incurred by a state for the illegal use of its sovereignty.

If the foregoing observations be correct, it will then follow that the state may be liable for purely private acts of individuals in situations not exclusively dependent upon the element of fault. Certainly, the

[42] A. Ross, *op. cit.*, p. 256.
[43] H. W. Briggs, *op. cit.*, p. 618.
[44] Cf. D. Anzilotti, *op. cit.*, Vol. I, pp. 466, 467.
[45] L. Podestá Costa, *op. cit.*, Vol. I, p. 451.
[46] H. Lauterpacht, "Revolutionary Activities by Private Persons Against Foreign States," *Am. J. Int. Law*, Vol. 22, pp. 105, 126 (1928).
[47] D. W. Bowett, *Self-Defence in International Law*, pp. 39–40 (1958).
[48] See particularly U.N. Charter, art. 2, sec. 4.

responsibility of the state should not be made to depend upon subjective conceptions of fault, but rather upon the illicit nature of the act. If it be admitted that certain acts of private persons are illicit in that they harm foreign nations, then whether or not fault exists as regards the state would seem to be of no particular consequence. The point that must be stressed is that a private person has violated an international obligation and in addition to the criminal responsibility which is imputable to the individual, the state is similarly responsible, precisely because the illicit act took place within its jurisdiction.[49] This position has been admirably summarized by Professor Charles C. Hyde as follows:

> ...the society of nations imposes upon each of its members, with respect to places under its control, certain duties to prevent the occurrence of some acts therein that are themselves necessarily defiant of the principles of international law, or which may be productive of a situation at variance with what these principles appear to demand...[50]

This broader basis upon which state responsibility is predicated is admittedly innovatory rather than declaratory of existing law. But even granting such objections, it should be fairly clear that underlying the theory of objective or strict liability is the possibility of tightening up the obligations of the states in respect to acts of private persons which vitally engage the peace and security of mankind.[51] It is precisely in this respect that the doctrine of objective liability undertakes a successful attack upon the weaknesses of the existing law of international responsibility by virtually closing the various avenues by which states can frustrate attempts to impose responsibility for hostile acts of private persons.[52] These observations reveal a clear picture of what international law should be if the values of the world community are to be adequately safeguarded. And when the argument is thus reduced to a requirement of international order, the conclusion of law that states are responsible for the private acts of individuals inescapably emerges. Disregard of this prescription seriously prejudices international peace and security.

It may therefore be concluded that the responsibility of the states for hostile acts of private persons is a requirement of the world com-

[49] Cf. H. Kelsen, "Théories du Droit International," *Hague Recueil*, Vol. 84, III, 1953, p. 92 (1955).

[50] C. C. Hyde, *op. cit.*, Vol. I, p. 36. See also his remarks in p. 723.

[51] H. Lauterpacht, *International Law and Human Rights*, pp. 40–42 (1950).

[52] Cf. V. F. García-Amador, "State Responsibility in the Light of New Trends in International Law," *Am. J. Int. Law*, Vol. 49, p. 339 (1955).

munity deeply concerned with peace and security in international relations. Peace and security may become illusory should the states be able to escape responsibility for private acts by merely pleading lack of knowledge of these acts or impossibility of fulfilling the duty of prevention.[53] These defenses lose all their cogency and vitality when remembering that the present day government control over the movement and actions of persons is so pervasive and complete that any harmful action of a person against a foreign state is almost certain to be carried out under the moral approval and acquiescence of the state.[54] These are not fanciful assumptions but contemporary realities, and they certainly lend powerful support to the theory of absolute responsibility here suggested.[55]

AGGRESSION AND PRIVATE HOSTILE ACTS OF INDIVIDUALS

Assuming the correctness of the preceding observations, international law confronts the state with three levels of obligations by which its international responsibility is to be discharged. The first is the duty to enact measures of municipal law punishing offenders for unlawful acts against foreign states.[56] Measures of this kind are in the first instance measures of municipal law, but they must carefully operate within the authority granted by international law to each

[53] Thus, Professor C. C. Hyde said: "The underlying principle would seem to be that what a state claims the right exclusively to control, such as its own territory, it must possess the power and accept the obligation to endeavor so to control as to prevent occurrences therein from becoming by any process the immediate cause of such injury to a foreign state as the latter, in consequence of the propriety of its own conduct, should not be subjected to at the hands of a neighbor." C. C. Hyde, *op. cit.*, Vol. I, p. 723.

[54] Cf. A. Rougier, *Les Guerres Civiles et le Droit des Gens*, p. 418 (1903). It should be remembered that these considerations gave Pufendorf ample reason to presume the existance of fault. See S. Pufendorf, *op. cit.*, bk. VIII, ch. VI, sec. 12.

[55] It is admitted, though, that the *culpa* rule does not preclude the possibility that international law in certain cases recognize absolute responsibility, as for instance, the case of Article 3 of the Hague Convention IV of 1907 regarding Law and Customs of War on Land which says: "A belligerent party... shall be responsible for all acts committed by persons forming part of its armed forces." For text of the Convention, see W. W. Bishop, Jr., *International Law: Cases and Materials*, p. 604 (1953). For comments, see A. Ross, *op. cit.*, p. 258.

[56] In United States v. Arjona, 120 U.S. 479 (1887), involving the counterfeiting within the United States of currency issued by the Colombian Government, the Supreme Court said: "The law of nations requires every national government to use 'due diligence' to prevent a wrong being done within its own dominion to another nation with which it is at peace, or to the people thereof; and because of this the obligation of one nation to punish those who, within its own jurisdiction, counterfeit the money of another nation has long been recognized." P. 497.

state.[57] It is precisely within this common ground of international and municipal law that the international responsibility of the state can most accurately be viewed. And it is also in this sense that the legal order of the state is a part of the international legal order. Second, a most stringent duty requires the state to prevent, by the use of force if necessary, the activities being carried on by anyone or by any group within its jurisdiction.[58] Activities subject to this duty will subsequently be seen to include, partially, though not exclusively, the organization of hostile military expeditions, the departure of volunteers and the incursion of armed bands into foreign territory. Third, assuming its inability to fulfill this second duty, international law confronts the state with the alternative either to resort to a world or a regional authority capable of repressing these acts or to suffer enforcement actions as an aggressor.[59] The basic postulate underlying this third level of obligation is simple enough, namely, that inability to act similarly engages the peace and security of mankind and should not therefore be accompanied by inactivity or indifference on the part of the state to invoke organized community action. It is therefore submitted that even in terms of the traditional law, if a state has obviously used all the means at its disposal to prevent a hostile act of a person against a foreign nation but is physically unable to suppress it, it certainly has not discharged its international duty. This view of the matter sharply draws attention to the possibility that a state thus acting is guilty of an act of aggression.[60] This question is learnedly discussed by Professor Quincy Wright, who in describing acts of ag-

[57] This assertion immediately brings into play the controversy as to whether international law gives the states competence. Thus, Judge Dionisio Anzilotti says that international law presupposes the state and, therefore, cannot be superior to it. See D. Anzilotti, *op. cit.*, Vol. I, p. 51. Also C. De Visscher, *Theory and Reality in Public International Law*, p. 103 (Transl. by P. E. Corbett, 1957). Professor Georges Scelle, on the other hand, believes that the competence of the state proceeds from a legal system superior to it. See, G. Scelle, *Précis de Droit des Gens: Principes et Systématique*, Vol. I, p. 80 (1932). See also to the same effect, P. Fiore, *International Law Codified*, p. 157 (Transl. by E. M. Borchard, 1918).

[58] Cf. H. Kelsen, *Principles of International Law*, p. 126 (1952).

[59] This is not only a responsibility of the state which is unable to suppress the acts, but also of any other state, since it is a matter which affects world peace. This can be done under Article 35 of the United Nations Charter. Also certain regional arrangements provide for a similar course of action. Thus, Articles 6 and 7 of the Inter-American Treaty of Reciprocal Assistance are pertinent in this regard. For text, see *Am. J. Int. L. Supp.*, Vol. 43, p. 53 (1949).

[60] We are not here concerned with the insoluble problem of defining aggression, but it is understood for our purposes that any use of force which results in a violation of the territorial integrity of a state thus endangering world peace is an act of aggression. For the difficulties in defining aggression, see J. Stone, *Aggression and World Order: A Critique of United Nations Theories of Aggression* (1958).

gression says that "... failure of a government to prevent armed bands or insurgents from organizing within its territory to engage in hostilities across a frontier, will make it responsible for aggression, if such hostilities actually occur."[61] As the learned writer nowhere says what he means by "failure to prevent," it is not at all unreasonable to suppose that it may take place in practice either by a deliberate omission on the part of the state to act or by its physical inability to do so. In the presence of the latter possibility, no one expects the authority of the world community to remain passive until such a time when and if the state is able to discharge its international responsibility. Conversely, Professor Josef L. Kunz, in speaking of the obligations of a neutral state, has advanced the thesis that "A neutral state which has used all the means at its disposal to prevent a violation of its neutrality but is *unable* to prevent it, has fulfilled its international duty, is not guilty of any violation of international law; hence, no sanctions, no military reprisals against this state are justified."[62] This statement has some relevance for the matter under consideration, for if in respect to harmful acts of private persons the international responsibility of the state is confined to using all the means at its disposal to prevent them, as the *Alabama Claims Arbitration*[63] clearly established, in Professor Kunz's view this responsibility is adequately discharged by simply doing so, completely irrespective of the adequacy of the measures taken. But Professor Kunz is apparently aware of some difficulty in this area, for he resorts to the United States Instructions in respect to the Law of Naval Warfare to the effect that:

> When the means at its disposal are clearly inadequate to fulfill its neutral obligations, it is recognized that a belligerent is not forbidden from taking, as an extreme measure, acts of hostility in neutral jurisdiction against an enemy making improper use of that jurisdiction.[64]

For the right embedded in this passage, the celebrated *Caroline Affair*[65] can be said to be indisputable authority. This case involved the incursion of British forces into American territory to suppress the organization of factions in the United States to help insurgents against

[61] Q. Wright, "The Prevention of Aggression," *Am. J. Int. L.*, Vol. 50, pp. 514, 527 (1956).

[62] J. L. Kunz, "Sanctions in International Law," *Am. J. Int. L.*, Vol. 54, pp. 324, 331–332 (1960). Italics are the author's.

[63] United States v. Great Britain (1871). For the record of this arbitration see J. B. Moore, *A Digest of International Law*, Vol. 7, pp. 1059–1067 (1906). This case is fully discussed in Chapter IV, *infra*.

[64] J. L. Kunz, *op. cit.*, p. 332.

[65] For the record of this case, see J. B. Moore, *op. cit.*, Vol. 2, pp. 409–414 (1906).

the British rule in Canada. As this case will be discussed in the chapter dealing with armed bands, for the present it is enough to say that the case stands for the right of self-defense of a state against hostile actions proceeding from another's jurisdiction. According to this view, the failure of a government to prevent harmful acts of private persons against foreign states can legally be met by the exercise of the right of self-defense on the part of the menaced community, and this right extends to the invasion of the territory in which the hostile act originated. It will subsequently be seen that the exercise of this right in the manner indicated is not a sanction of the world community and is in any event prohibited by obligations undertaken under the United Nations Charter.[66]

These observations are of critical importance in relation to proposals for a definition of aggresion. Without in any way pretending to solve a problem which has engaged the labor of outstanding minds,[67] it can nevertheless be observed that a general conviction appears to exist strongly suggesting that at least certain private acts of individuals, as for instance, the organization of armed bands and the undertaking of revolutionary activities, if carried out with impunity, make the state in whose territory these acts were committed guilty of an aggression.[68] Indeed, a number of international instruments afford a fruitful reflection in this regard. Thus, the Draft definition of aggression, drawn up in 1933 by the Committee on Security Questions of the League of Nations, included as an act of aggression "provision of support to armed bands formed in its territory which have invaded the territory of another state, or refusal, notwithstanding the request of the invaded state, to take in its own territory all the measures in its power to deprive those bands of all assistance or protection."[69] The substance of this provision was subsequently incorporated in the Convention Defining Aggression concluded between the Soviet Union and her neighbors in London on July 3, 1933.[70] Similarly, the many proposals defining aggression presented in 1956 to the United Nations General Assembly's Special Committee on the Definition of Aggression included

[66] Q. Wright, "United Nations Intervention in the Lebanon," *Am. J. Int. L.*, Vol. 53, pp. 112, 115 (1959).

[67] The question of a definition of aggression has occupied the minds of great jurists for over a half-century. For the difficulties involved, see C. Eagleton, "The Attempts to Define Aggression," *International Conciliation*, No. 264, p. 579 (1930).

[68] L. B. Sohn, "The Definition of Aggression," *Virginia L. R.*, Vol. 45, p. 677 (1959).

[69] For text, see J. Stone, *Aggression and World Order: A Critique of United Nations Theories of Aggression*, p. 35 (1958).

[70] Convention Defining Aggression, London, July 3, 1933, Article II, paragraph 5. For text, see *Am. J. Int. L. Supp.*, Vol. 27, p. 193 (1933).

the support of armed bands, and significantly added to the catalogue of aggressive acts, the encouragement of subversive activities as well as the publication of hostile propaganda against another state.[71] In like manner, the International Law Commission of the United Nations has considered draft definitions of aggression from several of its members in which support of armed bands and the promotion of civil strife in another state play a prominent role.[72] Also the Draft Declaration on Rights and Duties of States, prepared by the International Law Commission, provides in Article 4 that "Every state has the duty to refrain from fomenting civil strife in the territory of another state, and to prevent the organization within its territory of activities calculated to foment such civil strife."[73] It may be pertinent to add that the Draft Code of Offenses against the Peace and Security of Mankind, also prepared by the International Law Commission, gives a catalogue of acts, in which acts of private persons against foreign states are included, and which are considered as offenses against the peace and security of mankind.[74] Other illustrations could be given showing the consistent tendency to regard the failure to prevent the commission of hostile acts by private individuals as an act of aggression.[75] But the few international instruments here mentioned are perhaps enough to perceive the pattern running through international practice. In the face of all this, it must therefore be clear that the unwillingness or inability of a state to prevent private persons from committing offenses against another state is an international delinquency for which the former is responsible. Certainly, present international consensus would seem to be in agreement with this conclusion.

Additionally to the above comments, it is to be observed that the responsibility of the state for acts of private persons, when such has existed, has traditionally been regarded as a civil responsibility, which involves the double notion of a violation or non-observance of an international obligation and the corresponding duty of the state to

[71] For these proposals, see J. Stone, *Aggression and World Order: A Critique of United Nations Theories of Aggression*, pp. 201–202 (1958).

[72] For the various proposals, see *U.N. General Assembly, Official Records, Sixth Session, Supplement No. 9* (A/1858), p. 12 (1951).

[73] For text, see *Am. J. Int. L. Supp.*, Vol. 44, p. 16 (1950).

[74] See, in particular, Article II, sections (4), (5), and (6). For text, see Report of the International Law Commission, Covering the Work of Its Third Session, 16 May – 27 July, 1951, *U.N. General Assembly, Official Records, Sixth Session, Supplement, No. 9* (A/1858), p. 12 (1951).

[75] These will be discussed in the various chapters dealing with specific hostile acts of private individuals.

make reparation.[76] Though because of the absence of international tribunals endowed with proper jurisdictional requirements, it is at this stage hard to apply criminal responsibility to the state,[77] there are nevertheless certain situations where the criminal responsibility of the state is clearly established. Thus, the crime of genocide and other violations of human rights are not only illegal but also involve the criminal responsibility of the state.[78] Similarly, wars of aggression are regarded as an international crime and, thus, any act falling within this conception would surely make the state criminally liable.[79] Sanctions against this criminal conduct were provided for by orthodox international law. Measures of this kind were found in the permissible resort to war and reprisals in an attempt to rectify viot lations of international law by a state, and it is specially significan- that these measures went beyond the mere compensation for injuries received.[80] But these were sanctions applied by individual states in an era characterized by decentralization of the international community. With the centralization of this legal community by the creation of international organizations, special organs have been established for the enforcement of the law. Thus, the Covenant of the League of Nations provided in Article 16 for sanctions of a penal nature against a state which resorted to war in violation of the Covenant. It will be recalled that these measures ranged from the severance of all trade and financial relations to the use of military, naval or air force against the recalcitrant state. The United Nations Charter has similarly provided for sanctions, also penal in complexion, against a state threatening world peace or committing an act of aggression. These sanctions are specifically listed in Chapter VII of the Charter, and they range from the interruption of economic and diplomatic relations to the use of force against a delinquent state, as instructively illustrated by the Korean situation in 1950. Since certain offenses of private persons against foreign states are regarded as acts of aggression, there is no conceivable reason why the victim of such offenses could not resort to the United Nations in an effort to initiate organized community action.

[76] V. F. García-Amador, *op. cit.*, p. 345.

[77] In this connection, the Draft Statute for an International Criminal Court proposed by the Committee on Criminal Jurisdiction in 1951 rejected the conception of responsibility of states. For text of the Draft Statute, see *Report of the Committee on International Criminal Jurisdiction, U.N. General Assembly, Official Records, Seventh Session, Supplement No. 11, Annex I* (A/2136), pp. 21–25 (1952).

[78] L. Oppenheim, *op. cit.*, Vol. I, p. 355.

[79] In this category are of course included private acts against foreign states, as it has been seen that they may constitute aggression.

[80] L. Oppenheim, *op. cit.*, Vol. I, p. 356.

That this action is justified under Chapter VII of the Charter can scarcely be denied, for this Chapter clearly deals with action in respect to threats to the peace, breaches of the peace and acts of aggression. Support for these conclusions may be found in the conviction that since private acts of individuals have become a critical factor in the preservation of mankind's security and since nations have been known to avail themselves of these activities to promote their international objectives, the traditional principle of state criminal immunity retreats before the overriding demands of world peace.

CONCLUSION

The foregoing examination of the various kinds of responsibility of the state for hostile acts of private persons against foreign governments would seem to support the inescapable conclusion that the state ought to be made liable for private actions which engage the peace and security of mankind. This conclusion is reached irrespective of the doctrine of implied governmental complicity. The necessity for adequate protection of foreign nations and interest in the security of international relations would seem to require that states be internationally liable if the values of world peace and order are to be attained. These propositions reflect a broader principle of international law whereby it is just and necessary that states assume such responsibility, for the commission of these acts has taken place within their territory, which international law clearly protects against external violation. Thus, the protection of international law cannot be used to allow citizens to violate the rights of other nations in their territorial integrity, political independence and internal peace. Unless this alternative is erected into a legal postulate, the effectiveness of the rule of law in the world community will surely fall far behind reasonable expectations and might finally go down in history as a victim of the arbitrariness and political expediency of governments.

CHAPTER III

THE EMERGING CONCEPT OF INDIVIDUAL LIABILITY

A radical postwar development clearly marked the trend toward making individuals criminally responsible for international crimes. Included within the latter concept are offenses committed against foreign states. But to postulate this kind of international responsibility is really to pose two separate and yet intimately connected concepts. One is the criminal responsibility of the individuals who act as agents of the state; and the other concerns the criminal responsibility of private persons. It has been seen in the preceding chapter that international law has been almost exclusively concerned with the international responsibility of the state. The present trend of the law, however, poses the preliminary problem of adequately imposing criminal liability upon individuals under international law. Although it may still be too early to assert that as a general proposition of international law individuals are criminally liable for hostile acts directed against foreign states, there is respectable authority that claims precisely that.[1] These preliminary assertions may clearly show the difficulties attending any discussion of the international responsibility of individuals involving their own private actions. This point is indeed fundamental inasmuch as the responsibility here involved is based on different considerations.

BACKGROUND

The first concrete attempt to impose criminal liability upon individuals for violations of international law is historically traceable to Articles 227 and 228 of the Treaty of Versailles which provided, *inter alia,* for the prosecution of Kaiser Wilhelm II and other German leaders "for supreme offenses against international morality and the sanctity of treaties."[2] The obvious purpose of this provision was to make individuals bear the responsibility for an international confla-

[1] Cf. P. C. Jessup, *A Modern Law of Nations,* chap. 5 (1947).
[2] For text, see *Am. J. Int. L. Supp.,* Vol. 13, p. 151 (1919).

gration of their own making. It is a matter of recorded history, however, that this attempt ended in complete frustration.[3] Nevertheless, insofar as violations of international law had taken place, each injured belligerent was left free to deal with the offenders through its own tribunals and to impose punishment accordingly.[4] But this manner of dealing with offending individuals has no consequence whatever for the international criminal liability of individuals.

The problem engaged again the attention of governments and jurists during and after the Second World War.[5] The unparalleled murdering of the innocent population in the Nazi-occupied countries moved the conscience of mankind to demand responsibility from those responsible for such unprecedented atrocity. It is in this connection that the question of imposing criminal liability upon individuals emerged in full force. To this end, under an agreement of August 8, 1945,[6] the United States, the United Kingdom, France and the Soviet Union established an International Military Tribunal with jurisdiction to try the following crimes: (a) crimes against peace, consisting in "planning, preparation, initiation or waging a war of aggression, or a war in violation of international treaties, agreements or assurances, or participation in a common plan or conspiracy for the accomplishment of any of the foregoing"; (b) war crimes, consisting in "violations of the laws or customs of war [including but not limited to] murder, ill-treatment or deportation to slave labor or for any other purpose of civilian population of or in occupied territory, murder or ill-treatment of prisoners of war or persons on the seas, killing of hostages, plunder of public or private property, wanton destruction of cities, towns or villages, or devastation not justified by military necessity"; and (c) crimes against humanity, consisting in "murder, extermination, enslavement, deportation, and other inhumane acts committed against any civilian population, before or during the war; or persecution on political, racial or religious grounds in execution of or in connection with any crime within the jurisdiction of the Tribunal, whether or not in violation of

[3] It is generally known that when the demand for the extradition of the Kaiser was made to the Dutch Government, the latter refused it on the ground that "age-long tradition... has made this country always a ground of refuge for the vanquished in international conflicts." For comments, see J. W. Garner, "Punishment of Offenders Against the Laws and Customs of War." *Am. J. Int. L.*, Vol. 14, p. 70 (1920); Q. Wright, "The Legal Liability of the Kaiser," *Am. Pol. Sc. Rev.*, Vol. 13, p. 121 (1919).

[4] For the inadequacy of this procedure, see S. Glueck, "The Nürnberg Trial and Aggressive War," *Harvard L. R.*, Vol. 59, p. 396 (1945–1946).

[5] See Dept. of State, *Trial of War Criminals* (1945).

[6] For text, see *Trial of the Major War Criminals Before the International Military Tribunal*, Vol. I, pp. X, XI (1946–1947).

the domestic law of the country where perpetrated."[7] Though the recital of this provision clearly shows that the responsibility involved was that of the authorities of the state, the Nürnberg Charter, nevertheless, constitutes a useful precedent to get over the legal difficulties which up to that time had successfully blocked any attempt to impose responsibility upon individuals.[8] Insofar as criminal responsibility was attached to certain Nazi leaders at Nürnberg, international law was eminently successful in punishing individuals for the violations of its tenets. The Tribunal left no room for doubt when it said that "international law imposes duties and liabilities upon individuals as well as upon states..."[9] In thus clearing the way for the imposition of liability upon individuals, the Nürnberg judgment is a significant landmark in the history of the law of nations, and since this judgment may be a precedent for future legal action, it may confidently be asserted that international law imposes criminal liability upon individuals who plunge mankind into the scourge of war.

In recognition of the foregoing observations, and proceeding on the basis of the Nürnberg judgment that "Crimes against international law are committed by men, not by abstract entities, and only by punishing individuals who commit such crimes can the provisions of international law be enforced,"[10] the United Nations General Assembly in 1947 requested the International Law Commission (a) to formulate the principles of international law recognized in the Charter and in the judgment of the Nürnberg Tribunal, and (b) to prepare a Draft Code of Offenses Against the Peace and Security of Mankind, indicating clearly the place to be accorded to the above principles.[11] After laborious deliberations, the Commission adopted a Draft Code of Offenses against the Peace and Security of Mankind in its Third Session in 1951.[12] The main innovation of this Draft Code consists precisely in imputing criminal responsibility to individuals for acts which previously only engaged the responsibility of the state. After providing that

[7] Charter of the International Military Tribunal, Article 6, paragraphs (a), (b) and (c). For text, see note 6, *supra*.

[8] For these difficulties, see P. M. Carjeu, "Quelques Aspects du Nouveau Project de Statut des Nations Unies pour une Jurisdiction Criminelle Internationale," *Rev. Gén. de Droit Int. Public*, Vol. 50, pp. 401, 405 (France, 1956).

[9] See *Trial of the Major War Criminals Before the International Military Tribunal*, Vol. 22, pp. 465–466 (1948).

[10] *Ibid.*

[11] Resolution 177 (II), November 21, 1947.

[12] For text, see Report of the International Law Commission Covering the Work of its Third Session, 16 May – 27 July, 1951. *U.N. General Assembly, Official Records, Sixth Session, Supplement No. 9* (A/1858), pp. 10–14 (1951).

"Offenses against the peace and security of mankind, as defined in this Code, are crimes under international law, for which the responsible individuals shall be punishable,"[13] the Draft Code proceeds to enumerate the acts which fall into this forbidden category. From the standpoint of the individual, the responsibility here envisaged is of two kinds: one involves the responsibility of the authorities of the state, that is, of the individuals who act for the state, while the other engages the responsibility of private individuals participating in the unlawful acts. But, broadly, the Draft Code imputes criminal liability upon state authorities and private individuals for substantially similar acts.[14] It may perhaps be profitable to discuss separately these two types of responsibility under the Code.

RESPONSIBILITY OF THE AUTHORITIES OF THE STATE

In regard to the criminal responsibility of the authorities of the state, the Code follows closely on precedents supplied by the Nürnberg Charter and Judgment. In fact, in terms of its future possibilities, the Code represents an attempt to overcome the difficulties raised with respect to the retroactivity charge of the Nürnberg Charter.[15] Should the Code gain acceptance by governments, this stigma of the Nürnberg proceedings may be partially eliminated for future trials, for it carefully enumerates the offenses which will primarily engage the criminal responsibility of the authorities of the state. Included in this list are such offenses as acts of aggression,[16] any threat to resort to an act of aggression, preparation for the employment of armed forces against another state, fomenting civil strife and encouragement of terrorist activities against another state, destruction in whole or in part of a national, ethnical, racial, or religious group, and several other offenses. The comments attached to every one of these offenses specifically say that the offense thus defined can only be committed by the authorities of the state, though the criminal responsibility of private persons is

[13] This is Article 1 of the Draft Code.

[14] Judge Hersch Lauterpacht argued in favor of this combination of state and individual responsibility in 1950. See H. Lauterpacht, *International Law and Human Rights*, p. 41 (1950).

[15] J. Stone, *Legal Controls of International Conflict*. p. 370 (1954).

[16] Article 2, paragraph (1) defines an act of aggression as "the employment by the authorities of a state of armed force against another state for any purpose other than national or collective self-defense or in pursuance of a decision or recommendation by a competent organ of the United Nations."

also envisaged in a manner which will subsequently be discussed. It is interesting to observe that although these offenses primarily involve the criminal responsibility of the authorities of the state, such a responsibility is also postulated in respect to what might be regarded as private acts of individuals, such as, for instance, the incursion of armed bands into foreign territory.[17] In respect to this, the Code makes a criminal offense "The incursion into the territory of a state from the territory of another state by armed bands acting for a political purpose." And the comment following this provision clearly says that "The offense defined in this paragraph can be committed only by the members of the armed bands, and they are individually responsible. A criminal responsibility of the authorities of the state under international law may, however, arise under the provisions of paragraph (12) of the present article."[18] The Draft Code provides in Article 2, paragraph (12) that the following shall also constitute punishable offenses:

(i) Conspiracy to commit any of the offenses defined in the preceding paragraph of this article; or
(ii) Direct incitement to commit any of the offenses defined in the preceeding paragraphs of this article; or
(iii) Attempts to commit any of the offenses defined in the preceding paragraphs of this article; or
(iv) Complicity in the commission of any of the offenses defined in the preceding paragraphs of this article.

Again, the comment to this provision indicates that the notion of "conspiracy" was well known in the Charter of the Nürnberg Tribunal,[19] while the notions of "incitement," "attempt," and "complicity" are found in Article 3 of the Convention for the Prevention and Punishment of the Crime of Genocide adopted by the United Nations General Assembly on December 9, 1948,[20] and ratified by a substantial number of states.

The principle contained in Article 2 (12) is of considerable scope and importance, for its very inclusion is open to the view that the draftsmen of the Code accepted the legal possibility of imputing criminal responsibility to the authorities of the state for offenses of private individuals in situations not exclusively involving the traditional notion of implied governmental complicity. This broader basis upon which the criminal

[17] Article 2(4) of the Code. For modification of this provision, see note 37, *infra*.
[18] Report of the International Law Commission, *op. cit.*, p. 12.
[19] Charter of the International Military Tribunal, Article 6, paragraph (a). For text, see *Trials of War Criminals Before the Nürnberg Military Tribunal*, Vol. I, pp. X, XI (1946–1947).
[20] Article 3. For text, see *Am. J. Int. L. Supp.*, Vol. 45, p. 7 (1951).

responsibility of the state's authorities is predicated is admittedly innovatory rather than declaratory of existing law.[21] But even conceding such objections, it should be clear that underlying this innovation is the necessity of tightening up the obligations of the states in respect to unlawful individual acts vitally engaging the peace and security of mankind.[22]

It is of importance to realize that though the Nürnberg Trial seemed to have linked the criminal responsibility of individuals with the delinquent character of the activity engaged in by the state itself,[23] the Draft Code, on the other hand, clearly proceeds on a differentiation of state and individual responsibility. This would seem to be so for two reasons. First, though perhaps difficult to mark in practice, the Code foresees the possibility that the authorities of the state may become criminally responsible at a different stage at which state responsibility ensues.[24] In fact, the legal certainty arises that in respect to certain individuals criminal liability may be entirely absent. These assertions are instructively illustrated by the comment following Article 2, paragraph (12) of the Code, which says:

> In including 'complicity in the commission of any of the offenses defined in the preceding paragraphs' among the acts which are offenses against the peace and security of mankind, it is not intended to stipulate that all those contributing, in the normal exercise of their duties, to the perpetration of offenses against the peace and security of mankind could, on that ground alone, be considered as accomplices in such crimes. There can be no question of punishing as accomplices in such an offense all the members of the armed forces of a state or the workers in war industries.[25]

It is to be further noted that the criminal responsibility of the authorities of the state will not arise at all if it can be shown that the individual charged with state functions did not have a moral choice in fact opened to him.[26] It is therefore clear that a member of the government committing any of the offenses enumerated in the Code will only be responsible if in the prevailing circumstances it was quite possible

[21] It is on this and other grounds that the Draft Code has been criticized. See C. G. Fenwick, "Draft Code of Offenses Against the Peace and Security of Mankind," *Am. J. Int. L.*, Vol. 46, pp. 98–100 (1952); also P. B. Potter, "Offenses Against the Peace and Security of Mankind," *Ibid.*, p. 101.

[22] J. Paoli, "Contribution à l'étude des Crimes de Guerre et des Crimes Contre L'Humanité en Droit Penal International," *Rev. Gén. de Droit Int. Public*, Vol. 39, pp. 129–165 (France, 1944–1945).

[23] See on this, D. W. Bowett, *Self-Defense in International Law*, pp. 266, 267 (1958).

[24] Cf. Q. Wright, "The Prevention of Aggression," *Am. J. Int. L.*, Vol. 50, pp. 514–522 (1956).

[25] Report of the International Law Commission, *op. cit.*, p. 13.

[26] See Article 4 of the Code which is identical with Article 8 of the Charter of the Nürnberg Tribunal. See Report of the International Law Commission, *op. cit.*, p. 13.

for him to act contrary to superior orders.[27] In the absence of this showing, there can possibly be no individual obligation, though it is fairly clear that the criminal liability of the state still remains.

And, secondly, while, as it was seen, the criminal responsibility of the state is made effective by sanctions provided for by the Charter of the United Nations,[28] as regards the individual the penalty for any of the offenses defined in the Code is to be determined by the tribunal exercising jurisdiction over the accused.[29] In fact, the Code envisages international criminal jurisdiction over individuals, but pending its establishment, measures may be adopted for the application of the Code by national courts.[30] It is highly relevant to note that according to the Draft Statute for an International Criminal Court, drafted by the United Nations Committee on International Criminal Jurisdiction in 1951, in the trial of persons accused of crimes against international law, the Court is to apply international criminal law and, when appropriate, national law.[31] This would seem to suggest that the trial of persons is to take effect without any reference to principles of state responsibility.[32] The combined operation of these principles would seem to establish beyond any reasonable doubt that a criminal individual liability may exist without any degree of connection with state responsibility.[33]

CRIMINAL RESPONSIBILITY OF PRIVATE PERSONS

The most significant innovation of the Draft Code lies in the imposition of criminal responsibility upon private persons, who are not acting as authorities of the state, for the commission of any of the offenses listed therein. In so doing, the Draft Code goes beyond the Nürnberg precedent, for the latter was exclusively concerned with the individual responsibility of those acting for the state. The Code thus envisages criminal responsibility of private persons side by side with

[27] This is brought out in the Comment on Article 4. See Report of the International Law Commission, *op. cit.*, pp. 13–14.

[28] U.N. Charter, Chapter VII.

[29] Article 5 of the Draft Code.

[30] Report of the International Law Commission, *op. cit.*, p. 11.

[31] Article 2 of the Draft Statute for an International Criminal Court. For text, see *Am. J. Int. L. Supp.*, Vol. 46, p. 1 (1952).

[32] In fact, it has been said that the International Law Commission significantly erred "when it resolved to deal with the criminal responsibility of the individual only, and not with that of the state." See D. H. N. Johnson, "The Draft Code of Offenses Against the Peace and Security of Mankind," *Int. & Comp. L.Q.*, Vol. 4, pp. 445, 454 (1955).

[33] Cf. D. W. Bowett, *op. cit.*, p. 268.

the criminal responsibility of the authorities of the state. The Code seems to rest upon the firm conviction that certain actions of private persons have international repercussions and they lend themselves to the furtherance of aggressive designs without openly engaging the responsibility of the state. Looking comprehensively at its provisions, it may be said that the criminal responsibility of private persons may arise under three possible situations. First, there are some offenses which give rise to a simultaneous responsibility on the part of the authorities of the state and of private individuals. These offenses include genocide,[34] inhuman acts against any civilian population which in the Nürnberg Charter were known as "crimes against humanity,"[35] and acts in violation of the laws or customs of war.[36] Secondly, there is only one offense which gives rise to the primary responsibility of private persons, though the responsibility of the authorities of the state arises under paragraph 12 of Article 2 previously discussed. This offense is defined in Article 2, paragraph (4) and refers to "The incursion into the territory of a state from the territory of another state by armed bands acting for a political purpose."[37] And, finally, there are offenses which primarily give rise to the criminal liability of the authorities of the state, but which may also engage the responsibility of private individuals under the conditions enumerated in Article 2, paragraph 12. In this group are included acts of aggression, threat to resort to acts of aggression, fomenting civil strife in another state and many others. It is instructive to recall that paragraph 12 of Article 2 makes a punishable offense conspiracy, direct incitement, attempt and complicity in the commission of any of the offenses defined in Article 2 of the Code. It should similarly be remembered that under the comment on paragraph 12 of Article 2 "there can be no question of punishing as accomplices in such an offense [complicity] all the members of the armed forces of a state or the workers in war industries."[38]

Though the International Law Commission's proposal has been presented *de lege ferenda,* even on this level the Draft Code raises substantive questions in two area. First, in the area concerning the

[34] Article 2, paragraph (9).
[35] Article 2, paragraph (10).
[36] Article 2, paragraph (11).
[37] For comments upon this provision, see Report of the International Law Commission, *op. cit.*, p. 12. This text was modified in 1954 in an attempt to widen the scope of the provision. For text of the new article see L. B. Sohn, *Cases on United Nations Law.*, p. 999 (1956).
[38] See the Comment on Article 2, paragraph (12). Report of the International Law Commission, *op. cit.*, p. 13.

requirements of the world community is the fundamental question whether this proposal by thus imposing criminal responsibility on private individuals has accordingly increased the possibility of controlling offenses of this nature against foreign states. And, secondly, in the area of strict legal technicalities is the question of whether the Draft Code has presented a coherent and adequate statement of the law of international responsibility of private persons.

Strictly concerning legal technicalities, though there can be no doubt that the Code has undertaken a frank and unprecedented attack upon the deficiencies of traditional theories in that the state is no longer alone made liable for international crimes, the formulation of individual responsibility is too narrowly confined to offenses of a political nature.[39] It has been the conclusion of certain authors that no real progress in this area of the law is really possible until a more comprehensive code is formulated which would include offenses aimed at the corruption of the mind through hostile propaganda as well as against the international economic order.[40] This conclusion must be accepted if it be considered that the peace and security of mankind is placed in danger by false propaganda, counterfeiting of foreign currency and documents,[41] and boycott of foreign goods, and not exclusively by direct incitement to civil strife or any of the actions specifically included in the Code.[42] Even as to the specified offenses, other acts of a clear political complexion have regrettably been left out. Thus, the organization of hostile military expeditions against a state and the departure of volunteers to enlist in belligerent or insurgent forces are conspicuously absent. Subsequent discussions of these acts will reveal their explosive nature in specific cases. It is in recognition of this possibility that the International Law Commission of the United Nations has suggested that a definition of aggression should include the sending of volunteers to engage in hostilities against a friendly nation.[43] The absence of these offenses from the Draft Code may well be due to the

[39] The Commission itself said that it decided to deal with offenses which contain a political element and which endanger or disturb the maintenance of international peace and security. See Report of the International Law Commission, *op. cit.*, p. 11.

[40] Cf. C. Parry, "Some Considerations upon the Content of a Draft Code of Offenses Against the Peace and Security of Mankind," *Int. L.Q.*, Vol. 3, pp. 208, 224–226 (1950). Also J. Paoli, *op. cit.*, pp. 129, 146.

[41] Professor Vespasian V. Pella regarded counterfeiting as an offense against the peace and security of mankind. See V. V. Pella, *La Coopération des États dans la 'Lutte contre le Faux Monnayage*, p. 106 (1928).

[42] As to the economic sources of friction between the states, see G. Hornsey, "Foreign Investment and International Law," *Int. L.Q.*, Vol. 3, p. 552 (1950).

[43] See U.N. General Assembly, Official Records, Sixth Session, Supp. No. 9 (A/1858 1951); *Am. J. Int. L., Supp.*, Vol. 45, pp. 103, 121 (1951).

International Law Commission's design to follow closely on the precedent supplied by the Nürnberg Judgment, and to its apparent purpose to eliminate the substantive questions regarding the criminality of individuals under international law which were raised against the Nürnberg Trial.[44] It may nevertheless be said that under the Draft Code international law has asserted such control over the customary liberty of private persons that should they commit any of the enumerated offenses they would be liable to criminal punishment.

When the Draft Code is viewed in the light of the requirements of the world community the possibility that it will effectively increase the control over hostile acts of private persons would seem to be plagued with doubts.[45] Though the Commission apparently was not aware of this difficulty, it seems clear that the majority confidently expected that, by imposing criminal responsibility upon private individuals, an additional level of responsibility would be added, thus closing the gap existing in situations where individuals remain unpunished by their own national law for the commission of acts which seriously endanger the peace and security of mankind.[46] The expectation that private persons may be held internationally liable would in principle increase the effectiveness of controlling private offenses against the international order. It is therefore believed that the imposition of responsibility upon individuals may serve as a deterrent to the commission of private offenses, even when the private person in question is merely used as a tool of his government. Yet this expectation can only be sustained on the assumptions (1) that individuals have loyalty toward the world community; (2) that there is a large measure of individual moral judgment by which each person can freely determine the morality of the actions of his own government; and (3) that should the individual find that a state policy is contrary to the requirements of peaceful international life, he must further have the necessary moral courage to act according to his loyalty to the world community and, if necessary, against his own government.[47] To assert the existence of individual obligations under the Draft Code is to acknowledge the validity of these assumptions. Though a respectable authority finds these assumptions utterly lacking in the contemporary world,[48] still the im-

[44] Cf. J. Stone, *Legal Controls of International Conflict*, p. 370 (1954).
[45] Cf. C. G. Fenwick, *op. cit.*, p. 98.
[46] P. M. Carjeu, *op. cit.*, p. 401.
[47] J. Stone, *Aggression and World Order: A Critique of United Nations Theories of Aggression*, pp. 147–148 (1958).
[48] J. Stone, *Legal Controls of International Conflict*, pp. 370–371 (1954).

plicit purpose of the Draft Code is precisely to give expression to the values of the world community, thus helping to create loyalty toward this community. It may perhaps be safely said that the Draft Code is the most direct and sustained appeal for a world community of men bound by shared convictions of social solidarity,[49] and it is precisely on the realization of this hope that the wellbeing of mankind largely depends. While it is true that by accepting its compulsive obligations, a state is surrendering to the world community the trial and punishment of individuals for acts clearly falling within its jurisdiction, compelling considerations of world peace and order would seem to justify sufficiently this derogation of state sovereignty. Confronted with the possibility of anarchy and destruction, mankind demands a more effective legal order, which is only possible by a more integrated world community. And the latter can only be attained if states and individuals are constantly made aware that the values of the international community will scrupulously be enforced by the establishment of a criminal law reaching individuals.[50] This may be a slow and painful process, but in the end it may make it possible for national loyalties to yield to the requirements of the world community.[51] Within these modest goals the Draft Code may receive a happier acceptance by the states.

CONCLUSION

In conclusion it may be stressed that the emerging type of criminal responsibility here discussed is calculated to promote a more integrated world community where individuals have an unmistakable responsibility for the promotion and preservation of peace and security. Since presently international law does not hold the state responsible for the actions of private persons against foreign states, the criminal responsibility of private persons would clearly close a loophole presently existing in the law of international responsibility. This conception is indeed inescapable if world peace is ever to be attained on firmer grounds.

[49] Cf. P. E. Corbett, *Law in Diplomacy*, p. 253 (1959).
[50] Q. Wright, "Proposal for an International Criminal Court," *Am. J. Int. L.*, Vol. 46, pp. 60, 64 (1952).
[51] Cf. P. E. Corbett, *Law and Society in the Relations of States*, p. 47 (1951).

PART TWO

SOME HOSTILE ACTIONS OF PRIVATE PERSONS AGAINST FOREIGN STATES

CHAPTER IV

ORGANIZATION OF HOSTILE MILITARY EXPEDITIONS

International law unmistakably postulates that a neutral state must maintain an attitude of strict impartiality toward belligerents in the presence of a war.[1] Included in this obligation is the duty of a neutral government not only to abstain from participating in the conflict but also to refuse the use of its territory and resources for the organization of military expeditions against states with which it is at peace.[2] A similar obligation exists in the presence of a civil war or an insurgency in the territory of a foreign state.[3] It can thus be seen that the duty to prevent the formation of military expeditions is not in any way limited by the relations of neutrality. It is a duty which exists in peacetime as well. Though the law in this regard is relatively clear, it is believed that its somewhat narrow construction has made it susceptible of violations by the states. For present purposes it is important to emphasize that a military expedition is organized by private persons seemingly without the participation of the government. A critical examination of this act may therefore bring out the deficiencies of the law and the urgent necessity for its revision.

THE TRADITIONAL LAW

Present international consensus regards the law of hostile military expeditions as specifically applying to the act of organizing in neutral territory an expedition for the purpose of engaging in military operations against a state with which the former is at peace.[4] It seems similarly agreed that the rules against hostile military expeditions are

[1] For a full discussion of this duty of impartiality, see G. H. Hackworth, *Digest of International Law*, Vol. 7, pp. 372–79 (1943).

[2] C. C. Hyde, *International Law Chiefly as Interpreted and Applied by the United States*, Vol. 3, pp. 2254 (2d ed., 1945).

[3] The application of the law of hostile military expeditions in respect to civil war is not always well observed, and most discussions take place within the context of neutral-belligerent relations. See C. G. Fenwick, *International Law*, p. 303 (3d ed., 1948).

[4] "Corps of combatants cannot be formed nor recruiting agencies opened on the territory of a neutral Power to assist the belligerents." Convention Respecting the Rights and Duties of Neutral Powers and Persons in War on Land, Oct. 18, 1907, Second International Peace Conference, No. V, art. IV (hereinafter cited as Hague

applicable *mutatis mutandis* to naval[5] and aerial[6] expeditions organized for similar ends. Though initially developed in connection with neutrality, this branch of the law is only a phase of the general duty of a government to prevent the commission of injurious acts against foreign countries.[7] It is therefore equally applicable to a civil strife or simply to acts threatening the peace and security of a foreign state.[8] In regard to a civil strife, however, the law has its foundation on the obligation of every government to respect the independence of other nations.[9] Thus, while in the presence of war the obligation of a neutral is one of impartiality, as applied to a civil war the duty is one of noninterference in the conflict,[10] irrespective of whether a status of belligerency has been recognized.[11]

But whether the state is confronted with a duty of impartiality or with one of noninterference, the obligation to prevent hostile military expeditions from departing from its jurisdiction remains essentially the same.[12] The duty involved has been summarized as one of pre-

Convention No. V). For text, see W. M. Malloy, *Treaties, International Acts, Protocols and Agreements Between the United States of America and Other Powers*, Vol. 2, p. 2290 (1910).

[5] C. Wiesse, *Droit International Appliqué Aux Guerres Civiles*, p. 169 (1898).

[6] See Article 46 of the Hague Air Rules of 1923. For text, see *Am. J. Int. L. Supp.*, Vol. 32, p. 38 (1938).

[7] R. E. Curtis, "The Law of Hostile Military Expeditions as Applied by the United States," *Am. J. Int. L.*, Vol. 8, p. 1 (1914).

[8] A. Rougier, *Les Guerres Civiles et le Droit des Gens*, pp. 415, 417 (1903). He seems to believe that this principle applies to a civil war when belligerency has been recognized. Dr. Luis A. Podestá Costa, on the other hand, believes that if the expedition is to help the legitimate government, there is no obligation to prevent it, for this obligation only arises if the expedition is organized with the purpose of aiding the insurgents. See L. A. Podestá Costa, *Derecho Internacional Público*, Vol. 2, p. 265 (3d ed., 1955).

[9] H. Lauterpacht, *Recognition in International Law*, p. 229 (1947).

[10] This duty of noninterference was clearly laid down by Mr. Justice Joseph Story in the case The Santissima Trinidad, 20 U.S. (8 Wheat.) 283, at 337 (1822), where he said: "The government of the United States has recognized the existence of a civil war between Spain and her colonies, and has avowed a determination to remain neutral between the parties, and to allow to each the same rights of asylum, and hospitality and intercourse. Each party is, therefore, deemed by us a belligerent nation, having, so far as concerns us, the sovereign rights of war, and entitled to be respected in the exercise of those rights. We cannot interfere, to the prejudice of either belligerent, without making ourselves a party to the contest, and departing from the posture of neutrality." Despite these commendable words, it has been proved that this duty of noninterference is rather deceptive, for in fact it amounts to intervention on behalf of the one or the other in the rebellion. See N. J. Padelford, *International Law and Diplomacy in the Spanish Civil Strife*, p. 119 (1939).

[11] L. Oppenheim, *International Law*, Vol. 2, p. 532 (6th ed. by H. Lauterpacht, 1944).

[12] A. Rougier, however, believes that there is a difference, namely, that in case of war the obligation is of a strictly legal nature, while noninterference in a civil strife is simply a moral obligation which can be disregarded with impunity. See A. Rougier, *op. cit.*, p. 418, n.2. It may be answered, however, that since intervention violates the sovereignty and independence of a state, this is in itself a legal obligation imposed by general international law. See H. Lauterpacht, *op. cit.*, p. 229.

vention,[13] and it proceeds largely upon the theory that since international law confers upon every state a power of exclusive control over its territorial domain,[14] concurrent with this is the correlative duty to protect within its territory the rights of other states.[15] This is, therefore, a prescription resulting from the exercise of territorial sovereignty and unmistakably falling within the competence of the territorial state. Underlying these principles is the recognition of a community of interests existing in the world society imperatively demanding the suppression within each country's territory of harmful activities directed against foreign nations.

With this background in mind, it may readily be perceived that the violation of the foregoing obligation engages the international responsibility of the state precisely because governmental inactivity in preventing the organization of a military expedition amounts to complicity in the hostile attack and can logically be regarded as actual governmental participation in the conflict.[16] It would seem, therefore, that state tolerance raises a presumption of governmental complicity which amounts to an international delinquency.[17]

By thus acknowledging that the principle of international law rendering hostile military expeditions criminal is based upon a failure of a government to fulfill its duty towards another, there is an express recognition of the individualistic nature of international law accordingly concerned with defining the rights and jurisdiction of a state *vis-à-vis* those of other states and with the possibility of their successful reconciliation.[18] To pose the matter exclusively in terms of an injury to the state is to simplify the nature of the problem, for the fact will have to be faced that under a modern law of nations deeply concerned with social cooperation, the duties of the state towards the world community are also vitally at stake.[19] In particular, hostile military expeditions

[13] A. Rougier, *op. cit.*, p. 423.

[14] P. Fauchille, *Traité du Droit International Public*, Vol. 1, pp. 3–10 (8th ed., 1925). Mr Justice J. Story referred to this principle as follows: "Every nation possesses an exclusive sovereignty and jurisdiction within its own territory." J. Story, *Conflict of Laws*, sec. 18 (8th ed., 1883).

[15] U.N. Secretariat, *Survey of International Law*, U.N. Doc. No. A/CN4/1 Rev. 1, pp. 34–35 (1949).

[16] R. E. Curtis, *op. cit.*, pp. 34–37.

[17] See J. Dumas, *De La Responsabilité Internationale des Etats*, pp. 57–64 (1930).

[18] C. W. Jenks, "The Scope of International Law," *Brit. Y. B. Int. L.* 1954, Vol. 31, pp. 1–3 (1956).

[19] A. Alvarez, "The Reconstruction and Codification of International Law," *Int. & Comp. L.Q.*, Vol. 1, p. 469 (1947). See also Judge Alejandro Alvarez' dissenting opinion in the Advisory Opinion of the International Court of Justice concerning the International Status of South-West Africa, (1950) *I.C. J. Reports*, pp. 174, 176. See also

seriously injure the legitimate expectations of the peoples of the world, for it is a value of the international community to localize wars to minimize the danger of their spreading to other nations, and to prevent a civil strife from becoming an actual testing ground for the forces and weapons of potential belligerents.[20] The problem is even more acute with the establishment of the United Nations, for in so far as a military action against a state by the United Nations might be involved, the member states are not only obliged to assist the United Nations in carrying out its lawful action but also to refrain from giving any assistance to the state against which enforcement action is undertaken.[21] If the foregoing observations be correct, the interests of the world community will adequately be served if the states effectively refrain from augmenting the fighting forces of the belligerents in an international war, or the insurgents in a civil strife, or of an aggressor against whom the world organization takes enforcement action. The force of this suggestion reveals itself with all its cogency if it is considered that international conflagrations often have their roots in local conflicts between minor powers or in civil wars apparently confined to the territory of one state.[22] In situations where the United Nations might be involved, the intervention of the Chinese Communists in the Korean conflict in 1950 shows only too well that but for the United Nations' self-restraint the matter might well have developed into an international war of the greatest dimensions threatening the existence of the world organization itself. This also instructively illustrates the proposition that as long as a strong centralized authority is not yet developed, the obligation to prevent hostile expeditions will have to remain as a fundamental principle of the law.

However, in dealing with this branch of the law, the interaction of law and politics is at once perceivable, and it may not be an exaggeration to say that the law of hostile military expeditions is a principle of international law only by virtue of national policies seeking to support wars or revolutions where it is politically most advantageous

Hon. Viscount Jowitt, "The Value of International Law in Establishing Cooperation Among Nations," *Int. & Comp. L.Q.*, Vol. 1, p. 295 (1947); K. Loewenstein, "Sovereignty and International Cooperation," *Am. J. Int. L.*, Vol. 48, p. 222 (1954).

[20] Thus, in respect to the Spanish Civil War, the Portuguese Government stated in 1936 that "the civil war in Spain is an international war." G. Schwarzenberger, *Power Politics – A Study in International Relations*, p. 229 (2d ed., 1951).

[21] U.N. Charter, art. 2, paragraph 5.

[22] E.g., some writers maintain that World War II actually began in Spain in 1936. See N. D. Palmer and C. Perkins, *International Relations: The World Community in Transition*, p. 553 (1953). This assertion illustrates vividly the urgent necessity for the effective regulation of hostile military expeditions.

to do so.[23] Underlying the law, therefore, is the pursuit of self-interest neatly garbed in a deliberate state policy.[24] Moreover, the impact of the outbreak of war or civil strife is so vast and complicated that the law of hostile military expeditions can be adequately treated only in the context of the interplay of domestic law and politics. A phase of the broader law of neutrality and noninterference which has proved to be peculiarly vulnerable to the vicissitudes of political demands, the law of hostile military expeditions is bound to meet a similar fate. Because of national policies, this branch of the law exhibits a high degree of instability. These deficiencies are strengthened by the unquestionable fact that international law gives to each state discretion to enforce the duty of prevention as it sees fit.

With this consideration in mind, it is interesting but not at all surprising to note that the legal practice of nations in this area is governed by a variety of rules dependent upon a disturbing number of factors. These will be seen in the substantive treatment of the law of the various states and the frustrated attempts of international law at effective regulation.

THE LAW AND PRACTICE OF THE UNITED STATES

Municipal statutes enforcing the international duty of preventing military expeditions are historically traceable to the Act of June 5, 1794 making it a misdemeanor for any person, within the jurisdiction of the United States, to "prepare the means for any military expedition or enterprise... against the territory or dominions of any foreign prince or state with whom the United States are at peace..."[25] Although this act was enacted initially as a temporary measure owing to the difficulties experienced by the United States in maintaining a strict neutrality in the wars of the French Revolution, it was perpetuated by the Act of April 24, 1800.[26] However, with the increased emphasis upon neutral duties arising out of the Napoleonic wars, the prohibition of military expeditions was incorporated in a more effective neutrality law enacted in 1818, which, *inter alia*, made it a crime:

[23] R. Strausz-Hupé and S. T. Possony, *International Relations In the Age of Conflict Between Democracy and Dictatorship*, pp. 354–355 (2d ed., 1954).

[24] P. C. Jessup, *Neutrality – Today and Tomorrow*, p. 209 (1936).

[25] Act of June 5, 1794, ch. 50, sec. 5, 1 Stat. 381, 384.

[26] Act of April 24, 1800, ch. 35, 2 Stat. 54.

> if any person shall, within the territory or jurisdiction of the United States, begin or set on foot, or provide or prepare the means for any military expedition or enterprise, to be carried on from thence against the territory or dominions of any foreign prince or state ... with whom the United States are [at] peace...[27]

This provision was subsequently incorporated in the Revised Statutes in substantially similar form.[28] In 1909 the provisions of the statute were enacted in the revision and codification of the criminal law,[29] and by section 8 of the Act of June 15, 1917,[30] the pertinent provision of the Criminal Code was amended by adding to the punishable acts not only the preparation but also the furnishing of money for military or naval expeditions, and also by providing that the penalties of fine and imprisonment may be imposed concurrently. The present provision thus states:

> Whoever, within the United States, knowingly begins or sets on foot or provides or prepares a means for or furnishes the money for, or takes part in, any military or naval expedition or enterprise to be carried on from thence against the territory or dominion of any foreign prince or state, or of any colony, district, or people with whom the United States is at peace, shall be fined not more than $ 3,000 or imprisoned not more than three years, or both.[31]

The foregoing provision represents the standard treatment of the law of hostile military expeditions in American law. A cursory reading of this provision will show clearly that its injunction is not limited to situations where in the course of a war the United States chooses to remain neutral.[32] More generally, the brief history of American legislation here outlined shows remarkably well the consolidation of the law of hostile military expeditions in the domestic legislation of a state interested and willing to make it work. It is largely for this reason that there is ample justification in the double assertion that American legislation in this regard has been a model followed by other nations,[33] and that much of international law on the subject is unmistakably traceable to American experience.[34]

[27] Act of April 20, 1818, ch. 88, sec. 6, 3 Stat. 449.

[28] Rev. Stat. sec. 5286 (1875).

[29] Act of March 4, 1909, ch. 321, sec. 13, 35 Stat. 1090.

[30] Act of June 15, 1917, ch. 30, sec. 8, 40 Stat. 223.

[31] Foreign Relations Act, 18 U.S.C., sec. 960 (1952). For the application of this provision, see G. H. Hackworth, *op. cit.*, Vol. 7, sec. 664. See also the recent indictment, under this provision, of a former President of Cuba and others. N.Y. Times, Feb. 14, 1958, sec. 1, p. 1, col. 1.

[32] C. C. Hyde, *op. cit.*, Vol. 3, p. 2254, n. 2.

[33] J. Stone, *Legal Controls of International Conflict*, p. 384, n. 25 (1954).

[34] Authors on the subject cite American cases and practice with approval. See C. Wiesse, *op. cit.*, pp. 169–74.; J. Dumas, *op. cit.*, p. 58.

Turning now to the practical application of the statute, it will shortly be seen that to determine the acts which fall within its province is one of the most acute problems of the law. The language of the statute, "military or naval expedition or enterprise," suggests a distinction between an expedition and an enterprise and one main source of confusion is the frequent failure to distinguish between the two.[35] Though their line of demarcation may sometimes be rather shadowy, in reality two different offenses have been established whose exact make-up consists of entirely different elements. It seems clear that to constitute a military expedition two basic factors need be present. First, there must be an association or an organization of a military character within the United States.[36] This condition seems most naturally to assume that unless an actual organization is in operation, a potential injury to a foreign state can hardly be deemed to exist.[37] Behind this condition there is the further supposition that an individual acting alone cannot seriously threaten the peace and security of a foreign state.[38] On this plane, the departure of single individuals or of unorganized groups for the purpose of joining the forces of the belligerents is not a violation of the law and a duty of prevention need not be acknowledged.[39] Thus, during the revolutionary years, when the Mexican Government complained of military expeditions allegedly formed in the United States with the purpose of overthrowing the existing regime, the State Department called attention to the distinction "on the one hand, between the passage of men singly or in small groups across our frontier and into another country, or the sailing of individuals or small groups in the ordinary course of events from one of our ports, and on the other hand, the departure from our territory of organized groups of men avowing the purpose of undertaking belligerent activities in foreign territory,"[40] vigorously asserting that

[35] This distinction, however, has been unequivocally endorsed by the courts. See Wiborg v. United States, 163 U.S. 632 (1896), and subsequently, United States v. Sander, 241 Fed. 417 (S.D.N.Y. 1917).

[36] See the note of Secretary of State Marcy to Mr. Escalente, May 8, 1856. J. B. Moore, *A Digest of International Law*, Vol. 7, p. 927 (1906).

[37] United States v. Tauscher, 233 Fed. 597, pp. 599–600 (N.D. Cal. 1917).

[38] However in the United States v. Ram Chandra, 254 Fed. 635, 636 (N.D. Cal. 1917), the court said: "I see no reason, however, why a single individual may not begin or set on foot a military expedition or enterprise, and more especially why a single individual may not well provide or prepare the means for such an expedition or enterprise."

[39] See the note of the Counselor of the State Department to the German Ambassador in the United States, Oct. 6, 1914, G. H. Hackworth, *op. cit.*, Vol. 7, p. 412. See also the note of Secretary of State Jefferson to the Minister of France, November 30, 1793, J. B. Moore, *op. cit.*, Vol. 7, p. 917.

[40] Note of Secretary of State Knox to the Mexican Chargé d'Affaires, June 7, 1911. G. H. Hackworth, *op. cit.*, Vol. 7, p. 410. It is also well known that in 1870, during the

a duty of prevention only existed in the presence of the latter. This distinction is a basic postulate of American law in this area and has been applied with impeccable consistency. As early as 1793, Thomas Jefferson, then Secretary of State, addressed a note to the Minister of France forcibly stating that "the Government of the United States will not at the request of a foreign government intervene to prevent the transit to the country of the latter of persons objectionable to it unless they form part of a hostile military expedition."[41] This curious paradox of not compromising a state's responsibility even if its territory is being used as a basis of operations by unorganized individuals can only be understood in the light of *laissez faire* conceptions, more particularly the deep conviction that wars were matters between states and that therefore the freedom of the individual should not suffer in his relations with belligerents.[42] It may be added in passing that such assumptions of the American law were faithfully reflected in Article VI of the Hague Convention Number V of 1907 which states: "The responsibility of a neutral Power is not engaged by the fact of persons crossing the frontier separating to offer their services to one of the belligerents."[43] To appreciate the full impact of this provision, it should be compared with Article IV of the same Convention which says that "corps of combatants cannot be formed nor recruiting agencies opened on the territory of a neutral Power to assist the belligerents."[44] When these two provisions are viewed together, the neutral state must prevent its frontier from being crossed by corps or bands which have already been organized on its territory, but may remain indifferent in respect to individuals acting in an isolated manner.[45] Though in thus providing, international law has shown its greatest weakness as will be subsequently seen, for present purposes it is only necessary to emphasize that the American distinction in this regard conforms exactly to the requirements of the law of nations.

The second factor necessary for the existence of a military expedition is the presence of a common design of hostile operation against

Franco-German War, 1200 Frenchmen were allowed to depart from New York in two French vessels for the purpose of joining the French Army. The United States Government did not interfere with their departure on the ground that the men were not organized in a body. See L. Oppenheim, *op. cit.*, Vol. 2, p. 565, n. 4.

[41] Note of Secretary of State Jefferson to the French Ambassador, November 30, 1793, J. B. Moore, *op. cit.*, Vol. 7, p. 917.

[42] J. Stone, *op. cit.*, p. 384.

[43] Hague Convention No. V, art. VI, W. M. Malloy, *op. cit.*, Vol. 2, p. 2298.

[44] Hague Convention No. V, art. IV, W. M. Malloy, *op. cit.*, Vol. 2, p. 2298.

[45] J. B. Scott, *The Proceedings of the Hague Peace Conferences – Meetings of the Second, Third and Fourth Commissions*, Vol. 3, pp. 51–52 (1921).

a friendly state.[46] This condition would seem to follow logically and naturally, for if a hostile criminal intent is lacking, no injury to the foreign state in question can be said to have been committed. Broadly, then, it may be said that under the relevant statute and case law, if these two factors are not present, the United States is unwilling to recognize the existence of a military expedition and, consequently, a duty of prevention does not arise.[47]

In marked contrast with a military expedition, a military enterprise is more comprehensive in scope. The United States Supreme Court has defined it as "a martial undertaking, involving the idea of a bold, arduous and hazardous attempt."[48] Clearly, then, while a military expedition might conceivably be herein embraced, the concept of a military enterprise gives a wider sweep to the statute and may consequently include various undertakings not only by a number of persons but by a single individual as well.[49] Thus, generally, but not exhaustively, the miscellaneous acts of sending spies from the United States,[50] furnishing munitions to rebels,[51] participating in a scheme to start a revolution in a possession against the mother country,[52] and conspiring to blow up tunnels between the United States and Canada[53] have all been characterized by the courts as falling within the purview of a military enterprise and, therefore, punishable under the statute. It is highly significant that these activities would not have qualified as military expeditions simply because the existence of an organization of a strictly military character was absent.[54] It should be manifestly clear, however, that even though the United States would seem to go beyond the requirements of Articles IV and VI of the Hague Convention Number V of 1907 previously cited, in that it prohibits and penalizes a number of acts not embraced in those provisions, nevertheless these acts are prohibited by general international law which imposes the duty to prevent any kind of injurious acts directed against foreign states.

In recognition of the preceding considerations, the United States has

[46] Wiborg v. United States, 163 U.S. 632, 653–654 (1896).
[47] C. C. Hyde, *op. cit.*, Vol. 3, p. 2255.
[48] Wiborg v. United States, 163 U.S. 632, 650 (1896).
[49] United States v. Sander, 241 Fed. 417, 419–420 (S.D.N.Y. 1917).
[50] *Ibid.*
[51] Gandara v. United States, 272 Fed. 399 (7th Cir. 1920), *cert. denied*, 256 U.S. 703 (1921).
[52] Jacobsen v. United States, 272 Fed. 399 (7th Cir. 1920), *cert. denied*, 256 U.S. 703 (1921).
[53] United States v. Bopp, 230 Fed. 723 (N.D. Cal 1916).
[54] United States v. Sander, 241 Fed. 417, 419–420 (S.D.N.Y. 1917).

enforced its neutrality laws, in which the prohibition of military expeditions is included, in cases of insurgency in which recognition of belligerency has not been granted. Thus, on June 12, 1895, and July 27, 1896, the President of the United States issued two proclamations noting that Cuba was the seat of serious civil disturbances and admonishing all persons within the jurisdiction of the United States to refrain, *inter alia*, from forming or taking part in military expeditions in violation of the neutrality laws.[55] American courts considered these proclamations as sufficiently authoritative for the application of the United States neutrality laws. Thus, in *The Three Friends* the Supreme Court said:

> We are thus judicially informed of the existence of an actual conflict of arms in resistance of the authority of a government with which the United States are on terms of peace and amity, although acknowledgment of the insurgents as belligerents by the political department has not taken place; and it cannot be doubted that, this being so, the act in question [the neutrality statute] is applicable.[56]

A similar proclamation was issued on March 2, 1912, in respect to the Mexican Civil War.[57] These instances strikingly illustrate the proposition that the prohibition of hostile military expeditions is of a permanent character not exclusively dependent upon the existence of an international war. Particularly instructive is the proclamation of June 6, 1886, against a military expedition to Canada, which said that such proceedings "Constitute a high misdemeanor forbidden by the laws of the United States as well as the law of nations."[58] The significance of this proclamation lies in the fact that the prohibition of hostile military expeditions was regarded as a duty stemming from accepted principles of international law.

THE LAW AND PRACTICE OF OTHER COUNTRIES

Following the American example closely, Great Britain enacted the Foreign Enlistment Act in 1819[59] which remained in force until 1870. As the Act failed to prevent adequately the organization of hostile expeditions as evidenced by the *Alabama* controversy, it was subse-

[55] F. Deák and P. C. Jessup, *A Collection of Neutrality Laws, Regulations and Treaties of Various Countries*, Vol. 2, pp. 1195–1196 (1939).
[56] 166 U.S. 1, 65–66 (1896).
[57] F. Deák and P. C. Jessup, *op. cit.*, Vol. 2, p. 1200.
[58] F. Deák and P. C. Jessup, *op. cit.*, Vol. 2, p. 1183.
[59] Foreign Enlistment Act, 1819, 59 Geo. 3, c. 69.

quently replaced by a new Foreign Enlistment Act enacted on August 9, 1870.[60] The pertinent provision of this act is as follows:

> If any person within the limits of Her Majesty's dominions, and without the license of Her Majesty, –
>
> Prepares or fits out any naval or military expedition to proceed against the dominions of any friendly state, the following consequences shall ensue:
>
> (1) Every person engaged in such preparation or fitting out, or assisting therein, or employed in any capacity in such expedition, shall be guilty of an offence against this Act, and shall be punishable by fine and imprisonment, or either of such punishments, at the discretion of the court before which the offender is convicted; and imprisonment, if awarded, may be either with or without hard labour.
>
> (2) All ships, and their equipments, and all arms and munitions of war, used in or forming part of such expedition, shall be forfeited to Her Majesty.[61]

The most authoritative early statement of the conditions under which the statute would apply is that contained in the judgment of the House of Lords in *Regina v. Sandoval*[62] relating to purchases of goods and munitions in Great Britain for the purpose of aiding an insurrection in Venezuela. As to the elements of the offense provided for by the Act, the court said that the act of "fitting out" an expedition includes its preparation as well. The court thus concluded that any act which "contributes in any material degree towards setting on foot an expedition fitted for warlike purposes... is the preparation of that expedition."[63] Similarly, in *The Queen v. Jameson*,[64] involving a British subject accused of assisting to prepare a military expedition to proceed against the South African Republic without the license of Her Majesty, the court advanced a step forward in holding that if there be an unlawful preparation of an expedition by some person within Her Majesty's dominions, any British subject who assists in such preparation will be guilty of an offense even though he renders the assistance from a place outside Her Majesty's dominions.[65]

In striking similarity to the American practice, the British Government has also applied the Foreign Enlistment Act of 1870 to civil strifes without the existence of a declaration of belligerency. Thus, by

[60] Foreign Enlistment Act, 1870, 33 & 34 Vict., c. 90.

[61] Foreign Enlistment Act, 1870, 33 & 34 Vict., c. 90, sec. 11. This and other provisions of the Act have been substantially embodied in Article 955 of the King's Regulations and Admiralty Instructions, 1926. For text, see F. Deák and P. C. Jessup, *op. cit.*, Vol. 1, pp. 150–53.

[62] 56 L.T.R. (n.s.) 526 (1887), per J. Wills.

[63] *Ibid.*

[64] [1896] 2 Q.B. 425, per Lord Russell, C. J.

[65] *Ibid.*, p. 430.

a declaration of January 1937, the Foreign Enlistment Act was declared to be applicable to the Spanish Civil War.[66] Though this declaration specifically referred to the provisions of the Act prohibiting persons to enlist in the service of either side to the conflict,[67] it is generally accepted that section 11 of the Act which deals with hostile military expeditions is probably the only section which is so worded as to make it unmistakably clear that it applies to situations where a formal war has not been recognized.[68] This interpretation clearly indicates that the operation of the Foreign Enlistment Act, like its American counterpart, is not at all dependent upon the existence of war in the technical legal sense.[69]

The adoption by other countries of substantially similar provisions prohibiting the formation of hostile military expeditions shows remarkably well the full measure of agreement existing on the subject. Thus, the French Penal Code, though not specifically referring to military expeditions, more generally prohibits any hostile action which exposes the state to a declaration of war.[70] Pursuant to this provision, measures of a temporary character have been enacted in the presence of particular wars.[71] In applying this legislation, the Civil Tribunal of the Seine held in *In re Florsheim*[72] that a contract made with a view to forming a hostile military expedition against a foreign state is null and void and, thus, unenforceable in court. This case compares with the early American case, *Kennett v. Chambers*,[73] involving a contract between citizens of the United States and an inhabitant of Texas whereby the latter agreed to convey land in Texas to the former in consideration of advances of money to enable him to raise and procure men to carry on the war with Mexico. The Supreme Court held the contract to be contrary to the United States policy toward Mexico and, therefore, unenforceable in the federal courts.[74]

[66] L. Oppenheim, *op. cit.*, Vol. 2, pp. 532–33.

[67] Foreign Enlistment Act, 1870, 33 & 34 Vict., c. 90 secs. 4, 5.

[68] A. D. McNair, "The Law Relating to the Civil War in Spain," *L.Q. Rev.*, Vol. 53, pp. 471, 494–496 (1937).

[69] H. Lauterpacht, *Recognition in International Law*, pp. 235 n. 4, 273 n. 7 (1947).

[70] Code Pénal, art. 84 (Fr. 1810). For text, see F. Deák and P. C. Jessup, *op. cit.*, Vol. 1, p. 583.

[71] See Article 5 of the Declaration of Neutrality in the American Civil War, June 10, 1861, and the Law of January 21, 1937, authorizing the Government to take the necessary measures to prevent the departure of volunteers for Spain. For text of these documents, see F. Deák and P. C. Jessup, *op. cit.*, Vol. 1, pp. 590, 603.

[72] *Annual Digest*, 1931-1932, p. 31 (H. Lauterpacht ed., 1938).

[73] 55 U.S. (14How.) 38 (1852).

[74] *Ibid.*, p. 50. The court at p. 49 also stated that the contract was not only void, but the parties who advanced the money were liable to punishment in a criminal prosecution.

One could, of course, cite other countries' legislation and case law prohibiting the formation of hostile military expeditions within their jurisdiction.[75] It suffices to say that so general is this domestic position that one can experience no difficulty in inferring a general principle of law recognized by civilized nations which the Statute of the International Court of Justice regards as a source of international law.[76] This assertion is bolstered by the fact that these domestic principles merely enforce a duty which international law imposes on the states to respect within their territory the rights of other states.

MEASURES OF PREVENTION

Much of the uncertainty touching the application of the preceding rules arises not only from the doubts and indeterminacies affecting their interpretation, but also from the fact that international law nowhere prescribes the test by which a duty of prevention must be enforced. Accordingly, many writers as well as much of state practice proceed on the assumption that each state can determine by its own national standards the nature and extent of the measures of exertion.[77] Though various attempts have been made to determine exactly the obligations of a neutral in this regard, perhaps the most comprehensive statement of the obligation is contained in the celebrated "Three Rules" of the Anglo-American Treaty of Washington of May 8, 1871.[78] These rules were accepted by the parties as a legal guide in the arbitration of the *Alabama Claims*,[79] involving the international liability of Great Britain for her alleged failure to prevent the building and equipping in its ports of naval expeditions in the service of the Confederate States in the American Civil War. The first and third rules bound a neutral Government: "First to use due diligence to prevent the fitting out, arming, or equipping, within its jurisdiction, of any vessel which it has reasonable ground to believe is intended to cruise or to carry on war against a power with which it is at peace; and also

[75] See, e.g., Article 10 of the Canadian Act Respecting Foreign Enlistment enacted on April 10, 1937, see F. Deák and P. C. Jessup, *op. cit.*, Vol. 1, p. 239; Art. 10, Venezuela Penal Code, 1926.

[76] Statute of the International Court of Justice, art. 38, paragraph C.

[77] L. Oppenheim, *op. cit.*, Vol. 2, p. 530; C. C. Hyde, *op. cit.*, Vol. 3, p. 2327.

[78] Treaty With Great Britain, May 8, 1871, art. VI, 17 Stat. 863, T.S. No. 133, Text of the treaty is also in W. M. Malloy, *op. cit.*, Vol. 1, p. 700.

[79] United States v. Great Britain (1871). For the record of this arbitration, see J. B. Moore, *op. cit.*, Vol. 7, pp. 1059–67.

to use like diligence to prevent the departure from its jurisdiction of any vessel intended to cruise or carry on war as above, such vessel having been specially adapted, in whole or in part, within such jurisdiction, to warlike use" and "thirdly, to exercise due diligence in its own ports and waters, and, as to all persons within its jurisdiction, to prevent any violation of... [these] obligations and duties." Though the United States and Great Britain agreed upon the "Three Rules," they failed to agree upon their interpretation. The crux of the difficulty lay in the true construction of the phrase "due diligence." While Great Britain contended that due diligence "signifies that measure of care which the government is under an obligation to use for a given purpose," the United States, on the other hand, suggested that it must be a diligence "proportioned to the magnitude of the subject, and to the dignity and strength of the power which is to exercise it."[80] Without in any way adopting either of these interpretations, the tribunal decided that it must be a diligence exercised by neutrals "in exact proportion to the risks to which either of the belligerents may be exposed, from a failure to fulfill the obligations of neutrality on their part..."[81] The rule has therefore developed that the responsibility of the state in cases of military or naval expeditions departing from its territory is to be determined by the degree of "due diligence" that it has shown in discharging its international obligations. However, dissatisfaction with the standard established by the term "due diligence" has led international conventions to adopt a different terminology believed to yield more satisfactory results. Thus, Article VIII of the Hague Convention Number XIII of 1907,[82] while reproducing the first of the "Three Rules" in almost identical terms, replaces the phrase "to use due diligence" with the admittedly less ambiguous "to employ the means at its disposal." Similarly, the Pan American Convention on the Duties and Rights of States in the Event of Civil Strife signed at Habana on February 20, 1928,[83] binds the parties "to use all means at their disposal to prevent the inhabitants of their territory, nationals or aliens, from participating in, gathering elements, crossing the boundary or sailing

[80] T. J. Lawrence, *Principles of International Law*, pp. 633, 634 (6th ed., 1915).

[81] J. B. Moore, *op. cit.*, Vol. 7, p. 1067.

[82] Convention Concerning the Rights and Duties of Neutral Powers in Naval War, Oct. 18, 1907, Second International Peace Conference, No. XIII, art. VIII. For text, see J. B. Scott, *The Proceedings of the Hague Peace Conferences – Meetings of the Second, Third and Fourth Commissions*, Vol. 3, p. 497 (1921).

[83] Convention With other American Republics, Feb. 20, 1928, 46 Stat. 2749, T.S. No. 814. For text, see *The International Conferences of American States 1889–1928*, p. 435, (J. B. Scott ed., 1931).

from their territory for the purpose of starting or promoting civil strife."[84] Finally, Article 1 of the rules adopted by the Institute of International Law on August 13, 1875,[85] imposes upon the neutral Government the obligation "to exercise vigilance to prevent its territory from becoming a center of organization or point of departure for hostile expeditions against one or both of the belligerents."

The foregoing exposition would seem to make it fairly clear that the criterion of "due diligence" has been abandoned in favor of supposedly more ascertainable standards. But, apart from these modifications, there can be no doubt that the obligations contained in the "Three Rules" of the Treaty of Washington were declaratory of existing international law[86] and that whether one refers to "due diligence" or to "the means at its disposal" as a standard of obligation, these terms are limitative in nature and do not impose upon the state an absolute obligation of prevention.[87] It may be argued accordingly that the responsibility of the state will not be involved unless it is unequivocally established that the state has neither exercised due diligence, nor employed all the means at its disposal in preventing the organization of military expeditions. This interpretation is highly questionable, for it reflects the indefensible assumption that a duty of prevention cannot be exercised at all times. If one starts with the proposition that a state in discharging its obligations must do so faithfully and in good faith, then it cannot reasonably be doubted that whether the duty of prevention will be effectively discharged depends wholly upon the willingness to do so.[88] But the present law clearly says that whether a state is to prevent the formation of a hostile expedition is inevitably limited by the capacity of the state, which must be interpreted as being as far as possibilities will reasonably permit.[89]

It is perhaps for this reason that the Institute of International Law said that "the mere fact that a hostile act has been committed upon neutral territory is not sufficient to make the neutral state responsible.

[84] Convention With other American Republics, Feb. 20, 1928, art. 1, para. 1, 46 Stat. 2749–50.

[85] For text, see *Resolutions of the Institute of International Law*, p. 12 (J. B. Scott ed. 1916).

[86] J. Stone, *Legal Controls of International Conflict*, p. 391 (1954); H. Accioly, *Manual de Direito Internacional Público*, p. 416 (1948); C. Rousseau, *Droit International Public*, p. 692 (1953). *Contra:* L. Oppenheim, *op. cit.*, Vol. 2, p. 577.

[87] A. V. W. Thomas and A. J. Thomas, Jr., *Non-Intervention – The Law and Its Import in the Americas*, p. 217 (1956).

[88] A. Rougier, *op. cit.*, p. 425.

[89] B. Cheng, *General Principles of Law as Applied by International Courts and Tribunals*, p. 221 (1953).

Before it can be admitted that it has violated its duty it must be shown that there was a hostile intention (*dolus*), or manifest negligence (*culpa*)."[90] Similar sentiments had already been expressed by Secretary of State Cass in a communication to the Central American governments as follows: "A Government is responsible only for the faithful discharge of its international duties, but not for the consequences of illegal enterprises of which it had no knowledge, or which the want of proof or other circumstances render it unable to prevent."[91] In a somewhat similar vein, the Government of Chile refused to accept responsibility for the departure from its territory of an expedition directed against Bolivia in 1872 on the ground that it was not sufficiently informed of the existence of the expedition.[92] This domestic position was unequivocally endorsed by an international arbitral tribunal in the *St. Albans Claims*,[93] where the United States sought to hold the British Government responsible for the attack in 1864 upon the town of St. Albans, Vermont, by a small party of persons who, acting in the interests of the Confederate States, prepared their expedition in Canadian territory. The arbitral tribunal unanimously disallowed the claims on the ground that the expedition was conducted with such secrecy that no care or diligence which one nation might reasonably require of another would have been sufficient to discover it. It would seem, therefore, that the international responsibility of a neutral government is engaged only if it is at fault, and fault is to be determined according to the circumstances of each individual case.[94] The doctrine of no liability without fault is therefore the standard of responsibility.

Though generally accepted, this conception of no responsibility without fault is clearly an archaic law and not at all consistent with modern morality. It has already been shown that recent developments seem to favor the theory of liability based on objective risk rather than on fault.[95] There is, accordingly, one area where the duty of

[90] See the Resolution dealing with the International Duties of Neutral States; Rules of Washington, Article 5. For text, see *Resolutions of the Institute of International Law*, pp. 12, 13 (J. B. Scott ed. 1916). It would seem, therefore, that the principle of no liability without fault is accepted in this area as well.

[91] November 26, 1860, J. B. Moore, *op. cit.*, Vol. 7, p. 928.

[92] C. Wiesse, *op. cit.*, p. 176; A. Rougier, *op. cit.*, p. 425, n. 2.

[93] For the record of this arbitration, see J. B. Moore, *Digest of International Arbitrations*, Vol. 4, pp. 4042–54 (1898).

[94] C. Wiesse states that if the participants of an expedition move about publicly, the duty of the state is to apprehend them immediately without waiting for their formal denunciation. See C. Wiesse, *op. cit.*, p. 177.

[95] Theodor Meron, "International Responsibility of States for Unauthorized Acts of their Officials," *Brit. Y.B. Int. L.*, 1957, Vol. 33, pp. 85–114 (1958).

exertion on the part of a neutral seems to be more exacting and stringent. This refers to aircrafts which, because of their potential for offensive action, undoubtedly constitute a greater danger to the opposing belligerent than military or naval expeditions departing from neutral territory. It is precisely for this reason that the unratified Hague Air Warfare Rules of 1923[96] have laid down more strict rules on the part of neutrals. Particularly, Article 46 binds the neutral government to use the means at its disposal:

1. To prevent the departure from its jurisdiction of an aircraft in a condition to make a hostile attack ... if there is reason to believe that such aircraft is destined for use against a belligerent Power.
2. To prevent the departure of an aircraft, the crew of which includes any member of the combatant forces of a belligerent Power.

While there can be little doubt that the first duty incorporates the spirit of the first of the "Three Rules" of the Treaty of Washington, the second provision imposes upon the neutral an additional obligation which, though considered by some as wholly unnecessary and superfluous,[97] reinforces the obligation to prevent the possibility of its territory being converted into a military base for hostile expeditions against a belligerent. Following closely this international standard in regard to aircraft, the Danish Rules of Neutrality of May 27, 1938,[98] provide in Article 15, paragraph 2, that "any aircraft in a condition to commit an attack against a belligerent, or which carries apparatus or material the mounting or utilization of which would permit it to commit an attack, is forbidden to leave Danish territory if there is reason to presume that it is destined to be employed against a belligerent Power." It is submitted that this provision illustrates well the manner in which international obligations ought to be observed.

CONCLUSION

In this chapter an attempt was made to point out the inefficiencies of the present law of hostile military expeditions. It has been made abundantly clear that the domestic legislation of some states is far ahead of

[96] Rules of Aerial Warfare, Feb. 10, 1923, The Hague. For text, see *Am. J. Int. L., Supp.*, Vol. 32, p. 12 (1938).
[97] See L. Oppenheim, *op. cit.*, Vol. 2, p. 578.
[98] For the text of this provision, see F. Deák and P. C. Jessup, *op. cit.*, Vol. 1, p. 479. Actually, almost identical rules were adopted by Finland, Iceland, Norway and Sweden pursuant to a declaration signed on May 27, 1938, adopting uniform rules of neutrality. For the text of this declaration, see F. Deák and P. C. Jessup, *op. cit.*, Vol. 2, p. 1518.

the requirements of general international law. Therefore, the revision of the law which is advocated clearly applies to the body of conventional international law which presently regulates the subject. But the problem cannot be solved in terms of simple formulas which endeavor to restore to the law of neutrality the nineteenth century dichotomy of the individual and the state.[99] Rather, the solution of the problem must be focused against the background of twentieth century conditions. As such, it demands a frank recognition that in respect to the law of neutrality the state must be made to answer for the private actions of individuals. In so doing, the glaring paradox of allowing a state to remain neutral while at the same time permitting its citizens to participate individually in the conflict will to a great extent be eliminated. It is hoped that this step will in turn remove the loophole which so far has rendered the law rather ineffective. Perhaps it may not be an exaggeration to say that the law of hostile military expeditions is destined to occupy a pivotal position in the present reorganization of the world society.

[99] For a general plea in this connection, see H. J. Morgenthau, "The Dilemmas of Freedom," *Am. Pol. Sci. Rev.*, Vol. 51, p. 714 (1957).

CHAPTER V

RECRUITMENT AND DEPARTURE OF VOLUNTEERS

Technically different from military expeditions, which are characterized by some kind of organization, is the practice of private individuals to cross the frontiers of their own state, either singly or in greater numbers, in order to join the forces of a belligerent power or to participate in a foreign civil war. As in the case of military expeditions, however, these persons are nationals of a state which is on peaceful terms with the government against which they enlist, thus posing the interesting question whether the former has the obligation to prevent their departure. Largely because these individuals presumably join the foreign force without the intervention and compulsion of their government, international practice has referred to them as volunteers. But, since recent events unmistakably demonstrate that these volunteers are used by states as instruments of aggression, their impact upon the peace and security of mankind can no longer be ignored.[1]

VOLUNTEERS AND NEUTRALITY

While the departure of volunteers from neutral territory has not traditionally engaged the responsibility of a neutral,[2] their use in substantial numbers as an instrument of governmental policy produces a situation which imperatively calls for the revision of the old law.[3] The customary rule in this connection is found in Article VI of the Hague Convention No. V of 1907, which provides that "the responsibility of a neutral Power is not engaged by the fact of persons crossing

[1] In October and November, 1956, when Israeli forces invaded Egypt, and France and Great Britain joined them, the Soviet Government threatened to permit "volunteers" to act in behalf of Egypt. See Q. Wright, "Intervention, 1956," *Am. J. Int. L.*, Vol. 51, pp. 257, 259 (1957).

[2] N. J. Padelford, *International Law and Diplomacy in the Spanish Civil Strife*, p. 74 (1939).

[3] For a treatment of this matter, see I. Brownlie, "Volunteers and the Law of War and Neutrality," *Int. & Comp. L.Q.*, Vol. 5, pp. 570–580 (1956).

the frontier separately to offer their services to one of the belligerents."[4] The only prohibition imposed is the formation of combatant corps to assist any of the belligerents as found in Article IV of the Convention.[5] It has been seen quite clearly that this Article really prohibits the organization of military expeditions in neutral territory, and that the obligation contained in it does not go beyond the prevention of such expeditions in the manner indicated.[6] As previously submitted, the cardinal distinction embodied in these two articles reflected the nineteenth century *laissez faire* philosophy whereby a line of demarcation was drawn between the sphere of the government and that of the individual, thus implicitly assuming that purely private actions of the individual could not be imputed to the state.[7] It has thus resulted that while in respect to military expeditions the neutral state has the obligation to prevent their departure, in respect to volunteers the state has remained singularly free from any legal obligation. However, the totalitarian character of wars and the almost complete government control of the activities of the individual in time of war have made the individual-state dichotomy for the law of neutrality factually nonexistent.[8] Therefore, it is the measure of the inadequacy of the nineteenth century *laissez faire* philosophy that the assumptions on which Article VI of the Hague Convention was founded no longer have any conceivable basis. Consequently, in respect to volunteers, there is no adequate legal obligation under conventional international law. The present status of the law is succinctly described by Judge John B. Moore in the following terms:

> No act, for example, could be more clearly unneutral than that of a citizen of a neutral country in going abroad and enlisting in the military or naval service of a belligerent; and yet this is an act which a neutral government is not obliged to prevent, and neutral governments do not in fact undertake to prevent it.[9]

This statement of the law in respect to the neutral state does not, however, mean that the individual volunteer has no status in international law. Under international law, volunteers have been assimilated

[4] Hague Convention No. V, Art. VI. For text, see W. M. Malloy, *Treaties, International Acts, Protocols and Agreements between the United States of America and Other Powers*, Vol. 2, p. 2298 (1910).

[5] Hague Convention No. V, Art. IV. For text, see W. M. Malloy, *op. cit.*, Vol. 2, p. 2298. See also A. C. Raja Gabaglia, *Guerra Direito Internacional*, p. 321 (1949).

[6] This was fully discussed in Chapter IV, *supra*.

[7] J. Stone, *Legal Controls of International Conflict*, p. 384 (1954).

[8] Cf. P. E. Corbett, *Law and Society in the Relations of States*, pp. 242–243 (1951).

[9] As quoted in C. C. Hyde, *International Law Chiefly as Interpreted and Applied by the United States*, Vol. 3, p. 2306 (2d ed., 1945).

to the insurgents or belligerents they join.[10] In this connection, Emerich de Vattel's treatment of this matter is illustrative of this position. Thus, Vattel considered the practice of enlisting volunteers as commendable, but said that if they are captured, they should "be treated by the enemy as if they formed part of the army in which they are fighting... for they are in fact part of that army, and they support the same cause; and it matters little whether they do so from obligation or of their own free will."[11] This statement represents the standard treatment of volunteers in the practice of nations. But even this conception, proceeding from one of the fathers of international law, left the states virtually free from the legal obligation to prevent its citizens from joining insurgent and belligerent forces, though it did foreshadow the responsibility of private persons which has presently emerged in full force.

Frail as the *laissez faire* conceptions have thus become in the presence of contemporary realities, three considerations still remain which seem to give some support to the older law. The first is the conviction, still apparently existing, that individuals crossing the frontier to enlist in the army of a belligerent or of an insurgent, do not seriously endanger the position of the opposing belligerent so as to constitute a violation of the neutrality or the duty of non-intervention of the government that permits their departure.[12] Deeply embedded in this conviction is the supposition that the security of a state is only endangered when there is a military organization, since only an organization of this kind can provide the necessary strength to augment the forces of one of the belligerents. It is of some significance to add that this assumption has been adhered to with impeccable consistency, even in cases where a number of individuals simultaneously cross the frontier thus constituting a substantial body of prospective fighters.[13] Secondly, the rather attractive thesis has been advanced that since the formation of corps of volunteers is exclusively due to private initiative, it is quite possible to keep it from any governmental knowledge or interference.[14] This argument loses all its cogency and validity when considering that the

[10] D. P. Myers, "Contemporary Practice of the United States Relating to International Law," *Am. J. Int. Law*, Vol. 54, pp. 632, 656 (1960).

[11] E. de Vattel, *Le Droit des Gens*, bk. III, ch. XV, sec. 230 (Transl. by C. G. Fenwick, 1916).

[12] This apparently was at one time the position of the United States, as seen in the Rules of Land Warfare, 1917, No. 400, note 1. Quoted in C. C. Hyde, *op. cit.*, Vol. 3, p. 2306 n. 3.

[13] See the note of Secretary of State Knox to the Mexican Chargé d'Affaires, June 7, 1911. G. H. Hackworth, *Digest of International Law*, Vol. 7, p. 410 (1943).

[14] Cf. A. Rougier, *Les Guerres Civiles et le Droit des Gens*, p. 418 (1903).

present state organization is so pervasive that the government counts on adequate means to control the movement of people within its jurisdiction. Finally, it has strongly been suggested that the prohibition of the departure of volunteers would presently violate Article 13, paragraph 2, of the Universal Declaration of Human Rights, which guarantees to each individual the right to leave his country and return to it at will.[15] It is respectfully submitted that this argument seriously misconceives the purposes of the Universal Declaration of Human Rights, for any casual observer of the situation would immediately realize that the Declaration guarantees the lawful exercise of the rights therein contained and in a manner not endangering the peace and security of mankind. It is reasonable to assume that the framers of the Declaration intended the rights thus guaranteed to be subordinated to the requirements of world peace.[16] This assertion is supported by the Declaration itself, for it provides in the Preamble for the necessity "to promote the development of friendly relations between nations."[17] One needs no great effort to realize that the departure of volunteers from a state with the purpose of participating in a war or civil strife in foreign territory scarcely tends to develop friendly relations between the nations concerned. Thus, the act of leaving the country to join belligerent or insurgent forces is so patently at variance with the requirements of the world community as to render it wholly incapable of becoming the source of a legal right.

INTERNATIONAL AND NATIONAL REGULATIONS

Rejecting the fictions and assumptions upon which the older rules rested, there are some conventions of a rather limited character which modify somewhat the law in respect to both international war and civil strife. Thus, as regards civil strife, the General Treaty of Peace and Amity of the Central American States of 1923[18] provides in Article 14 that "none of the Contracting Parties will permit the persons under its jurisdiction to organize armed expeditions or *to take part in any hostilities which may arise in a neighboring country.*"[19] Similarly, Article

[15] I. Brownlie, *op. cit.*, p. 579.

[16] Cf. H. Lauterpacht, *International Law and Human Rights*, ch. 17 (1950).

[17] For text of the Declaration, see *Am. J. Int. L. Supp.*, Vol. 43, p. 127 (1949).

[18] For text, see Conference on Central American Affairs, Washington, December 4, 1922 – February 7, 1923, p. 287 (1923).

[19] General Treaty of Peace and Amity of Central American States, February 7, 1923. Italics supplied.

1, paragraph 1 of the Pan American Convention on the Rights and Duties of States in the Event of Civil Strife adopted at Habana in 1928[20] binds the contracting states "to use all means at their disposal to prevent the inhabitants of their territory, nationals or aliens, from participating in, gathering elements, crossing the boundary or sailing from their territory for the purpose of starting or promoting civil strife."[21] In respect to a foreign war, the Habana Convention on Maritime Neutrality of 1928,[22] while providing in Article 23 that "neutral states shall not oppose the voluntary departure of nationals of belligerent states even though they leave simultaneously in great numbers," further says that "they may oppose the voluntary departure of their own nationals going to enlist in the armed forces." Finally, in the General Declaration of Neutrality of the American Republics approved at the Meeting of Foreign Ministers held at Panama on October 3, 1939,[23] it was provided in paragraph 3(c) that the American Republics:

> shall prevent on their respective territories the enlistment of persons to serve in the military, naval, or air forces of the belligerents; the retaining or inducing of persons to go beyond their respective shores for the purpose of taking part in belligerent operations; the setting on foot of any military, naval or aerial expedition in the interests of the belligerents...

The matter has also been regulated by bilateral agreements. Thus, the Treaty of Brotherhood and Alliance between Iraq and Trans-Jordan, signed on April 14, 1947,[24] says in Article 6:

> In the event of the outbreak of disturbances or disorders in the territory of one of the High Contracting Parties, each of them undertakes reciprocally as follows:
>
> (a) To take all possible measures or actions:
>
> 1. To make it impossible for the insurgents to utilize his territory against the interests of the other High Contracting Party, and
>
> 2. To prevent his subjects from taking part in the disturbances or disorders, or from helping or encouraging the insurgents...

[20] Convention with Other American Republics, February 20, 1928, 46 Stat. 2749, T.S. No. 814. For text, see *The International Conferences of American States* 1889–1928, p. 435 (J. B. Scott ed., 1931).

[21] Convention with Other American Republics, February 20, 1928, 46 Stat. 2749–50. See also L. A. Podestá Costa, "La Revisión de la Convención Interamericana sobre Derechos y Deberes de los Estados en caso de Luchas Civiles," *Inter-Amer. J. Y.B.* 1949, p. 9 (1950).

[22] Pan American Maritime Neutrality Convention, February 20, 1928, 47 Stat. 1889–94, T.S. No. 845. For text, see *The International Conferences of American States* 1889–1928, p. 428 (J. B. Scott ed., 1931).

[23] For text, see *Am. J. Int. L. Supp.*, Vol. 34, p. 9 (1940).

[24] *U.N. Treaty Ser.*, Vol. 23, I, No. 345.

In addition to the above provisions, the legislation of a number of states similarly forbids the departure of volunteers from their jurisdiction. Thus, the United States Criminal Code provides as follows:

Whoever, within the United States, enlists or enters himself, or hires or retains another to enlist or enter himself, or to go beyond the jurisdiction of the United States with intent to be enlisted or entered in the service of any foreign prince, state, colony, district, or people as a soldier or as a marine or seaman on board any vessel of war, letter of marque, or privateer, shall be fined not more than $ 1,000 or imprisoned not more than three years, or both.[25]

This provision acquired a special significance during the Spanish Civil strife of 1936 when some three hundred Americans joined the Loyalist forces, while a smaller number served with the Nationalists.[26] Since such enlistment took place outside the jurisdiction of the United States, it is believed that the provisions of the Code were wholly inapplicable.[27] However, the State Department officially warned American citizens that serving "in either of the opposing forces in Spain is unpatriotically inconsistent with the American Government's policy of the most scrupulous non-intervention in Spanish internal affairs."[28]

In like vein, the British Foreign Enlistment Act of 1870[29] prohibits the enlistment of British subjects in the foreign armed forces of belligerents without the permission of the Crown.[30] During the Spanish Civil War the British Foreign Office issued a warning to the effect that the Foreign Enlistment Act was applicable to the conflict in Spain and, accordingly, it was "an offense for any British subject to accept or agree to accept any commission or engagement in the military, naval, or air service of either party to the present conflict, or for any person within the United Kingdom to induce any other person to accept or agree to accept any such commission or engagement."[31]

Also the French Law of January 21, 1937,[32] authorized the govern-

[25] Foreign Relations Act, 18 U.S.C. sec. 959 (a) (1952). It would seem that the "Flying Tigers," organized and recruited by Colonel Chennault in the United States for the war of China against Japan, was a violation of this provision as well as of the neutrality of the United States.

[26] N. J. Padelford, *op. cit.*, p. 186.

[27] *Ibid.*, p. 185.

[28] *Ibid.*, p. 185, n. 25.

[29] 33 & 34 Vic., c. 90.

[30] 33 & 34 Vic., c. 90, sections 4–7. In 1940, following the League of Nations Resolution, permission was granted to British subjects to enlist in the Finnish Forces fighting against the Soviet Union. See I. Brownlie, *op. cit.*, p. 579.

[31] For text, see N. J. Padelford, *op. cit.*, p. 317.

[32] For text, see F. Deák and P. C. Jessup, *A Collection of Neutrality Laws, Regulations and Treaties of Various Countries*, Vol. I, p. 603 (1939).

ment to take the necessary measures to prevent the departure of volunteers to participate in the Spanish Civil War. More particularly, the law prohibited in Article 1, Section 1, paragraph (a) "the enlistment or other acts tending to enlist persons in the forces which presently fight in Spain or in Spanish possessions, including the sphere of influence of Spain in Morocco." This provision, however, appeared to have been narrowly interpreted, for in the case *Public Prosecutor v. Ledkowski and Others*,[33] involving three White Russians, residing in Paris, who admitted having left Paris with the intention of crossing the frontier and enlisting in Franco's army, the court held that their journeying within the country "with the ultimate intention of crossing into Spanish territory is not the commencement of a 'departure' within the meaning of the law, but should be considered as a mere preparatory act, which under the penal law is not liable to punishment."[34] According to the court, therefore, departure only takes place upon leaving French territory, which would seem to make the law rather ineffective to prevent the movement of persons within the country, even though such movement is a link in the journey which would ultimately enable the volunteer to reach his foreign destination.

The legislation of other countries may be cited which similarly prohibits the departure of volunteers. Thus, the decree of El Salvador regarding the neutrality of the country in a foreign or civil war enacted on October 9, 1912,[35] prohibits in Article 3 the recruiting of volunteers and the organization of military expeditions. Finally, the East German Law on the Defense of Peace enacted on December 16, 1950,[36] provides in Section 2, paragraph 1, that: "whoever... recruits, induces, or incites Germans to take part in warlike actions which serve to subjugate another people, shall be punished by imprisonment or, in grave cases, by imprisonment at hard labor."

It follows from the preceding exposition that even if no universally binding convention imposes upon the states the duty to prevent the departure of volunteers from their territory, the domestic legislation of the state may explicitly prohibit it.[37] These provisions, concurrent

[33] *Annual Digest* 1935–1937, p. 278 (1941).
[34] *Ibid.*
[35] For text, see F. Deák and P. C. Jessup, *op. cit.*, Vol. 1, p. 566.
[36] Law on Defense of Peace, December 16, 1950. For text, see *Am. J. Int. L. Supp.*, Vol. 46, p. 99 (1952).
[37] It is conceded, however, that the enactment of this legislation is not due to any duty imposed by international law, but is rather a matter of convenience to avoid external complications. See in this connection L. A. Podestá Costa, *Derecho Internacional Público*, Vol. 2, pp. 172–173 (3d ed., 1955).

with the conventions previously quoted, show that there is a firm conviction among governments that the departure of volunteers should be made an international delinquency, and that Article VI of the Hague Convention Number V falls short in this regard.[38] It is indeed a matter of the gravest doubt whether the large influx of volunteers during the Spanish Civil War or of the Chinese volunteers at the time of the Korean conflict in 1950 could really proceed without such organization as to avoid the application of Article IV of the Hague Convention.[39] One needs no great effort to realize that any considerable amount of volunteers would almost certainly have to proceed through an organization of some sort.[40] To insist on calling them "volunteers" in an attempt to exempt them from the application of Article IV of the Hague Convention amounts to concealing the reality of the situation, thereby permitting a state to participate covertly in a conflict without in any way changing its privileged status as a neutral. Continuous adherence to this outmoded concept seriously impairs the possibility of effective regulation of the subject. It is therefore submitted that no real progress is possible in this area until such verbal illusions are abandoned. Once this is done, the hard fact will have to be faced that the departure of volunteers violates the independence of the state against whom they are directed,[41] thus constituting an act of aggression.[42] Certainly, the Spanish Government, in a note to the United States Secretary of State, characterized the influx of German and Italian volunteers as "acts of invasion and aggression" and desperately appealed to the principles embodied in Pan American Conventions and the Kellogg-Briand Pact of 1928.[43] In respect to the intervention of the Chinese

[38] P. C. Jessup, *A Modern Law of Nations*, p. 200 (1947).

[39] Professor Julius Stone persuasively argues this point. See J. Stone, *op. cit.*, p. 389. A. Rougier said sometime ago that though the formation of corps of volunteers is surely due to private initiative and not to state initiative, its importance is such that it is impossible to keep it from the knowledge of the government and when this is the case, it must be prevented. See A. Rougier, *op. cit.*, p. 418.

[40] J. Stone, *op. cit.*, p. 389. For the boldness with which governments act, see note 1, *supra*.

[41] Thus, Article 4 of the Draft Declaration on Rights and Duties of States, prepared by the International Law Commission of the United Nations, provides: "Every State has the duty to refrain from fomenting civil strife in the territory of another State, and to prevent the organization within its terrritory of activities calculated to foment such civil strife." International Law Commission, Report, U.N. General Assembly, Official Records, Fourth Session, Supp. No. 10 (A/925), (1949). For text, see *Am. J. Int. L. Supp.*, p. 16 (1950).

[42] This would be an aggression which is not an armed attack. See "The Question of the Definition of Aggression," Memorandum submitted by Ricardo J. Alfaro to the International Law Commission of the United Nations, A/CN.4/L.8, May 30, 1951.

[43] Note from the Spanish Ambassador to the Secretary of State, *U.S. Foreign Rel.*, 1938, Vol. I, p. 180 (1955).

Communist volunteers in the Korean conflict, the General Assembly Resolution of February 1, 1951, found that "by giving... assistance to those who were already committing aggression in Korea and by engaging in hostilities against the United Nations forces there," the Central People's Government of the People's Republic of China had itself engaged in aggression.[44] It may be pertinent to add that the International Law Commission of the United Nations has suggested that a definition of aggression should include within its terms the sending of volunteers to engage in hostilities against another state.[45] As the relationship between volunteers and aggression became fairly clear in the Communist intervention in the Korean situation in 1950, it may be profitable to discuss it in more detail.

THE CHINESE INTERVENTION IN KOREA

As previously indicated, volunteers joining belligerent forces have been assimilated to those forces, thus acquiring a belligerent status in international law.[46] As long as volunteers were confined to a few isolated individuals, the situation remained fairly free from doubt. However, with the advent of totalitarian governments claiming ideological followers in other states, a situation has arisen which has severely put to a test the validity of the present law. The crucial question in its simplest terms is therefore the responsibility of the state from which volunteers depart. This situation first came to the attention of mankind during the Spanish Civil War, when substantial bodies of Communists, Nazis and Fascists coming from the Soviet Union, Germany and Italy respectively, joined the forces more in line with their ideologies.[47] The situation arose again in an even more acute form in 1950, when the so-called "Chinese People's Volunteers" entered the Korean hostilities against the United Nations forces. Though technically speaking, these volunteers were regarded as distinct from the forces of the People's Republic of China,[48] behind these

[44] U.N. General Assembly, Official Records, Fifth Session, Sup. No. 20, p. 1 (A/1775) (1951). It should be noted, however, that this conclusion could be reached because the original movement of North Korea into the Republic of Korea had already been characterized as an aggression.

[45] For text, see U.N. General Assembly Official Records, Sixth Session, Supp. No. 9 (A/1858) (1951); *Am. J. Int. L. Supp.*, Vol. 45, pp. 103, 121 (1951).

[46] D. P. Myers, *op. cit.*, pp. 632, 656.

[47] N. J. Padelford, *op. cit.*, pp. 73–77.

[48] In fact, the Armistice Agreement signed on July 27, 1953, was signed between

legal niceties the fact still remained that they were subordinated to, and supplied by, the Chinese Communist Government. This interpretation was possible because of the narrow construction given to Article VI of the Hague Convention No. V according to which the "responsibility of a neutral Power is not engaged by the fact of persons crossing the frontier separately to offer their services to one of the belligerents."[49] Wholly apart from the fact that the Chinese Communist forces were engaged in action against lawful United Nations forces in the area, this intervention offers a contemporary illustration of the totally inadequate range of Article VI of the Hague Convention.

Much debate surrounded the question regarding the legal position of the Chinese Communist forces, but the body of opinion in the Political and Security Committee of the General Assembly[50] clearly indicated that in any event Article VI of the Hague Convention was obsolete and that the Chinese intervention fell more properly within the provision of the United Nations Charter which prohibits its members from giving any "assistance to any state against which the United Nations is taking preventive or enforcement action."[51] While this argument is admittedly open to question since the Chinese Communist regime is not represented in the United Nations, a more defensible position would proceed on the theory that Article VI of the Hague Convention is exclusively limited to volunteers crossing the frontier individually and singly,[52] and not those crossing the frontier *en masse*, for the presumption immediately arises that they form part of a fighting organization or unit.[53] This presumption is aided by the fact that it is scarcely possible for a substantial number of persons to cross the frontier without some sort of organization.[54] Moreover, the present day state control over the movement of persons is so pervasive and complete that the departure of a vast number of individuals to participate in a foreign or civil war must necessarily count upon the approval of

the United Nations Command, on the one hand, and the Supreme Commander of the Korean People's Army and the Commander of the Chinese People's Volunteers, on the other. For the text of the Armistice, see *Am. J. Int. L. Supp.*, Vol. 47, p. 186 (1953).

[49] For text, see note 4, *supra*.

[50] See U.N. General Assembly, Official Records, Fifth Session, First Committee, p. 401 (1950).

[51] U.N. Charter, art. 2, paragraph 5. This argument was maintained by the Turkish Delegate and supported by other representatives. See U.N. General Assembly, Official Records, Fifth Session, First Committee, p. 405 (1950).

[52] A. P. Higgins, *The Hague Peace Conferences and Other International Conferences Concerning The Law and Usages of War*, p. 280 (1909).

[53] See in this connection the remarks of the Cuban Representative. See U.N. General Assembly, Official Records, Fifth Session, First Committee, pp. 409–411 (1950).

[54] The amount was estimated at 268,000 Chinese troops. *Ibid.*, p. 410.

the state, thus engaging its international responsibility.[55] It is perhaps worth mentioning in this connection that when the situation as to the threat of the political independence and the territorial integrity of Greece was discussed in the General Assembly of the United Nations, the French Delegate pointedly commented that so much assistance had been furnished Greek guerrillas in Albania, Bulgaria and Yugoslavia "that it was hard to believe that the Governments of those countries were unaware of it or even that they had not fostered it."[56] And, specifically, as to the Communist intervention in Korea, the Government of the United States offered to prove by competent evidence that "the Chinese authorities in control of the territory of Manchuria and other Chinese territories, calling themselves the Central People's Government of the People's Republic of China, were active participants in the military aggression then being waged in the Korean theater against the Republic of Korea..."[57]

The Chinese intervention forces thus afford an instructive example of volunteers that ceased to be so within the meaning of the Hague Convention because their disproportionate number made it reasonable to assume the existence of a military organization.[58] Though the arguments of the representatives of the Soviet and Iron Curtain countries put forth before the Political and Security Committee of the General Assembly were well worn and emotionally charged,[59] they are nevertheless useful in showing the inadequacy of applying the 1907 Hague Convention, founded on nineteenth century conceptions, to wholly different conditions. It is indeed of some significance to observe that the Soviet Union representative might have been keenly aware of this situation, for in proposals for a definition of aggression, permitting volunteers to depart from a state's territory has been included within its terms.[60] It is only by a persistent display of bad faith that one can

[55] For development of this thesis, see J. Stone, *op. cit.*, p. 411.

[56] See U.N. General Assembly, Official Records, Third Session, First Committee, 172d Meeting, p. 271 (1948).

[57] Quoted in D. P. Myers, *op. cit.*, p. 657.

[58] "Volunteers" have been adequately described by the Delegate of Israel to the First Committee of the General Assembly as "war by power of attorney... [which] has become a feature of strategy since the end of the Second World War." See Complaint of the Union of Burma regarding aggression against it by the Government of the Republic of China, U.N. General Assembly, Official Records, Seventh Session, First Committee, 608th Meeting, p. 669 (1953).

[59] For some of these views, see U.N. General Assembly, Official Records, Fifth Session, First Committee, pp. 415–419 (1950). See also W. W. Kulski, "Soviet Comments on International Law and International Relations," *Am. J. Int. L.*, Vol. 45, pp. 556, 558 (1951).

[60] The International Law Commission of the United Nations has strongly recom-

consider the Chinese intervention forces as falling outside the scope of that definition.

It may be finally suggested that whether one considers the Chinese intervention forces as volunteers or not, the inevitable fact remains that in either case such forces were fighting against the forces of the world community engaged in a lawful undertaking. It would seem that when this is the case, the exemption provided for by Article VI of the Hague Convention loses all its useful meaning, for, technically speaking, it could not be applied to states hindering organized community action. That this interpretation was adopted is clearly borne out by the Resolution of the General Assembly of February 1, 1951, branding the Chinese Communist Government an aggressor for its unlawful intervention.[61] This resolution, moreover, stands as a living reminder that though the matter has been settled for the present, the future possibility of legally imputing international responsibility to a state for allowing large numbers of volunteers to depart from its territory is still to be determined by a revision of the existing conventional law. Because of its urgency and vitality, the formulation of this principle in a revised convention can no longer be deferred.

CONCLUSION

In conclusion it may be said that in the area of volunteers, as in the case of hostile military expeditions, it is absolutely necessary, if any progress is to be made, that obsolete conceptions be discarded in favor of a more realistic understanding of the world situation as it affects the effectiveness of the law. The years that have elapsed since the adoption of the Hague Conventions have made it crystal clear that volunteers are really instruments of international policy and not simply innocent foreigners who for ideological reasons join belligerent forces. The stark clarity of this situation should not be concealed by the legal obscurities invoked by the Soviet representative in an attempt to justify the intervention of the Chinese Communist forces in the Korean situation.[62] In the analysis of the legal standing of these forces, itit was shown to exist grave technical obstacles to regarding the Chinese Communist forces as included within Article IV of the Hague Convention,[63] prohi-

mended that a definition of aggression should include the sending of volunteers "to engage in hostilities against another State." For text, see note 45, *supra*.

[61] For text, see note 44, *supra*.

[62] See J. Stone, *Aggression and World Order: A Critique of United Nations Theories of Aggression*, p. 20, n. 11 (1958).

[63] See note 5, *supra*.

biting the formation of combatant corps to aid any of the belligerents. But it was also shown, contrary to the Soviet view, that the so-called Chinese volunteers could not be included in Article VI of the Convention, for this article applies to volunteers crossing the frontier singly and individually, and not to those crossing in such great numbers as to presume the existence of some kind of organization.[64] Certainly, this second view of the Chinese volunteers avoids dangerous and impossible overstrain of Article VI. Yet it may be essential to bear in mind that to get out of this inextricable dilemma resort was had to the provisions of the United Nations Charter which prohibits its members from giving any "assistance to any state against which the United Nations is taking preventive or enforcement action."[65] It should be kept in mind, however, that the invocation of the United Nations Charter in no way removes the need for amending the Hague Conventions, for events have shown the necessity of considering volunteers, either singly or in great numbers, as a threat to good relations between nations and, thus, seriously affecting the peace and security of mankind. In such a case, a frank recognition of the obligation of the state to prevent the departure of volunteers would seem to be eminently desirable. It is therefore hoped that future international legislation in this area will firmly implant this legal duty with as much clarity and precision as it can reasonably muster. Under such a development, one more source of friction between governments would accordingly be eliminated.

[64] L. A. Podestá Costa, *op. cit.*, Vol. 2, p. 173.
[65] U.N. Charter, art. 2, paragraph 5.

CHAPTER VI

REVOLUTIONARY ACTIVITIES AND HOSTILE PROPAGANDA

It is a fairly well established legal proposition that subversive activities or revolutionary propaganda stemming from official sources is an international delinquency and, thus, redressable under international law.[1] However, an area of controversy is entered when dealing with revolutionary activities or hostile propaganda proceeding from private individuals. The preliminary problem thus arises of adequately imposing international responsibility on the state for hostile acts committed by private persons under the protection of its territorial sovereignty and directed against the peace and security of a foreign state. While it is generally agreed that revolutionary acts of private persons are liable to be punished by the criminal law of the state against which they are directed under the so-called protective jurisdiction principle,[2] international law becomes equally involved when the menaced state is unable to punish such activities thereby frustrating its possibilities of maintaining internal peace.[3] It is the purpose of this chapter to explore the position of international law on this subject.

THE PRINCIPLES OF INTERNATIONAL LAW

Private revolutionary activities against foreign states present the initial and vital questions concerning the competence of international law to deal with them and the existence of a duty of prevention on the part of the territorial state. Though the rules of international law on this matter have not been considered as sufficiently precise to insure international cooperation,[4] it may be quite possible to suggest a control

[1] C. Rousseau, *Droit International Public*, p. 374 (1953).
[2] For a full discussion of this principle, see Chapter IX, *infra*.
[3] H. Lauterpacht, "Revolutionary Activities by Private Persons Against Foreign States," *Am. J. Int. L.*, Vol. 22, p. 105 (1928).
[4] See in this connection the Resolution of the Council of the League of Nations of December 10, 1934, in respect to the alleged terrorist activities of Yugoslav nationals in Hungary. *Publications of the League of Nations*, p. 219 (1934).

of private revolutionary activities both by international law and by the law of each individual state.

As matters stood prior to the legal transformation following World War II, the rules of customary international law not only failed to impose upon the territorial state the duty to prevent subversive activities on the part of the individual against foreign governments, but also denied to the affected nation a corresponding right to redress.[5] More precisely, the international law position of this period seemed to indicate that the international responsibility of the state was not engaged in so far as private revolutionary activities were concerned.[6] The right of the aggrieved community could scarcely exceed one of vigorous protest. The net result of this legal position was the lack of a legal duty of the territorial state to enforce observance thereof upon citizens and aliens alike. International law, therefore, did not itself make the toleration of private revolutionary activities an international delinquency. What it did was to grant the liberty to the wronged state to deal with offending individuals who came into its jurisdiction. It thus became almost generally accepted that persons threatening a state's political institutions from foreign territory were amenable to the jurisdiction of the aggrieved state.[7] In so doing, international law made available to the state the so-called protective ground upon which to exercise jurisdiction.[8]

The failure of international law to bring private hostile activities against foreign states within its regulation can be broadly attributed to three factors. The first is that, while the authority of international law is generally conceded, in principle that authority has stopped short in matters stemming from the exercise of territorial sovereignty inasmuch as the latter is not only exclusive but is also a right protected by international law itself. It is, therefore, possible to argue, as Judge Dionisio Anzilotti apparently did,[9] that in so far as territorial supremacy exists, "international law presupposes the state" and, thus, the state cannot be held accountable by international law unless it should neglect its duties specifically emanating from a treaty.[10] The

[5] L. Preuss, "International Responsibility for Hostile Propaganda against Foreign States," *Am. J. Int. L.*, Vol. 28, p. 649 (1934).

[6] L. Oppenheim, *International Law*, Vol. 1, p. 293 (8th ed. by H. Lauterpacht, 1955).

[7] D. H. De Vabres, *Les Principes Modernes du Droit Pénal International*, p. 87 (1928).

[8] Research in International Law under the Auspices of the Harvard Law School, "Jurisdiction With Respect to Crime," *Am. J. Int. L. Supp.*, Vol. 29, p. 543 (1935).

[9] D. Anzilotti, *Cours de Droit International*, Vol. 1, p. 51 (French transl. by G. Gidel, 1920).

[10] *Ibid.*, pp. 466, 467.

central core of this doctrine really proceeds from a conception of sovereignty singularly exempted from any legal regulation.[11] Second, revolutionary actions by private individuals against foreign governments are usually classed as political offenses for which the state has competence to grant asylum under international law.[12] On this view, states are naturally reluctant to punish individuals for the commission of political offenses. This fact is particularly heightened in a conflict of ideology where the asylum state may not feel any special sympathy towards the political institutions of the state of which refugees are nationals and, thus, the suppression of revolutionary propaganda coming from these sources may be viewed with particular antipathy. This argument on principle would still afford no legal warrant for a state's failure to suppress revolutionary propaganda by refugees, for, though there is no question about a nation's right to harbor political refugees, it would seem that consistently with the obligations of friendship between states, such persons may not be permitted to plot against the institutions of their native country.[13] The third factor can best be explained in terms of the dilemma posed by a democratic society in preventing subversive propaganda against foreign governments while at the same time preserving its constitutional liberties.[14] Even if in practice this problem may be real, the obligations of the state on the international plane cannot be avoided by invoking difficulties of internal constitutional order.[15]

[11] Apparently, Judge Charles De Visscher held similar views. See C. De Visscher, *Theory and Reality in Public International Law*, pp. 103–104 (Transl. by P. E. Corbett, 1957). See also G. Scelle, *Précis de Droit des Gens: Principes et Systématique*, Vol. 1, p. 80 (1932).

[12] Cf. M. R. García-Mora, *International Law and Asylum as a Human Right*, ch. 4 (1956).

[13] In fact, this is one obligation that the state granting asylum has to fulfill. Thus, when in March 1960, the United Nations Human Rights Commission urged all governments to extend asylum to any refugee whose life was in danger, it added that "persons enjoying asylum should not engage in activities contrary to the purposes and principles of the United Nations." Cited by Q. Wright, "Subversive Intervention," *Am. J. Int. L.*, Vol. 54, pp. 521, 532, n. 34 (1960).

[14] Upon complaint of the Mexican Government that publications appearing in the United States incited anarchism against Mexico, the State Department answered in part that "free speech and freedom of the press are two of the most sacred rights guaranteed by the Constitution of this country; ...they are absolutely inviolable rights; and... although it may for a moment appear that such rights should be to a greater or less extent curtailed, a continous national growth and development of more than a century and a quarter demonstrates beyond the possibility of a doubt that the public intelligence necessary to a firm and permanent stability and progress requires that such rights shall remain inviolate." Note of Secretary of State Knox to the Mexican Ambassador De Zamacona, June 7, 1911, G. H. Hackworth, *Digest of International Law*, Vol. 2, p. 142 (1941).

[15] In this connection, the Permanent Court of International Justice said: "While on the one hand, according to generally accepted principles, a state cannot rely, as against

It can be readily seen, therefore, that traditional juristic interest was primarily concerned with preserving the rights involved in territorial sovereignty and not at all with the function of international law or with laying a foundation for international cooperation.[16] The difficulty with the problem arises from narrow and oversimplified interpretations which have obscured the issue by formulating it exclusively in terms of territorial sovereignty and, in so doing, international law faithfully reflected the absence of an international community of shared values and social solidarity. In addition, the constructive role which can be played by the development of international cooperation in this area has been in large measure blocked by the extent to which political considerations have been permitted to hold the center of the scene. Parallel with all this, writers on the subject have reflected international sentiment by classifying states into the categories of "liberal" or "reactionary" depending upon whether or not their internal legislation provided for the punishment of revolutionary activities against foreign governments. As late as 1928, Judge Hersch Lauterpacht regarded the Russian Penal Code of 1903 as "the most reactionary of all" because it punished all attempts, conspiracies and preparations within Russian territory designed to overthrow a foreign government.[17] Such a statement may have been largely motivated by the belief that no democratic government could safely extend protection to political systems at variance with the democratic ideology. Since international law until recently was essentially European and the European countries largely subscribed to the democratic ideology, it was relatively simple to conclude that international law imposed no obligation whatsoever to protect foreign states whose political ideology was particularly distasteful. This argument, however, has lost all its useful meaning today when over a hundred states of diverse political systems have come to play a vital role in the world community process, thus transforming the exclusive European nature of international law into a world wide system.[18] The peaceful coexistence of these states in the world com-

another state, on the provisions of the latter's constitution, but only on international law and international obligations duly accepted, on the other hand and conversely, a state cannot adduce as against another state its own Constitution with a view to evading obligations incumbent upon it under international law or treaties in force." Advisory Opinion on Treatment of Polish Nationals in Danzig, *P.C.I.J.* Ser. A/B, No. 44, p. 24 (1932).

[16] A. Alvarez, "The Reconstruction and Codification of International Law," *Int. L.Q.*, Vol. 1, pp. 469, 471 (1947).

[17] H. Lauterpacht, *op. cit.*, p. 117; see also Q. Wright, "The Crime of War-Mongering," *Am. J. Int. L.*, Vol. 42, pp. 128, 134 (1948).

[18] C. W. Jenks, *The Common Law of Mankind*, ch. 2 (1958).

munity would seem to suggest that their governments be secured against revolutionary activities and hostile propaganda coming from other jurisdictions.

It can of course be argued that to accept the above analysis would amount to asserting that the international community may become a system of mutual assistance, thus helping to perpetuate tyrannical governments.[19] Though there may be substance in this view, it should be recalled that because of the concentration of power in the modern state popular revolutions are doomed to failure[20] and that, therefore, the interest of the world community in the maintenance of peace is greater than the well intentioned desires of sporadic groups of individuals to overthrow an existing totalitarian government. It certainly runs counter to justice to plunge the world society into a conflagration because of the toleration of private activities designed to overthrow the government of another state. Peace is the first duty of the world community that every state must promote and cultivate. This is an overriding moral obligation.

Even from the standpoint of territorial sovereignty, it must be recognized as axiomatic that the rights inherent in this concept must be exercised in a manner consistent with the equally protected rights of other nations. In this connection, there can be no doubt that a state has a right to independence and to the peaceful enjoyment of its institutions and that this is a right protected by international law. But it so happens that this right is put in danger by revolutionary acts stemming from private individuals under the protection of another country's sovereignty. It is, therefore, a reasonable expectation of every state that the territorial sovereignty of another should not be used in a manner which seriously threatens the former's safety and independence.[21] It would indeed be highly inconsistent with the independence of nations if the citizens of one state were allowed to plot against the institutions of a friendly nation. The force of this argument reveals itself with all its cogency when considering that if a state does not suppress revolutionary actions and subversive propaganda taking

[19] P. C. Jessup, *A Modern Law of Nations*, pp. 184–87 (1947).

[20] Cf. H. J. Morgenthau, *In Defense of the National Interest*, p. 59 (1951).

[21] Thus, Article 2 (6) of the Draft Code of Offenses Against the Peace and Security of Mankind prepared by the International Law Commission of the United Nations in its third session in 1951, makes an offense against the peace and security of mankind "The undertaking or encouragement by the authorities of a State of terrorist activities in another state, or toleration by the authority of a state of organized activities calculated to carry out terrorist acts in another state." For text, see Doc. A/CN.4/48, July 30, 1951 and *Am. J. Int. L. Supp.*, Vol. 45, pp. 103, 128 (1951).

place within its jurisdiction, the customary right of intervention on the part of the menaced government is readily conceded.[22]

The foregoing observations, though usually overlooked, are in the present view the most satisfactory ones, for a world community of states, where the rights of sovereignty and equality are postulates of the law, would of necessity imply a mutual obligation to suppress revolutionary acts directed against a friendly foreign nation. The real issue is, therefore, whether a state values the interest of the world community in peaceful coexistence sufficiently to impose upon itself the obligation to prevent and punish revolutionary activity which endangers good relations between nations.[23] This is clearly an obligation derived from a mutual duty to promote justice between nations.[24]

It would seem, therefore, that in a world community deeply concerned with order and justice, the state ought to be bound to prevent anything which constitutes a danger to foreign nations. This is not to imply that the state has the duty to protect actively the constitution of a foreign government, however distasteful that government may be to its own citizens. What it does imply is a duty of prevention, that is, of preventing injurious acts against foreign governments regardless of whether such acts proceed from official sources or from private individuals.[25] The international responsibility of the state is in either case engaged. If friendly relations between nations be the international common good, then it is essential that the international society constitute a cohesive and integrated whole by insisting upon a system of rights and mutual obligations, instead of being divided into a multiplicity of societies with diverse loyalties and contrasting sentiments, shattering the conception of a community of interests.

Looking comprehensively at the manner in which states fulfill their obligations in this area, three criteria immediately emerge, which suggest the classification of the states into three clearly defined categories. One group, which includes the United States and Great Britain, restricts the duty to prevent subversive acts to obligations arising under the laws of neutrality. The other group, which includes Continental European and South American countries, bases the duty of

[22] Cf. A. V. W. Thomas and A. J. Thomas, Jr., *Non-Intervention: The Law and Its Import in the Americas*, p. 274 (1956).

[23] A. K. Kuhn, "The Complaint of Yugoslavia Against Hungary With Reference to the Assassination of King Alexander," *Am. J. Int. L.*, Vol. 29, pp. 87, 89 (1935).

[24] It will be recalled that Emerich de Vattel thus founded the obligation to prevent injurious acts against a foreign state. See E. de Vattel, Le *Droit des Gens*, bk. II, ch. VI, sec. 72 (Transl. by C. G. Fenwick, 1916).

[25] H. Kelsen, *Principles of International Law*, p. 126 (1952).

prevention on the security of the state by avoiding complications with foreign nations. And, finally, the third group, which includes recent legislation from the Soviet Union and other Iron Curtain-countries, considers subversive acts and propaganda against foreign states as an offense against the peace and security of mankind. The application of these principles will be discussed in dealing with the legislation and case law of the various countries.

THE PRINCIPLE OF NEUTRALITY

The Law of the United States

The Law of the United States in respect to subversive acts planned or being committed against a foreign state by private individuals is exclusively confined to obligations resulting from the laws of neutrality relating to an international or a civil war. It is not surprising, therefore, that political plots against foreign nations are made punishable in the United States only when such acts adopt the form of a military or naval expedition or enterprise against a state with which the United States is on friendly terms.[26] The American position in this regard leaves no room for doubt. Thus, in 1885 when the British Government inquired whether participating in the Irish National League, an organization to promote revolutionary movements in Ireland, was an offense against the sedition statutes of the United States, the State Department succinctly answered that "treason and sedition made punishable under those statutes are treason and sedition against the United States, and they do not make punishable treason and sedition against foreign sovereigns."[27] Similarly, in 1907 the Mexican Government protested that revolutionary plots were being fomented in the United States for the purpose of launching attacks in Mexican territory. The Attorney General, while admitting that there had been publications in this country, by citizens of Mexico residing in the United States, of newspapers and circulars directed against the administration of President Díaz and intended to incite uprisings and foment revolutionary movements in Mexico, declined to act on the ground that there was not yet any evidence that the persons involved had violated the neutrality laws of the United States by initiating a military expedition to be

[26] See Chapter IV, *supra*.

[27] See Note from Secretary of State Bayard to the British Representative, Mr. Harris, April 2, 1885. J. B. Moore, *A Digest of International Law*, Vol. 2, pp. 431–432 (1906).

carried on from the United States against Mexico.[28] In a communication of July 31, 1885, addressed to the Spanish Minister, relating to revolutionary activities of the supporters of the Cuban insurrection, the State Department expressed similar views in an even more definite form: "It [the United States] does not assume to visit with penalty conduct, which if committed within a foreign jurisdiction, might be punished therein."[29] Finally, President Grover Cleveland's fourth message to Congress, in referring to the revolutionary activities of Cubans in the United States, deplored that "the spirit of our institutions and the tenor of our laws do not permit [revolutionary activities] to be made the subject of criminal prosecution."[30]

The body of evidence thus far gathered would seem to make it clear that in American law three conditions must exist in order to convert an otherwise unpunishable revolutionary act into a criminal offense. First, the purpose of the alleged offense must be an attack or invasion against a foreign country; second, it must proceed from the territory of the United States; and, finally, it must take the form of a military or naval force. In the absence of these conditions, the United States is reluctant to extend the restrictions placed upon its residents and declines to punish revolutionary activities confined to incitement to revolt or to foment uprisings in a foreign state.

The foregoing point is also applicable to libel and seditious publications against foreign governments.[31] For in so far as these are private publications, governmental action in this area is likely to give rise to difficulties involving the Constitutional guarantee of freedom of speech and of the press.[32] Concurrently with this is the fact that in the United States there is no federal common law of crimes and, thus, federal crimes must be established by statute.[33] Inasmuch as no federal statute exists providing punishment for the defamation of foreign govern-

[28] Note of Ambassador Creel to Secretary of State Root, March 4, 1907, G. H. Hackworth, *op. cit.*, Vol. 2, pp. 337–38. It should be added that subsequently the persons involved were convicted for violations of the neutrality statutes when they pleaded guilty to the charge of beginning and setting on foot a military expedition against Mexico. *Ibid.*, pp. 338–39.

[29] Note of Secretary of State Bayard to Minister Valera, July 31, 1885, *U.S. Foreign Rel.* 1885, p. 776 (1886).

[30] *U.S. Foreign Rel. 1896*, p. xxxi (1897).

[31] E. D. Dickinson, "The Defamation of Foreign Governments," *Am. J. Int. L.*, Vol. 22, p. 840 (1928), dealing specifically with the alleged defamation of the Mexican Government by the Hearst Newspapers in 1927.

[32] See the note of Secretary of State Knox to the Mexican Ambassador De Zamacona, June 7, 1911, G. H. Hackworth, *op. cit.*, Vol. 2, p. 142.

[33] United States v. Hudson & Goodwin, 11 U.S. (7 Cranch) 32 (1813). See also for discussion, R. von Maschzisker, "Common Law and Our Federal Jurisprudence," *U. Pa. L. R.*, Vol. 74, pp. 109, 270, 367 (1925–1926).

ments, a criminal prosecution in such cases would only be cognizable in the courts of the states.[34] Most of these principles are well illustrated in the communications of the State Department answering complaints of foreign governments for libelous propaganda published in newspapers in the United States. On such occasions, the State Department, in explaining the inability of the United States to act, has invariably referred to freedom of speech and of the press which is, "under the Constitution of the United States, absolutely assured to those dwelling within its jurisdiction,"[35] while at the same time calling to the attention of the foreign government in question that an action against the publisher could possibly be maintained in the proper state court.[36]

It is to be immediately observed that such assertions of the State Department can scarcely meet the international obligations of the United States to afford foreign governments adequate protection against revolutionary propaganda and libelous publications. Moreover, as Professor Percy E. Corbett might say, they can hardly be expected to promote a sense of community among the peoples of the world.[37] As propositions of law, their validity is dubious. It certainly is no argument to assert that a state is not bound to accede to requests from foreign nations which are incompatible with its laws and constitution. For not only can the federal government act under the constitutional power of Congress "To define and punish... Offenses against the Law of Nations,"[38] but it is common learning that statutes in the United States have imposed criminal liability for seditious utterances and publications injurious to public morals, and such statutes have been upheld by the courts against attacks grounded upon freedom of speech and of the press.[39] The operation of this type of legislation, how-

[34] J. B. Moore, *op. cit.*, Vol. 2, p. 432. It seems, however, that the laws of the United States make a penal offense the secret transportation of explosives from the United States to any foreign country. *Ibid.*, p. 431. See also the case Daeche v. United States, 250 Fed. 566 (2d Cir. 1918), involving the conviction of a person for attempting to blow up ships leaving the port of New York loaded with munitions for the Allied Powers in World War I.

[35] Note of Secretary of State Knox to the Mexican Ambassador De Zamacona, June 7, 1911, G. H. Hackworth, *op. cit.*, Vol. 2, p. 142.

[36] Note of Secretary of State Knox to the Mexican Chargé d'Affaires, February 15, 1911, G. H. Hackworth, *op. cit.*, Vol. 2, p. 142.

[37] P. E. Corbett, *Law in Diplomacy* (1959).

[38] *U.S. Constitution*, art. I, sec. 8.

[39] See in this connection, Schenck v. United States, 249 U.S. 47 (1919), affirming a conviction under the Federal Espionage Act, 40 Stat. 217 (1917), for causing or attempting to cause insubordination in the military forces of the United States by sending to men, who had been newly drafted into the army, pamphlets denouncing conscription and urging them to assert their rights in opposition to the draft. Also Dennis v. United States, 341 U.S. 494 (1951), affirming a number of convictions for violation of section 2

ever, has been carefully circumscribed, for the courts have explicitly required that it must meet the "clear and present danger" rule, which essentially means that before an utterance can be penalized by the government it must ordinarily have occurred "in such circumstances" or have been of "such a nature as to create a clear and present danger" that it would bring about "substantive evils" within the power of the government to prevent.[40] Thus viewed, it is difficult to see why legislation penalizing revolutionary activities and hostile propaganda against foreign governments could not be applied within the same limits.[41] It must be added that it is most questionable on grounds of public policy whether the United States can remain totally passive in the presence of activities calculated to create hostile feelings in foreign states and, more specifically, to cause a breach of peace between nations.[42] This last argument commends itself most cogently in practice, for it is indissolubly linked with the respect which nations owe each other at all times.

The Law of Great Britain

Like its American counterpart, the law of Great Britain has been predominantly based on the principle of neutrality and, therefore, does not punish revolutionary plots and treasonable acts against foreign states unless they form part of a military or naval expedition.[43] But despite this substantial similarity between the two laws, significant differences may nevertheless be observed.

First, when revolutionary activities assume the character of publications against the person of a foreign sovereign the English law treats them as criminal libel and punishable as such. The *raison d'être* of this rule is the well founded apprehension that if such hostile publications are permitted to go unpunished, peaceful relations with foreign nations may thereby be disturbed.[44] Thus, when in 1762 the King of Denmark

of the Smith Act, 54 Stat. 670 (1940), for advocating, advising and teaching the desirability of overthrowing the government by force. And, finally, Gitlow v. New York, 268 U.S. 652 (1925), dealing with a similar sedition law of New York.

[40] Schenck v. United States, 249 U.S. 47, 52 (1919).

[41] Q. Wright, *op. cit.*, p. 134.

[42] It should be observed that when the First Committee of the General Assembly discussed measures to be taken against propaganda and the inciters of a new war, the majority of the delegates felt that defamation of leaders of foreign governments was a form of war propaganda. See in particular the opinion of the Australian Delegate, Dr. Evatt. U.N. General Assembly, Second Session, First Committee, 79th Meeting, pp. 184–88 (1947).

[43] Foreign Enlistment Act of 1870, 33 & 34 Vic. ch. 90.

[44] L. Oppenheim, *op. cit.*, Vol. 1, p. 283.

complained of a scandalous and indecent publication contained in the *London Chronicle*, the Attorney-General emphatically stated:

> [S]candalous and injurious reflections published in derogation of the Honour and Dignity of Foreign States and Princes in Amity with his Majesty may be punished criminally by Information or Indictment as libel, because such Reflections tend to interrupt the Harmony and Confidence which subsists between the Crown of Great Britain and Its Allies...[45]

The English courts have been similarly strict in dealing with cases of defamation of a foreign sovereign. In this connection, in *King v. Vint*, involving a libelous publication against the Emperor of Russia, the Lord Chief Justice declared:

> I can only say, that if one were so to offend another in private life in this country, it might be made the subject of an action; and when these papers went to Russia and held up this great sovereign as being a tyrant and ridiculous over Europe, it might tend to his calling for satisfaction as for a national affront, if it passed unreprobated by our government and in our courts of justice.[46]

In a somewhat similar vein, in *King v. Peltier*, involving a libel against Napoleon Bonaparte as First Consul, the court unmistakably laid down as a proposition of law that "any publication which tends to degrade, revile, and defame persons in considerable situation of power and dignity in foreign countries may be taken to be and treated as a libel, and particularly where it has a tendency to interrupt the pacific relations between the two countries."[47]

It seems likely, however, that the liberal conceptions of freedom of the press and of expression of opinion which obtained in the twentieth century have somewhat limited the above holdings to the special circumstances of their origin.[48] This proposition is instructively illustrated by the more recent case of *King v. Antonelli & Barberi*, involving a libel in the form of a pamphlet, attempting to justify the crimes of assassination and murder, and to incite persons to commit those crimes upon the sovereigns and rulers of Europe. The significance of this decision lies in the fact that, contrary to previous rulings, the court held that "a document published in this country, which is calcu-

[45] Cited by A. D. McNair, "Aspects of State Sovereignty," *Brit. Y.B. Int. L.* 1949, Vol. 26, pp. 6, 27 (n.d.).

[46] 27 Howell's State Trials 627, 641 (1799), per Lord Kenyon, C. J.

[47] 28 Howell's State Trials 529, 617 (1803), per Lord Ellenborough, C. J. See also King v. Lord George Gordon, 22 Howell's State Trials 175 (1787), involving a libel against the Queen of France and the French Ambassador.

[48] English writers seem to agree on this point. See A. D. McNair, *International Law Opinions*, Vol. 1, pp. 10–14 (1956), and H. Lauterpacht, *op. cit.*, pp. 114–15.

lated to disturb the government of some foreign country, is not a seditious libel, nor punishable as a libel at all."[49]

Secondly, incitement to assassinate the head of a foreign government is also rigorously punishable under English law. Thus, the Act of 1861 dealing with Offenses Against the Person provides in its pertinent provision:

> All persons who shall conspire, confederate, and agree to murder any person, whether he be a subject of Her Majesty or not, and whether he be within the Queen's dominions or not, and whosoever shall solicit, encourage, persuade or endeavour to persuade, or shall propose to any person, to murder any other person, whether he be a subject of Her Majesty or not, and whether he be within the Queen's dominions or not, shall be guilty of a misdemeanor...[50]

The foregoing provision has occasionally come before the courts. The leading case in this connection is *Regina v. Most*,[51] involving the publication and circulation of an article, written in German in a newspaper in that language in London, exulting in the murder of the Emperor of Russia and commending it as an example to revolutionists throughout the world. In affirming the defendant's conviction, the court held that the publication and circulation of a newspaper article might be an encouragement to persuade to murder, within the statute, although not addressed to any person in particular.[52] A similar principle was applied in *King v. Antonelli & Barberi* previously cited.[53] There the court, in deciding upon the sufficiency of the indictment in regard to the contention that no prospective victim of the act had been specifically mentioned, held that "sovereigns of Europe" specified a sufficiently definite class and, therefore, that the counts of the indictment were good. It should be added that the Act is clearly applicable to subjects and aliens alike,[54] within and without the realm,[55] as long as there exists a permanent or temporary allegiance to the Crown.

[49] 70 J.P. 4 (1905), 14 The English and Empire Digest 99 (1956).

[50] Offenses Against the Person Act of 1861, sec. 4, 24 & 25 Vic. ch. 100.

[51] [1881] 7 Q.B. 244.

[52] See also the Opinion of the Law Officers of the Crown in respect to a complaint of the Turkish Ambassador relating to an alleged incitement to assassinate the Sultan. The Opinion is printed in A. D. McNair, "Aspects of State Sovereignty," *Brit. Y. B. Int. L.*, 1949, Vol. 26, pp. 28–29 (n.d.).

[53] See note 49, *supra*. It is significant that the same principle was applied in King v. Bowman, 76 J.P. 271 (1912), 15 *The English and Empire Digest* 781 (1957), dealing with an incitement to munity. The court held that "an indictment framed under the Incitement to Mutiny Act, 1797 (c. 70), need not specify any particular person or persons serving in His Majesty's forces by sea or land who have been approached by accused in contravention of the above Act."

[54] Regina v. Sandoval, 56 L.T.R. (n.s.) 526 (Q.B. 1887), per J. Willis.

[55] Regina v. Jameson, [1896] 2 Q.B. 425, per Lord Russell, C.J.

It is of some interest to note that the Canadian Criminal Code follows closely the principles of the English law. Its pertinent provision states that "Everyone is guilty of an indictable offense and liable to one year's imprisonment who, without lawful justification, publishes any libel tending to degrade, revile or expose to hatred and contempt in the estimation of the people of any foreign state, any prince or person exercising sovereign authority over such state."[56] It is quite obvious that this provision is calculated to punish libels against foreign governments and not revolutionary acts of a treasonable character. As to the latter, the Canadian law seems to follow the traditional Anglo-American law in that such acts must be a part of a military or naval expedition.[57]

THE PRINCIPLE OF SECURITY

Unlike Anglo-American law, the legislation of a number of states has regarded private revolutionary acts as well as hostile publications against foreign states as criminal offenses. The underlying motive behind this type of legislation appears to be a firm desire to avoid complications with foreign governments rather than a recognition of an international obligation towards foreign states. The security of the legislating state is therefore of paramount significance, though occasionally some legislative provisions made reference to the maintenance of friendly relations between nations.

In line with the foregoing considerations, the French Penal Code clearly provides that a person shall be liable to punishment for "any hostile act which exposes the State to a declaration of war, or the State or a French citizen to reprisals."[58] It seems generally agreed that this provision is only designed to prevent the commission of revolutionary and subversive acts within French territory. However, the Act Concerning the Freedom of the Press of July 29, 1881,[59] punishes hostile utterances against heads of foreign states and foreign diplomatic agents. More specifically, Article 36 of this law punishes "Insults uttered publicly against the Heads of Foreign States, Heads of Foreign Governments and Ministers of Foreign Affairs of Foreign Govern-

[56] *Can. Rev. Stat.* c. 36 sec. 135 (1927).
[57] See Canadian Act Respecting Foreign Enlistment, April 10, 1937, art. 10, F. Deák and P. C. Jessup, *A Collection of Neutrality Laws, Regulations and Treaties of Various Countries*, Vol. 1, pp. 236, 239 (1939).
[58] Code Pénal art. 84. For text, see F. Deák and P. C. Jessup, *op. cit.*, Vol. 1, p. 583.
[59] For text of this Act, see *U.N. Freedom of Information: A Compilation*, Vol. 2, pp. 30, 34 (1950).

ments." Similarly, Article 37 punishes "Insults uttered publicly against Ambassadors and Plenipotentiary Ministers, Envoys, *Chargés d'Affaires* or other diplomatic agents accredited to the Government of the Republic."[60]

The Italian law on the subject seems to apply exclusively to revolutionary acts and there seems to be no specific provision dealing with hostile propaganda against foreign governments.[61] Thus, the pertinent provision of the Italian Penal Code stipulates that "any person shall be liable to punishment who by enlistment or other hostile acts unauthorized by the government exposes the State to the danger of war or reprisals, or, in general, who disturbs the friendly relations between the Italian Government and a foreign State."[62] The corresponding provision of the Swiss Penal Code establishes that "If a person attempts, from Swiss territory, to disturb the political order of a foreign State by violence, he shall be liable to imprisonment."[63] But the Code is not exclusively confined to revolutionary activities, for Article 296 punishes hostile propaganda in the following terms: "If a person publicly insults a foreign State in the person of its Head, its diplomatic representative or its Government, he shall be liable to imprisonment or a fine." The interpretation of this last provision clearly indicates that attacks in the press are included.[64] It should be observed, however, that prosecution under these two articles can only be undertaken at the request of a foreign government and only if reciprocity is assured.[65]

In addition to the above provisions, the laws of a small number of states punish libelous publications by individuals against foreign

[60] These two provisions were included in articles 92 and 93 of the Act Regulating the Press, of June 30, 1947. For text, see *Ibid.*, pp. 44, 45. Though the articles are substantially the same, Article 92 merely increases the fine to 10,000 to 5,000,000 francs instead of the former 1,000 to 1,000,000 francs in regard to insults against the heads of foreign states.

[61] This appears from the reply which the Italian Government gave the United Nations Secretariat, Department of Social Affairs, as found in *U.N. Freedom of Information: A Compilation*, Vol. 1, pp. 10–11 (1950). In any event, the Act of February 8, 1948, establishing Provisions Concerning the Press, does not have any provision dealing with hostile propaganda against foreign states. For this law, see *U.N. Freedom of Information: A Compilation*, Vol. 2, pp. 67–69 (1950).

[62] Italy, Penal Code, art 113, as quoted in H. Lauterpacht, *op. cit.*, p. 119.

[63] Switzerland, Penal Code, December 21, 1937, as amended, art. 299.

[64] See the reply of the Swiss government to inquiry from the United Nations Secretariat, Department of Social Affairs, *U.N. Freedom of Information: A Compilation*, Vol. 1, pp. 214–15 (1950).

[65] Switzerland, Penal Code, December 21, 1937, as amended, art. 302. Though Switzerland is traditionally a land of refuge for the politically persecuted, hospitality is granted under the condition that refugees restrain from hostile acts against their own government. There have been many instances of deportation of political refugees for failure to abide by this condition. See J. Dumas, *De La Responsabilité Internationale des États*, p. 59 (1930).

states. Thus, the Iranian Act of February, 1908, Concerning the Press, punishes in Articles 40 and 41 "Attacks against the Sovereigns of Friendly States," and casting "slurs on the honor of foreign officials and members of foreign political assemblies."[66] In like manner, the Swedish Constitutional Act of March 23, 1949, Relating to the Freedom of the Press, prohibits in Article 4 utterances which are an "affront to the flag or shield of a foreign Power or to any other symbol of its sovereignty or libel or other defamatory act against the head or representative of a foreign Power here in the Kingdom."[67] Apparently, similar legislation is presently found in India,[68] Lebanon,[69] and Norway.[70]

Being much troubled by internal revolutions, the Central and South American countries have similarly enacted legislation punishing revolutionary activities emanating from their jurisdiction. Thus, Section 297 of the Penal Code of Peru of 1924 makes it an offense to violate the territorial sovereignty of a foreign state as well as to commit acts designed to alter by force the political order of other states. Also Article 115 of the Penal Code of Panama of 1922 punishes any one who within Panamanian territory commits an offense against the head of a foreign state, and adds that in such cases prosecution is to be had at the request of the foreign government in question. Similarly, Articles 367 and 368 of the Penal Code of the Dominican Republic of 1927 make it a criminal offense to libel and slander the head of a foreign friendly nation, while Articles 84 and 85 punish any hostile act disapproved by the Government which exposes the Republic to a declaration of war. It is of some interest to note in reference to these provisions that when in 1927 two journalists published libelous remarks against a deceased ex-president of the United States, a Dominican court interpreted them as applying to the head of a friendly nation and not to a deceased person who held the position when alive.[71] More recently, the Federal Supreme Court of Argentina denied habeas corpus to an Uruguayan citizen whose internment had been asked by the Uruguayan Government because of his seditious activities in Argentine territory to disturb the political order of Uruguay. The Supreme Court relied upon the Treaty of International Penal Law of

[66] For text, see *U.N. Freedom of Information: A Compilation*, Vol. 2, pp. 60, 63 (1950).
[67] For text, see *U.N. Freedom of Information: A Compilation*, Vol. 2, pp. 69, 74 (1950).
[68] India, Foreign Relations Act, 1932, as reported in *U.N. Freedom of Information: A Compilation*, Vol. 1, p. 212 (1950).
[69] Lebanon Government Decree of May 6, 1924, *Ibid.*, p. 212.
[70] Norway, Penal Code of May 22, 1902, chap. 23 *Ibid.*, p. 213.
[71] This case is anonymously reported in *U.N. Freedom of Information: A Compilation*, Vol. 2, p. 191 (1950).

Montevideo of January 23, 1889, which in guaranteeing the right of asylum, imposed upon the asylum state the duty to prevent "those taking asylum from carrying out on its territory acts which put in danger the public peace of the nation against which they have offended."[72]

The foregoing recital of municipal codes and legislation is a commendable recognition that friendly relations between states is a value of the world community and that these relations may be impaired by revolutionary activities and hostile propaganda on the part of individuals. Admittedly, the protection afforded foreign governments is motivated by considerations of security, thus being in reality incidental to the legislating nation's own interest.[73] As a practical matter, however, the line between the protection of the state's security and that of foreign states is not so very clear and in particular cases is fairly difficult to mark. It may be further noted that in this type of legislation there is at least an attempt to balance these interests so as to foster the development of reciprocal obligations along a course not wholly independent of the necessity for peaceful intercourse between nations. This requirement seems entirely proper, both in principle and policy, if revolutionary activities and hostile publications by private individuals against foreign states are to be adequately controlled. It may be entirely relevant to add that though a cloud of pessimistic gloom has been cast upon laws dealing with hostile propaganda,[74] this fact only emphasizes the urgency and necessity for their strict application.

AN OFFENSE AGAINST THE PEACE AND SECURITY OF MANKIND

Ironically enough, it is the legislation of the countries of the Soviet bloc that has emphatically classified private hostile activities against foreign states within the broader head of war propaganda and, thus, punishable as an offense against the peace and security of mankind. In this connection, Article 1 of the Peace Defense Act of the Soviet Union enacted on March 12, 1951, states that "war propaganda, in whatever form conducted, undermines the cause of peace, creates the

[72] *In re* Barreta, Argentina, Federal Supreme Court, *Annual Digest 1933–1934*, pp. 259, 260 (H. Lauterpacht ed. 1940).

[73] Research in International Law under the Auspices of the Harvard Law School, "Jurisdiction with Respect to Crime." *Am. J. Int. L. Supp.*, Vol. 29, p. 552 (1935).

[74] L. J. Martin, *International Propaganda*, p. 207 (1958); and J. B. Whitton, "Radio Propaganda – A Modest Proposal," *Am. J. Int. L.*, Vol. 52, pp. 739, 744–45 (1958).

danger of a new war and is therefore a grave crime against humanity."[75] More specific is the Czechoslovak Act on the Protection of Peace enacted on December 20, 1950, which provides in Section 1, paragraph 1 that "Any person who attempts to disturb the peaceful communion of nations by inciting in any way whatsoever to war, by propagating war or otherwise supporting war propaganda, shall commit a criminal act against peace."[76] Similarly, the East German Law on Defense of Peace enacted on December 16, 1950, states in Section 1 that "Whoever slanders other peoples and races, incites against them, and demands their boycott in order to disturb peaceful relations between them to involve the German people in a new war, shall be punished by imprisonment or, in grave cases, by imprisonment at hard labor."[77] The Albanian Law on Defense of Peace passed on January 10, 1951, provides in Section 1 that:

> Whoever directly or indirectly, orally or by means of the printed word, radio, or any other media, attempts to provoke an armed aggression of one state upon another; advocates the increase of armaments, the use of such weapons of mass destruction as the atom bomb, chemical and bacteriological weapons, and the like; advocates and propagates the doctrine of hatred among nations for the purpose of unleashing a new war; or commits any other acts aimed at the military and economic preparation of future aggression and causing in the minds of the people anxiety and fear of the possibility of a new war, shall be committing the crime of incitement to war and war propaganda.[78]

The Bulgarian Law on Defense of Peace enacted on January 12, 1951, states in Section 2 that "Instigation to war is committed by a person who endeavors directly or indirectly – by means of press, radio, speech, or other media – to provoke armed aggression by one state against another."[79] It must also be noted that strikingly similar laws have been enacted by Hungary,[80] Poland,[81] Rumania,[82] and the Outer Mongolian Republic.[83]

The above legislative provisions are very impressive indeed. Their approach is useful on two grounds. First, such legislation is directed against private hostile propaganda, thus implicitly assuming that the toleration of such activities engages the responsibility of the state.

[75] For text, see *Am. J. Int. L. Supp.*, Vol. 46, p. 34 (1952).
[76] For text, *Ibid.*, p. 35.
[77] For text, *Ibid.*, p. 99.
[78] For text, *Ibid.*, p. 101.
[79] For text, *Ibid.*, p. 102.
[80] Enacted on December 10, 1950, sec. 1. For text, *Ibid.*, p. 103.
[81] Enacted on December 31, 1950, sec. 1. For text, *Ibid.*, p. 103.
[82] Enacted on December 16, 1950, sec. 2. For text, *Ibid.*, p. 104.
[83] Enacted in 1951, art. 1. For text, *Ibid.*, p. 105.

Secondly, by adopting the broader concept of war propaganda, these legislative provisions make it reasonably clear that the interest violated is not that of the menaced state but, more significantly, an interest of the world community in the maintenance of peace. That incitement to commit aggression against another state is included in the crime of war propaganda can scarcely be denied. But the fact that the assumptions of the Communist legislation in defense of peace are in principle sound does not mean that their practical application must therefore be accepted. For the value of these provisions is partly deceptive both because of the use of carefully concealed language for the promotion of Communist objectives,[84] and because of the profound hostility of Communist policy towards all non-Communist states. This latter factor is not lightly to be set aside, for it is of some significance to observe that the preamble of the East German law specifically makes allusion to an alleged "aggressive policy of the imperialist governments of the USA, Great Britain, and France ..."

In view of the preceding observations and considering the Marxist social theory that the capitalist world is doomed to perish,[85] it follows logically that the Communist laws in defense of peace are only designed to protect countries having a Communist ideology, thus implicitly identifying threats to peace with the policy of the capitalist countries.[86] It is not at all surprising, therefore, that hostile propaganda against capitalist countries may be regarded by the Communist governments as merely hastening the inevitable process of their destruction.[87]

INTERNATIONAL REGULATION

Under the United Nations Charter

The traditional principle that states are under no obligation to suppress revolutionary activities and hostile publications by private individuals against foreign states breaks down altogether in the presence of obligations imposed by the United Nations Charter. For the Charter represents a turning point in efforts to suppress threats to peace coming from whatever source. It is pertinent to recall in this

[84] W. W. Kulski, "Soviet Comments on International Law," *Am. J. Int. L.*, Vol. 46, p. 131 (1952).

[85] H. Kelsen, *The Communist Theory of Law*, chs. 1, 3 (1955).

[86] K. Grzybowski and M. Pundeff, "Soviet Bloc Peace Defense Laws," *Am. J. Int. L.*, Vol. 46, pp. 537, 539 (1952).

[87] Cf. J. Stone, *Legal Controls of International Conflict*, p. 59 (1954).

connection that the Charter declares in paragraph 5 of its preamble that the peoples of the United Nations will "practice tolerance and live together in peace with one another as good neighbors." It is of capital importance to add that among the purposes of the United Nations as found in Article 1, paragraph 2, is the development of "friendly relations among nations based on respect for the principle of equal rights and self-determination of peoples, and to take other appropriate measures to strengthen universal peace." The twin assumptions concerning the equality of states and the rights of all peoples to choose the form of government under which they wish to live seem to have permeated this provision.[88] Since these assumptions are basic postulates of universal peace, it is not easy to see how the legality of a state's passivity in the presence of private revolutionary activities can be internationally admitted and the existence of a duty to prevent them be so emphatically denied.

The preceding argument is reflected quite explicitly in Resolution No. 2 adopted by the United Nations Conference on Freedom of Information held at Geneva in March and April of 1948. The pertinent part of the Resolution states that the Conference "Condemns solemnly all propaganda designed or likely to provoke or encourage any threat to the peace, breach of the peace, or act of aggression, and all distortion and falsification of news through whatever channels, private or governmental, since such activities can only promote misunderstanding and mistrust between the peoples of the world and thereby endanger lasting peace which the United Nations is consecrated to maintain."[89] It is also to be noted that in almost identical tones some governments expressed the belief that "all governments owe a duty not only to their own citizens but also to international law to suppress all activities which might prejudice international peace or law and order..."[90] Such assertions reveal a clear picture of what international law and the world community should be if the objectives of the United Nations Charter are to be attained. And when the argument is thus reduced to a requirement of the world community, the conclusion of law that private hostile activities prejudice international peace becomes, in turn, a demand that the states be required to suppress them. Such a

[88] L. M. Goodrich and E. Hambro, *Charter of the United Nations: Commentary and Documents*, pp. 61–62 (1946).

[89] *U.N. Conference on Freedom of Information*, Final Act, Doc. E/Conf. 6/79, April 22, 1948, p. 23.

[90] Cited by J. B. Whitton, "United Nations Conference on Freedom of Information and the Movement Against International Propaganda," *Am. J. Int. L.*, Vol. 43, pp. 73, 77 n. 19 (1949).

demand then falls naturally into place alongside the duties inherent in territorial sovereignty. Viewed in that position, its conclusiveness upon every state becomes fairly plain.[91]

If the foregoing observations be correct, the interesting question arises whether a state's tolerance of revolutionary activities and hostile propaganda by private individuals is such a threat to the peace of the world that the matter properly falls within the peace enforcement powers of the United Nations.[92] Clearly, the Security Council may, as Article 34 of the Charter makes explicit, "investigate any dispute, or any situation which might lead to international friction or give rise to a dispute, in order to determine whether the continuance of the dispute or situation is likely to endanger the maintenance of international peace and security." This broad phraseology roughly corresponds to Article 11 of the League of Nations Covenant which in paragraph 2, "declared to be the friendly right of each Member of the League to bring to the attention of the Assembly or of the Council any circumstance whatever affecting international relations which threatens to disturb international peace or the good understanding between nations upon which peace depends." Certainly, under the Charter the Security Council has broad authority to concern itself with any dispute or situation which is likely to endanger the maintenance of international peace and security. A close analysis of this proposition will immediately reveal that the power of the Security Council does not come into operation when the dispute or situation has already endangered international peace or security. The power of the Security Council is immediately operative upon the existence of a dispute or situation well in advance before it threatens the peace of the world. But under Article 34 the power of the Security Council is limited to two functions: (1) to investigate any dispute or situation; and (2) to determine whether its continuance is likely to endanger the maintenance of international peace and security.[93] Limited though these powers are, it nevertheless remains true that these are only preliminary to further action, and they in reality permit the Security Council to make determinations of fact precedent to the exercise of its peace enforcement functions.[94]

Against this background, revolutionary activities and hostile propa-

[91] P. C. Jessup, *op. cit.*, p. 178.

[92] *U.N. Charter* chs. VI, VII.

[93] The matter may be brought to the attention of the Security Council by any member of the United Nations, by a state which is not a member, or the Security Council itself may take notice of the dispute or situation. See in this connection *U.N. Charter* arts. 34 and 35.

[94] *U.N. Charter* art. 36.

ganda by private individuals against foreign states fall into proper perspective. For in terms of the kind of international peace and security which the United Nations seeks to achieve, toleration by a state of private hostile activities against nations with which it is presumably on friendly terms is probably a situation likely to endanger the maintenance of international peace, thus falling unmistakably within the provision of Article 34 of the United Nations Charter and clearly within the investigatory powers of the Security Council.[95] It may even consitute a danger to justice according to Article 2, paragraph 3 of the United Nations Charter, which forcibly commands the members of the United Nations to "settle their international disputes by peaceful means in such a manner that international peace and security, and *justice*, are not endangered."[96] It should be recalled in reference to this latter provision that Vattel regarded such a conduct as a violation of the mutual duty to promote justice between nations.

The foregoing analysis is powerfully supported by the experience of the League of Nations on the subject. For the legal problems involved were thoroughly explored in the complaint presented on November 22, 1934 by Yugoslavia against Hungary in respect to the assassination of King Alexander while paying an official visit to France.[97] Essentially, the Yugoslav Government maintained that the assassination of the King was the result of plots and terrorist activities by Yugoslav refugees in Hungarian territory. It is highly significant to point out that the Yugoslav complaint was squarely based on Article 11, paragraph 2, of the Covenant of the League of Nations which has been seen to

[95] Thus, the Mutual Security Act of 1951, enacted by the United States Congress has been said to be of doubtful character from the standpoint of international law, for Section 101 (a) of the Act appropriates up to $ 100,000,000 "for any selected persons who are residing in or escapees from the Soviet Union, Poland, Czechoslovakia, Hungary, Rumania, Bulgaria, Albania, Lithuania, Latvia, and Estonia, or the Communist dominated or Communist occupied areas of Germany and Austria, and any other countries absorbed by the Soviet Union either to form such persons into elements of the military forces supporting the North Atlantic Treaty Organization or for other purposes, when it is similarly determined by the President that such assistance will contribute to the defense of the North Atlantic Area and to the security of the United States." For text, see Public Law 165, 82nd Congress. 1st Sess. (H.R. 5113); 65 Stat. 373–74 (1951). For a discussion of the questionable character of this provision, see D. W. Bowett, *Self-Defense in International Law*, pp. 46–47 (1958). For the complaint against the United States by the Iron Curtain Countries, see U.N. General Assembly, Official Records, Sixth Session, First Committee, 472nd to 475th Meetings at pp. 99–121 (1951). Dr. C. G. Fenwick also believes that this act is violative of Article 2, paragraph (5) of the Draft Code of Offenses Against the Peace and Security of Mankind in that it undertakes and encourages activities calculated to foment civil strife in another state. See C. G. Fenwick, "Draft Code of Offenses Against the Peace and Security of Mankind," *Am. J. Int. L.*, Vol. 46, pp. 98, 99 (1952).

[96] Italics supplied.

[97] For a discussion of this case, see A. K. Kuhn, *op. cit.*

correspond substantially to Article 34 of the United Nations Charter. It should be similarly observed that the complaint did not invoke the first paragraph of Article 11, which referred to "any war or threat of war."[98] More specifically, the Yugoslav note asked the League to investigate "this situation, which seriously compromises relations between Yugoslavia and Hungary, and which threatens to disturb the peace and good relations between nations."[99] It can hardly be denied that such a situation was a danger to the maintenance of peace, for Czechoslovakia and Rumania associated themselves with Yugoslavia in almost identical notes, and the discussion in the Council of the League reached matters involving the peace settlement of 1919. This turn of events shows remarkably well that there was a growing conviction among the members of the League that the issue was not simply one of settling responsibility for the assassination of King Alexander. The more far-reaching question was presented whether a state is obligated by international law to suppress activities subversive of the political and social order of a foreign nation. That the Council answered this question in the affirmative is not seriously open to doubt, for it unanimously approved a resolution on December 10, 1934, clearly stating that "it is the duty of every State neither to encourage nor tolerate on its territory any terrorist activity with a political purpose"; and that "every State must do all in its power to prevent and repress acts of this nature and must for this purpose lend its assistance to governments which request it."[100] It would appear, therefore, that the League of Nations regarded the general principle concerning the duty of a state to protect other states from injurious acts originating within its jurisdiction, which is historically traceable to the *Alabama Claims Arbitration*,[101] as being susceptible of wider application. On this view, the widely applied distinction between organized

[98] Article 11, para. 1, provided: "Any war or threat of war, whether immediately affecting any of the Members of the League or not, is hereby declared to be a matter of concern to the whole League, and the League shall take any action that may be deemed wise and effectual to safeguard the peace of nations. In case such emergency should arise the Secretary-General shall on the request of any Member of the League forthwith summon a meeting of the Council."

[99] As quoted by A. K. Kuhn, *op. cit.*, p. 88.

[100] It should be pointed out that this resolution was based upon Article X of the Covenant which stated: "The Members of the League undertake to respect and preserve as against external aggression the territorial integrity and existing political independence of all Members of the League. In case of any such aggression or in case of any threat or danger of such aggression the Council shall advise upon the means by which this obligation shall be fulfilled." The corresponding provision of the United Nations Charter is art. 2, para. 4.

[101] United States v. Great Britain (1871). For the record of this arbitration, see J. B. Moore, *A Digest of International Law*, Vol. 7, pp. 1059–1067 (1906).

hostile expeditions which are condemned by international law and revolutionary acts by individuals which are not, has no defensible basis, for in either case there seems to be enough ground for liability.

If the experience of the League has any value, the Yugoslav-Hungarian dispute appears to be conclusive upon two points. First, the action of the League was essentially a recognition that as regards private revolutionary activities the state has a definite obligation to prevent them. Secondly, a state's tolerance of such activities engages its international responsibility amounting to an international delinquency. This conclusion is not only inescapable, but the United Nations cannot safely afford to ignore it.[102]

Under International Conventions

It was precisely because of the deep implications of the Yugoslav-Hungarian dispute that the Council of the League set up a committee of experts with a view to adopting an agreement for the suppression of terrorism. This committe drafted a Convention which was adopted at Geneva on November 16, 1937.[103] Though this Convention never entered into effect, it is believed that a recital of its pertinent provisions is in order, if only to show the conviction of the states that private terrorist activities ought to be suppressed. Thus, in Article 1, paragraph 1, the Convention "reaffirmed the principle of international law in virtue of which it is the duty of every State to prevent terrorist activities directed against another State and to prevent the acts in which such activities take shape," and imposed upon each state the obligation "to prevent and punish activities of this nature and to collaborate for this purpose." In Article 3, paragraph 2, the contracting parties agreed to enact legislation punishing "any incitement to commit" terrorism. It is of some significance to add that under the auspices of the League a Convention was adopted in November, 1937,[104] creating an International Criminal Court with jurisdiction to try persons accused of offenses dealt with in the Convention for the Prevention and Punishment of Terrorism. Under the United Nations system, the Draft Declaration on Rights and Duties of States, prepared by the International Law Commission, provides in Article 4 that

[102] In Resolution 380 (V) of November 17, 1950, the United Nations General Assembly declared that "fomenting civil strife in the interest of a foreign Power" is aggression. Cited in *Am. J. Int. L. Supp.*, Vol. 45, p. 128 (1951).

[103] Convention for the Prevention and Punishment of Terrorism. For text, see M. O. Hudson, *International Legislation*, Vol. 7, p. 862 (1941).

[104] For text of this Convention, see M. O. Hudson, *op. cit.*, Vol. 7, p. 878.

"Every State has the duty to refrain from fomenting civil strife in the territory of another State, and to prevent the organization within its territory of activities calculated to foment such civil strife."[105]

It is of some interest to observe that the Soviet Definition of Aggression presented to the Sixth Committee of the General Assembly included as an act of aggression the encouragement of subversive activities against another state as well as fomenting civil war within another nation.[106] Similarly, Article 2, paragraphs (5) and (6) of the Draft Code of Offenses against the Peace and Security of Mankind, also adopted by the International Law Commission, not only prohibits the fomenting of civil strife but also the undertaking or encouragement of terrorist activities in another state.[107] Though these offenses may be said to be committed by the authorities of the state, the International Law Commission itself has acknowledged that the criminal responsibility of private individuals under international law may arise under the provisions of paragraph 12 of Article 2, which considers as an offense against the Peace and Security of Mankind any act which constitutes conspiracy, incitement, attempt or complicity to commit the preceding offenses.[108]

In the field of international propaganda, the Convention Concerning the Use of Broadcasting in the Cause of Peace was adopted at Geneva on September 23, 1936.[109] It is highly interesting that this Convention imposes upon the contracting parties the obligation "to prohibit and, if occasion arises, to stop without delay the broadcasting within their respective territories of any transmission which to the detriment of good international understanding is of such a character as to incite the population of any territory to acts incompatible with the internal order or the security of a territory of a High Contracting Party."[110] It is clear from this provision that no distinction has been made between governmental and private propaganda. In the same area, it should be observed that a number of treaties of peace ending World War II contain a clause imposing upon the defeated nations the obligation to prevent hostile propaganda against the Soviet Union or any one of the

[105] For text, see *Am. J. Int. L. Supp.*, Vol. 44, p. 16 (1950).

[106] See L. B. Sohn, *Cases on United Nations Law*, p. 851 (1956).

[107] See Report of the International Law Commission Covering the Work of its Third Session, 16 May–27 July, 1951; U.N. General Assembly, Official Records, Sixth Session, Supplement No. 9 (A/1858) p. 12 (1951).

[108] *Ibid.*, p. 13.

[109] For text, see M. O. Hudson, *op. cit.*, Vol. 7, p. 409.

[110] Convention Concerning the Use of Broadcasting in the Cause of Peace, art. 1. See also arts. 2, 3, and 4, imposing more specific obligations in the presence of certain crises.

United Nations. Thus, the Peace Treaty with Finland signed in 1947[111] provides in Article 8 that "Finland, which in accordance with the Armistice Agreement has taken measures for dissolving all organizations of a Fascist type on Finnish territory, whether political, military or paramilitary, as well as other organizations conducting propaganda hostile to the Soviet Union or to any of the other United Nations, shall not permit in future the existence and activities of organizations of that nature which have as their aim denial to the people of their democratic rights." Almost identical provisions are found in the Peace Treaties with Bulgaria,[112] Hungary,[113] and Rumania.[114]

The foregoing international experience is powerfully reinforced by a similar experience of the Inter-American system, which has been deeply preoccupied with the problem both of revolutionary activities and of hostile propaganda. As early as 1889, the South American countries signed and adopted the Treaty of International Penal Law at Montevideo on January 23, 1889, which, in dealing with the right of asylum, in Article 16 provided: "Asylum is inviolable for those under prosecution for political crimes, but the nation of refuge has the duty to prevent those seeking asylum from carrying out on its territory acts which put in danger the public peace of the nation against which they have offended."[115] Subsequently, the General Treaty of Peace and Amity signed by the Central American States at Washington, D. C. on December 20, 1907,[116] provided in Article 17 that "Every person, no matter what his nationality, who, within the territory of one of the contracting Parties, shall initiate or foster revolutionary movements against any of the others, shall be immediately brought to the capital of the Republic, where he shall be submitted to trial according to law." It is of some interest to observe that this particular provision came before the Central American Court of Justice in 1908 when Honduras accused Guatemala and El Salvador of unneutral conduct in that refugees in the latter countries were permitted to foment revolution against Honduras.[117] After issuing an interlocutory decree in which the

[111] Signed on February 10, 1947. For text, see *Am. J. Int. L. Supp.*, Vol. 42, p. 203 (1948).

[112] Signed on February 10, 1947. Art. 4. For text, see *Am. J. Int. L. Supp.*, Vol. 42, p. 179 (1948).

[113] Signed on February 10, 1947. Art. 4. For text, see *Am. J. Int. L. Supp.*, Vol. 42, p. 225 (1948).

[114] Signed on February 10, 1947. Art. 5. For text, see *Am. J. Int. L. Supp.*, Vol. 42, p. 252 (1948).

[115] For text, see note 72, *supra*.

[116] See *Am. J. Int. L. Supp.*, Vol. 2, p. 219 (1908).

[117] See *Am. J. Int. L.*, Vol. 2, p. 835 (1908).

court ordered Guatemala, El Salvador and Nicaragua not to assist revolutionary movements within their territory and to confine to one place the political refugees from Honduras, final judgment was rendered on December 19, 1908, absolving the defendant governments of the charges brought against them.[118] The court seemed to have proceeded upon the theory that diplomatic negotiations between the parties had not been exhausted and that Honduras failed to maintain the burden of proof in respect to its allegations.

It is, however, in the area of hostile propaganda where more positive results seem to have been reached. Thus, the South American Regional Agreement on Radio Communications signed at Buenos Aires on April 10, 1935,[119] under Article 7, section 2, obliges the contracting parties to avoid broadcasts containing offensive or defamatory words or ideas against other signatory countries as well as "all kinds of transmissions which have an obvious tendency to jeopardize good international relations." Subsequently, the Inter-American Conference for the Maintenance of Peace held at Buenos Aires in 1936 approved several resolutions urging the American Republics to adhere to the Geneva Convention Concerning the Use of Broadcasting in the Cause of Peace of 1936, and to avoid broadcasting likely to disturb the peaceful relations between the signatories.[120] It may be added that the Charter of the Organization of American States adopted in Bogota in 1948 has a specific provision prohibiting the intervention of one state in the internal affairs of another.[121] It is submitted, however, that though this provision may be broad enough to include hostile propaganda,[122] it is addressed to governmental action and not to activities of private individuals. Of perhaps more significance is the resolution adopted at Bogota in 1948 in which the American Republics agreed to adopt measures against any kind of activities originating from abroad and designed to overthrow their political institutions, to foment internal disorder or to disturb "by means of pressure, subversive propaganda, threats or by any other means," the right of their peoples to govern

[118] See *Am. J. Int. L.*, Vol. 3, p. 434 (1909).
[119] For text, see M. O. Hudson, *op. cit.*, Vol. 7, p. 47.
[120] Cited by J. B. Whitton, "Radio Propaganda – A Modest Proposal," *Am. J. Int. L.*, Vol. 52, p. 739 (1958).
[121] This is article 15 which says: "No State or group of States has the right to intervene, directly or indirectly, for any reason whatever, in the internal or external affairs of any other State. The foregoing principle prohibits not only armed force but also any other form of interference or attempted threat against the personality of the State or against its political, economic and cultural elements." For text, see *Am. J. Int. L. Supp.*, Vol. 46, pp. 43, 46 (1952).
[122] A. V. W. Thomas and A. J. Thomas, Jr., *op. cit.*, p. 292.

themselves.[123] It may be significantly noted that in 1953 the Inter-American Council of Jurists adopted a Draft Convention on the Regime of Political Exiles, Asylees and Refugees, in which Article 6 stated:

> Freedom of expression of thought and of speech, granted by domestic law to all inhabitants of a State, may not be ground for complaint by a third State on the pretext of opinions expressed publicly against it or its government by political exiles, asylees, or refugees, *except when they constitute propaganda tending to incite to the use of force or violence against the complaining State.*[124]

As an added measure of protection, a number of states have entered into bilateral treaties binding themselves to suppress both revolutionary designs and hostile propaganda proceeding from each other's territory. One of the earliest treaties of this kind was the Treaty of Paris of October 8, 1801,[125] signed between France and Russia, which provided in Article 3:

> The two Contracting Parties... engage not to suffer their respective subjects to maintain any correspondence, direct or indirect, with the enemies of the present government of the two States, or to propagate principles contrary to their respective constitutions, or to foment disturbances, and that in consequence of this Agreement, every subject of one of those Powers inhabiting the States of the other, who shall do anything to its safety, shall be removed from the said country and transported beyond its frontiers without having any claim to the protection of its own government.

[123] As quoted by J. B. Whitton, "Radio Propaganda – A Modest Proposal," *Am. J. Int. L.*, Vol. 52, pp. 739, 743 (1958).

[124] Italics supplied. For text, see *Annals of the Organization of American States*, Vol. 5, p. 166 (1953). It is to be observed that two important cases have come before the Council of the Organization of American States which may throw some light on this problem. One case was that of Costa Rica against Nicaragua, in which Costa Rica charged Nicaragua with invading its territory. The investigation ordered by the Council showed that both governments were negligent for not having taken adequate measures to prevent the development in their respective territories of movements tending to overthrow each other's government. For a discussion of this case, see M. R. García-Mora, "The Law of the Inter-American Treaty of Reciprocal Assistance," *Fordham L.R.*, Vol. 20, pp. 1, 15–22 (1951). The other case was that of Haiti against the Dominican Republic, in which the Government of Haiti claimed that it was the victim of "moral aggression" in that a former colonel of the Haitian Army, having taken refuge in Santo Domingo, was engaged in the latter state in plots to overthrow the Haitian Government. After the matter had been submitted to the Council, the two states settled it amicably agreeing not to "tolerate in their respective territories the activities of any individuals, groups, or parties, national or foreign, that have as their object the disturbance of the domestic peace of either of the two neighboring Republics or of any other friendly Nation." *Annals of the Organization of American States*, Vol. 1, p. 326 (1949); see also *Ibid.*, pp. 217–19, 325–26 (1949). The significant point about these cases is that private subversive activities and propaganda in another state may constitute, according to the Inter-American Treaty of Reciprocal Assistance signed at Río de Janeiro in 1947, an aggression which is not an armed attack, thus falling within the provision of Article 6 of the Treaty. For text of this Treaty, see *Am. J. Int. L. Supp.*, Vol. 42, p. 53 (1949).

[125] As cited by H. Lauterpacht, *op. cit.*, p. 120.

In the inter-war period, the Soviet Union concluded a series of bilateral agreements with a number of states designed to suppress revolutionary activities against the Soviet Government abroad as well as to afford a similar protection to other governments in respect to revolutionary acts originating in Soviet territory. Thus, in the peace Treaty between the Soviet Union and Estonia signed on February 2, 1920,[126] both parties agreed in Article 7 "to prohibit the creation and presence in their territories of organizations and groups which claim to be the government of the territory, or a part of the territory of the other contracting party, or of representations and officials of such groups and organizations as aim at the overthrow of the government of the other contracting party." In the same category must be included the short-lived Roosevelt–Litvinov Agreement of November 16, 1933,[127] in which the Soviet Government undertook:

> Not to permit the formation or residence on its territory of any organization or group – and to prevent the activity on its territory of any organization or group, or of representatives or officials of any organization or group – which has as an aim the overthrow or the preparation for the overthrow of, or the bringing about by force of a change in, the political or social order of the whole or any part of the United States, its territories or possessions.

In a similar vein, the Tangier Agreement of 1929 signed between France, Great Britain, Italy and Spain[128] is of singular interest in that it provides in Article 10 that "any agitation, propaganda or conspiracy against the established order in any of the Zones of Morocco or in any foreign country is prohibited." Finally, it seems that since the end of World War II only one bilateral treaty has been entered into, namely, the Treaty of 1948 between India and Pakistan, in which the parties mutually promised to:

> ensure that their respective organizations handling publicity, including publicity through radio and the film, refrain from and control: (a) propaganda against the other Dominion, and (b) publications of exaggerated versions of news of a character likely to inflame, or cause fear or alarm to, the population, or any section of the population in either Dominion.[129]

[126] As cited by H. Lauterpacht, *op. cit.*, p. 120.

[127] Paragraph 4. For text, see G. H. Hackworth, *op. cit.*, Vol. 1, p. 305.

[128] For text, see *Am. J. Int. L. Supp.*, Vol. 23, p. 238 (1929).

[129] U.N. Doc. E/CN.4/Sub. 1/105, p. 29, and quoted in J. B. Whitton, "Radio Propaganda – A Modest Proposal," *Am. J. Int. L.*, Vol. 52, pp. 739, 741 (1958). Most recently, however, Tunisia and the United Arab Republic reached a compromise as regards a Tunisian refugee who in Egypt carried on revolutionary activities against Tunisia. The compromise provides that though asylum may be granted to political refugees, such refugees will be prevented from engaging in any political activity. See N.Y. Times, February 8, 1961, p. 9, col. 1.

These persuasive recitals would seem to be conclusive as to the obligation of a state to prevent revolutionary activities and hostile propaganda by private individuals against foreign states. In default of such a duty, the state has incurred an international responsibility. It is therefore concluded that the view that international law is not violated by private hostile actions against foreign governments may well have become an archaic hangover not at all consonant with international morality and must probably be regarded as unsound. It may be said to be a principle emerging from the international conventions here reviewed that a state's tolerance of private revolutionary activities and hostile propaganda against foreign nations is not only illegal under modern international law but it is also a disservice to the cause of international peace and security.

CONCLUSION

The body of international and domestic law above discussed would seem to establish beyond any reasonable doubt the existence of a duty to prevent the use of a state's territory for hostile private actions designed to change the political or social order of foreign states. While this proposition seems unquestioned, the argument may be advanced that such a duty exists among the states only on the basis of a treaty. On this view, it is readily concluded that even the multilateral conventions here reviewed seem to be based on the assumption that no such duty exists apart from treaty.[130] The validity of this argument is, however, highly deceptive, for this branch of the law is only a phase of the general duty of a state to prevent the commission within its jurisdiction of injurious acts against friendly foreign countries. This duty of prevention is a prescription resulting from the exercise of territorial sovereignty and unmistakably falling within the competence of general international law. It is therefore submitted that the inclusion of this duty in a number of conventions is a recognition on the part of the states of the existence of a rule of general international law, whose validity in terms of substantial justice and policy can scarcely be denied.

[130] This matter is brought out by Professor Julius Stone as regards hostile propaganda on the part of the government, but it is believed that the same observations are applicable to private propaganda. See J. Stone, *op. cit.*, p. 319.

CHAPTER VII

INVASION OF FOREIGN TERRITORY BY ARMED BANDS

Intermediate between the organization of hostile military expeditions and the encouragement of private revolutionary activities is the ever-recurring problem of invasion of a foreign state by armed bands formed within the jurisdiction of a friendly nation.[1] While the activities of armed bands may sometime be difficult to separate from those which fall into the categories of revolutionary activities, and the recruiting and departure of volunteers previously discussed, cases will be seen which do not exactly fit into any of these categories, thus requiring a separate treatment. One thing, however, appears fairly clear, namely, that armed bands differ substantially from hostile military expeditions in that there is in the former no formal organization, nor do they exhibit a strictly military character. There is the further distinction that the operation of armed bands does not require the existence of a state of war nor of an internal strife in the foreign state. They usually operate in time of peace and their activities may range from sporadic raids over frontiers by small groups of individuals to more dangerous threats to the political independence and territorial integrity of a foreign state. This partial catalogue of the activities in which armed bands may be engaged clearly indicates their specific character and the confusion which may result in treating them either as a revolutionary activity or merely as some kind of aggression.[2]

ARMED BANDS AND INTERNATIONAL RESPONSIBILITY

"Armed bands" is a term designating an irresponsible group of individuals who invade foreign territory and commit hostile acts upon persons and property by methods or in circumstances different from those of normal warfare. In this context, the practices of armed bands

[1] C. G. Fenwick, *International Law*, p. 301 (3d ed., 1948).
[2] For discussion of this problem, see I. Brownlie, "International Law and the Activities of Armed Bands," *Int. & Com. L. Q.*, Vol. 7, p. 712 (1958).

have had a long and continuous history. Though perhaps not known under their present name, their activities were apparently well known in antiquity. It is thus to be noted that Hugo Grotius' speculations on the subject were based on ancient sources. Quoting Saint Augustine with approval, he said that "To make war upon our neighbors, and thence to advance against others, and from the mere lust of ruling to crush peoples who have not troubled us, what we must call this but wholesale robbery?"[3] Similarly, quoting Agathias, he said: "They who for the sake of gain or unreasonable hatred, without any just pretext, *invade the territories of others and harm those who have done no wrong*, are both lawless and wicked."[4] It should also be noted that these actions were listed by Grotius among the unjust causes of war.[5] In like vein, Emerich de Vattel regarded the invasion of a nation's territory by the citizens of another as one instance in which a nation is held responsible for the acts of its citizens. He said:

> Finally, there is another case in which a Nation as a whole is responsible for the crimes of its citizens. This is when by its practices and by the principles of its government it accustoms and permits its citizens to rob and ill-treat foreigners at will, *to make inroads into neighboring territory*, etc. Thus the Usbecks as a Nation are guilty of all the robberies perpetrated by their members. The sovereigns whose subjects are robbed and murdered, and whose dominions are infested by these brigands, may justly lay the blame upon the whole Nation. Nay, more: all Nations may unite to repress such a Nation as the common enemy of the human race.[6]

Such assertions of the "fathers of international law" raise important points of substantive international law. For the attempts of international law to control resort to war are hopelessly frustrated by the efforts of the states to escape its regulations by engaging in actions legally outside of the concept of war. Aid to armed bands may be included in this type of action, for in its effect it is nothing more than an indirect and concealed technique of aggression aimed at undermining a state's internal political order without the resort to open hostilities.[7] It is precisely for this reason that the Draft Code of Offenses Against the Peace and Security of Mankind considers as one of such offenses "The incursion into the territory of a state from the territory of another state of armed bands acting for a political pur-

[3] H. Grotius, *De Jure Belli ac Pacis Libri Tres*, bk. II, ch. XXII, sec. 3 (2) (Trans. by F. W. Kelsey, 1925).

[4] *Ibid.*, n. 2. Italics supplied.

[5] *Ibid.*, bk. II c. XXII.

[6] E. de Vattel, *Le Droit des Gens*, bk. II, c. VI, sec. 78 (Trans. by C. G. Fenwick, 1916), Italics supplied.

[7] J. Stone, *Legal Controls of International Conflict*, p. 311 (1954).

pose."[8] In an attempt to widen the scope of this article, in 1954 the Commission modified the previous text as follows:

> The organization, or the encouragement of the organization, by the authorities of a state, of armed bands within its territory or any other territory for incursions into the territory of another state, or the toleration of the organization of such bands in its own territory, or the toleration of the use by such armed bands of its territory as a base of operations or as a point of departure for incursions into the territory of another state, as well as direct participation in or support of such incursions.[9]

Though this formulation is still a matter of future law, attention may nevertheless be drawn to its underlying conceptions. On the one hand, it is generally admitted that a state has a right to independence and to the integrity of its territory, and these are rights granted and protected by international law.[10] On the other hand, it is recognized as implicit in this very statement a corresponding duty of non-intervention on the part of other states, and this is a duty imposed by international law.[11] These postulates, whose mutual limits are difficult to mark in concrete situations, are also cut across by the requirements of the world community which imperatively demands compliance with this right-duty conception, for it is indissolubly linked with the peace and security of mankind.

If the above observations be correct, it will at once be seen that the problem of armed bands is not exclusively confined to the relations between states. It is a matter in which the world community has vital interests at stake. It is highly relevant to add that in so far as the world community is involved, there is the double responsibility of the state and of the individual. Support for this conclusion may again be found in the Draft Code of Offenses against the Peace and Security of Mankind, which regards the offense in respect to the incursion of armed bands as primarily giving rise to individual responsibility of the members of the bands, though a criminal responsibility of the authorities of the state also arises in the manner already fully discussed.[12] This reflects the general conviction that for the adequate suppression

[8] See Article II, paragraph (4), Report of the International Law Commission Covering Its Third Session, May 16–July 27, 1951, U.N. General Assembly, Official Records, Sixth Session, Supp. No. 9 (A/1858), p. 12 (1951).

[9] For text, see L. B. Sohn, *Cases on United Nations Law*, p. 999 (1956).

[10] Thus, Article 1 of the Draft Declaration on Rights and Duties of States says: "Every State has the right to independence..." For text, see *Am. J. Int. L. Supp.*, Vol. 44, p. 16 (1950).

[11] See in this connection Article 3 of the Draft Declaration on Rights and Duties of States. For text, see note 10, *supra*.

[12] See Chapter III, *supra*.

of activities of individuals against other nations some kind of personal liability must unequivocally be attached.

It can therefore be seen that the disturbing problems created by hostile acts which proceed from individuals cannot be isolated and treated as though the state alone is to be held responsible. A more compelling view requires constant efforts to ensure that even if the state cannot be held responsible for such activities, the private persons participating in them will not escape punishment. To do otherwise will only undermine respect for international law and will further depress the legitimate aspirations of the peoples of the world.

Although the preceding observations are compelling, a cursory glance at history will immediately reveal that international law has been conspicuously inadequate in its treatment of armed bands. As matters stood before the Nürnberg Trial, the individual was not personally liable for hostile acts carried out by armed bands. Under customary and treaty law the formation of armed bands was not a prohibited activity of individuals. It would seem not unnaturally to follow that the members of armed bands were not guilty of an offense against international law, even though international law left their punishment strictly to the invaded state's discretion. In respect to the responsibility of the state, since armed bands are formed by private individuals, the state has similarly avoided responsibility by simply pleading absence of fault.

One element which prevented an adequate approach to this broad question is that, historically, armed bands as an instrument of national policy did not really appear until the twentieth century. Under nineteenth century conditions activities of armed bands were regarded as purely private, though destructive, undertakings of individuals which, in the absence of prevention by the state of origin, could be legally punished by the victim through the exercise of the right of hot pursuit. This nineteenth century experience proved to be inadequate for twentieth century conditions, for it really sprung from a total misconception regarding the role of armed bands in international politics. For armed bands have today an ever-increasing political importance, and among its purposes may be included the preparation of a larger scale military invasion into foreign territory, the undermining of the morale of the people of the selected target and the establishment of bases in a foreign country for the purpose of eventual political annexation.[13]

[13] In discussing the threat to the political independence and territorial integrity of Greece before the First Committee of the General Assembly, the Greek representative

Since for all of these purposes armed bands constitute effective and concealed means of attack, they are invariably assured of support by the government in whose jurisdiction they are formed. It is precisely at this point that international law immediately becomes operative, for what international law has thus far required is that the government refrain from supporting or tolerating groups intending to invade foreign territory or to interfere in the affairs of other states.[14] There is ample evidence which gives foundation to the assertion that support to armed bands likely to make incursions into another state is an act of aggression for which the state is internationally responsible. Thus, the Convention for the Definition of Aggression of July 3, 1933, signed in London between the Soviet Union and its neighbors, regards as an aggressor in an international conflict the state which, *inter alia,* gives "support to armed bands formed on its territory, which have invaded the territory of another state," or has refused to take "in its own territory, notwithstanding the request of the invaded state, all the measures in its power to deprive those bands of all assistance or protection."[15] This definition was taken from the celebrated Politis Report submitted to the League of Nations Conference for the Reduction and Limitation of Armaments of 1933 and apparently was the first international instrument to include support of armed bands in the catalogue of acts of aggression.[16] Similarly, in the Seventh Pan American Conference held in Montevideo in 1933, the Mexican Government proposed a Code of Peace which described the aggressor as one who had committed a number of acts among which was included giving "aid to elements, which, having formed within its territory, should attack the territory of another country, or [rejected] the demand of the attacked country, that measures be taken to deprive those elements of support or defense."[17] Again, in the London Conference of 1945 the United States proposed a definition of aggression which included "provision of support to armed bands formed in its territory [of the state] which

called attention to this in the following terms: "At present new strategic conditions had widened the scope of the problem; aggression took less and less the form of direct attack, but more and more that of disguised subversive action. Therefore, the attitude which the First Committee would adopt towards the dealings of the neighbor states of Greece would be of historic importance." U.N. General Assembly, Official Records, Third Session, First Committee, 176th Meeting, p. 314 (1947).

[14] I. Brownlie, *op. cit.*, pp. 713–714.

[15] Convention Defining Aggression, July 3, 1933, art. II, paragraph 5. For text, see *Am. J. Int. L. Supp.*, Vol. 27, p. 193 (1933).

[16] See League of Nations, Conf. DC/CG 108, May 24, 1933.

[17] Draft Code of Peace, art. 2. For text, see R. A. Alfaro, "The Question of the Definition of Aggression," U.N. General Assembly, Official Records, International Law Commission, Third Session, May 30, 1951, p. 8 (1951).

have invaded the territory of another state."[18] The problem of armed bands has similarly appeared in the attempts of the United Nations International Law Commission to define aggression. Thus, proposals presented by Doctors Ricardo J. Alfaro of Panama,[19] Shuhsi Hsu of China,[20] and Jesús M. Yepes of Colombia[21] have all included the support of armed bands as an act of aggression. The general conviction thus exists that support to, and toleration of, armed bands likely to make incursions into foreign territory engage the international responsibility of the state amounting to an act of aggression.[22] It is highly significant that none of the instruments mentioned refers to the criminal responsibility of individuals. The fact is that the terms in which the status of armed bands continues to be discussed do not take account of the basic changes in their position, nor of the role which they are called upon to play in the foreign policy of their governments, and perhaps more important, of the changed conceptions regarding the position of the individual in international law. It is for this reason that the Draft Code of Offenses Against the Peace and Security of Mankind is reflective of these changes, for it lays down in categorical terms that the members of the armed bands who invade the territory of a state for political purposes are criminally liable.

Moreover, as pre-World War II international law was primarily concerned with imposing responsibility upon the state for the support and toleration of armed bands, the state injured by such activities was left free to deal with the members of these groups in any way it saw fit. It may be pertinent to add that since the international law of that era

[18] *Ibid.*

[19] *Ibid.*, p. 15. According to Dr. Alfaro "incursion by irregular bands" is a method of aggression, and is an element at the disposal of a state to commit aggression. *Ibid.*, pp. 15, 17.

[20] His draft says that "Aggression, which is a crime under international law, is the hostile act of a state against another state, committed by... (b) the arming of organized bands or of third states, hostile to the victim state, for offensive purposes." Report of the International Law Commission Covering Its Third Session May 16–July 27. 1951, U.N. General Assembly, Official Records, Sixth Session, Supplement No. 9, (A/1858), p. 9 (1951).

[21] His draft said: "Violence (force) exercised by irregular bands organized within the territory of a state or outside its territory with the active or passive complicity of the state shall be considered as aggression within the meaning of the preceding paragraph." *Ibid.*

[22] See also the Draft Definition submitted by Iran and Panama to the Ninth Session of the General Assembly, which is similar to the change made by the International Law Commission to Article 2, paragraph 4 of its Draft Code of Offenses against the Peace and Security of Mankind. For the Draft definition of Iran and Panama, see M. S. McDougal and F. P. Feliciano, "Legal Regulation of Resort to International Coercion: Aggression and Self-Defense in Policy Perspective," *Yale L.J.*, Vol. 68, pp. 1057, 1078 (1959).

was largely founded upon self-help, in enforcing the responsibility of the state the injured government could resort to measures of its own. Hence, when confronted with the invasion of its territory by bands organized in another country, the state affected has resorted to rights under international law allegedly based on self-defense and its corollary, hot pursuit. While the line of demarcation between these two rights may at times be rather shadowy, they nevertheless represent two distinct rights whose validity in the present context is cast into the gravest doubts. It may thus be beneficial to discuss them under separate headings.

ARMED BANDS AND THE RIGHT OF SELF-DEFENSE

The classical case in which the right of self-defense was exercised was the celebrated *Caroline Affair*[23] involving the incursion of British forces into American territory to suppress the organization in the United States of factions designed to help insurgents against the British rule in Canada. The record of this case unmistakably shows that despite the attempts of the United States Government to suppress any kind of hostile action by individuals against a foreign power, a substantial body of men was organized on the Canadian side and was constantly supplied from the United States with reinforcement of men and materials by the steamer *Caroline*. The critical stage of this case was reached when British forces entered into American territory with the intention of destroying the *Caroline*. Upon the successful completion of this mission and in answer to American protests, the British Government supported its position on three propositions whose validity under the circumstances of the case was vigorously disputed by the United States. The British Government essentially maintained (1) that the *Caroline* was engaged in piratical acts; (2) that the law of the United States was unable to suppress them; and (3) that the destruction of the ship was based on the right of self-defense.[24] It is of some significance to observe that at no time did the British Government suggest a breach of a duty of prevention by the United States.[25] In this context, the action of Great Britain in destroying the *Caroline* clearly revealed all

[23] For the record of this case, see J. B. Moore, *A Digest of International Law*, Vol. 2, pp. 409–414 (1906).

[24] *Ibid.*, p. 410.

[25] R. E. Curtis, "The Law of Hostile Military Expedition as Applied by the United States," *Am. J. Int. L.*, Vol. 8, p. 242 (1914).

the characteristics of necessity, thus making the exercise of the right of self-defense a justifiable course of action.[26] While the United States Government agreed that the requirement of self-defense might necessitate the use of force, it decisively rejected it in the present case. Instead, Secretary of State Webster forcibly maintained that "While it is admitted that exceptions growing out of the great law of self-defense do exist, those exceptions should be confined to cases in which the necessity of that self-defense is instant, overwhelming, and leaving no choice of means, and no moment for deliberation."[27] The matter was finally ended by the British Government justifying its action on these terms and by adding a suitable apology.[28]

The *Caroline Affair* is instructive for several reasons. The grounds on which both governments concurred would seem to leave no room for doubt that in the presence of hostile bands the state in whose territory they are formed not only must be willing but also able to suppress them.[29] Failing these two conditions, the right of territorial integrity must yield to the right of self-defense of the state against whom the bands are directing their activities. Implicit in this assertion is the recognition that the right of territorial integrity is by no means absolute but must give way to the apparently stronger right of self-defense of the threatened community. Self-defense in this context is exercised in derogation of the right of the territorial state, who apparently must acquiesce in the transgressions upon its sovereignty.[30] These propositions seem unquestioned, but they raise critical issues from the standpoint of the rule of law in the world community. It must of course be readily conceded that a state has the duty to prevent its sovereignty from being used by individuals to threaten seriously the peace and security of another nation. To allow such activities to go unpunished under the right of territorial sovereignty would certainly amount to an abuse of right for which the menaced community is entitled to redress.[31] The core of the difficulty lies, however, in that resort to measures of self-defense, even in the limited sense suggested by Secretary Webster, is an open invitation to the strong to be *judex*

[26] D. W. Bowett, *Self-Defense in International Law*, pp. 59–60 (1958).
[27] J. B. Moore, *op. cit.* Vol. 2,p. 412. Note of Secretary of State Webster to Lord Ashburton, British Minister, August 6, 1842.
[28] C. C. Hyde, *International Law Chiefly as Interpreted and Applied by the United States*, Vol. 1, p. 239 (2d ed., 1945).
[29] L. Oppenheim, *International Law*, Vol. 1, p. 298 (8th ed. by H. Lauterpacht, 1955).
[30] D. W. Bowett, *op. cit.*, p. 60.
[31] H. Lauterpacht, *The Function of Law in the International Community*, pp. 286, 303–304 (1933).

in causa sua[32] and, as Professor Julius Stone has well observed, it is really incongruous to think of such a measure as being functionally related to orderly world community processes.[33] However, the argument is irresistibly suggested that self-defense is frankly a legal sanction in an international society devoid of a centralized machinery to enforce the law.[34] Surely, as a proposition of power politics based on the questionable assumption that self-defense is a sanction of the law, it may be quite acceptable. As a proposition of law, however, it could scarcely find any justifiable foundation, for self-defense as an enforcement of the law can only operate in a situation involving a great power *vis-à-vis* a minor state.[35] But with any issue on which two great powers are opposed, it is certain that each will exercise the liberties which self-defense allows and, what is even more perplexing, each will identify its position with the supposed vindication of principles of international law. The resulting situation may be war against each other; but it would certainly be a curious paradox to regard such actions as emanating from the will of the world community.

The preceding observations merely underlie the important fact that measures of self-defense are not primarily questions of law but of the political relations between states. The valiant efforts of scholars[36] to treat self-defense in terms of law completely overlook the fact that resort to it remains a weapon of the strong against the weak. It can thus be suggested, as a basic task of a modern system of international law, to replace this anarchic liberty with a cooperative security arrangement reflecting more faithfully the values of the world community. Just and orderly processes are the essence of the law, and these objectives are not likely to be attained if conceptions of self-help dominate the international legal order. Echoing the incongruity of the right of

[32] *Ibid.*, p. 179.

[33] Cf. J. Stone, *Legal Controls of International Conflict*, p. 287 (1954).

[34] H. Kelsen, *Principles of International Law*, pp. 15–17 (1952).

[35] In this context, Professor Edwin D. Dickinson says that "Such devices, theoretically available to all, have actually been the remedy of the strong against the weak." See E. D. Dickinson, *Law and Peace*, p. 74 (1951). And Professor Josef L. Kunz, speaking of self-defense, says: "Under such a system a weak state can hardly go to war or take reprisals against a more powerful state, whereas the latter may abuse its power." J. L. Kunz, "Sanctions in International Law," *Am. J. Int. L.*, Vol. 54, pp. 324, 325 (1960).

[36] Thus, D. W. Bowett, *op. cit.* In the Preface to this book he says: "This work was written in the belief that the right of self-defense was capable of legal analysis and that in the present state of international law such an analysis is essential." On the other hand, Professor Percy E. Corbett asserts that resort to self-defense actually amounts to a negation of society for "the entity claiming the right also claims the exclusive power to determine when it comes into play." See P. E. Corbett, *Law and Society in the Relations of States*, p. 44 (1951).

self-defense, the Nürnberg Tribunal emphatically stated that "... whether action taken under the claim of self-defense was in fact aggression or defensive must ultimately be subject to investigation and adjudication, if international law is ever to be enforced."[37]

It is perhaps in recognition of the above considerations that the right of self-defense has been substantially restricted by the United Nations Charter. It must of course be readily admitted that though the Charter contains prohibitions against the threat or use of force,[38] it has not entirely precluded the exercise of the right of self-defense. Thus, Article 51, which provides for the right of self-defense, says:

> Nothing in the present Charter shall impair the inherent right of individual or collective self-defense if an armed attack occurs against a member of the United Nations, until the Security Council has taken the measures necessary to maintain international peace and security. Measures taken by Members in the exercise of this right of self-defense shall be immediately reported to the Security Council and shall not in any way affect the authority and responsibility of the Security Council under the present Charter to take at any time such action as it deems necessary in order to maintain or restore international peace and security.

That provision, contradictory as it is, would seem to be clear and simple in purpose, for it not only safeguards the traditional right of self-defense but also restricts it. This article narrows the field for the exercise of self-defense to circumstances involving an armed attack and only until such time when the Security Council has taken the measures necessary to maintain international peace and security. It should therefore be clear that self-defense is limited both as to the occasion which gives rise to its exercise and as to its duration. Though no authoritative definition of an armed attack has ever been suggested, it is at least generally agreed that an armed attack is a special type of aggression.[39] The line between armed attack and other kinds of aggression is in particular cases often difficult to mark; presumably, however, "armed attack" is narrower than the term "aggression."[40] It probably includes such acts as invasion of a state by the military forces of another state or some other grave breach of international peace.[41] It is highly questionable, however, that invasion of the territory by armed bands would make Article 51 operative unless the invasion is

[37] For text, see *Annual Digest*, 1946, pp. 203, 210 (1951).

[38] See in this connection article 2(4) of the Charter.

[39] J. L. Kunz, "The Inter-American Treaty of Reciprocal Assistance," *Am. J. Int. L.*, Vol. 42, pp. 111, 115 (1948).

[40] J. Stone, *op. cit.*, p. 244 n. 8.

[41] I. Brownlie, *op. cit.*, p. 731.

of such dimensions that the territorial integrity of the invaded state is seriously impaired. It has already been seen that, at most, toleration of armed bands by a state constitutes an act of aggression, which, under the Charter, does not warrant the exercise of the right of self-defense.

It has persuasively been suggested that since self-defense is strictly an anticipatory measure, it cannot be made to depend upon the existence of an armed attack.[42] There is implicit in this assertion the belief that a state threatened with a strong possibility of an armed attack may first attack in self-defense. Convincing as this argument may appear, it is, however, deceptive on all accounts, for it must be fairly apparent that in any exercise of self-defense there is imported into the issue the inevitable use of force, and it is precisely in prohibiting the use of force in any form that the Charter is clearly emphatic. Article 2(4) which would apply to such situations says:

> All Members shall refrain in their international relations from the threat or use of force against the territorial integrity or political independence of any State, or any other manner inconsistent with the Purposes of the United Nations.

Thus, the use of force in any form is clearly restricted to circumstances not violating the territorial integrity or political independence of any state or the purposes of the United Nations.[43] This is but one among many of the provisions of the Charter expressly narrowing the occasions for coercive action. Similarly pertinent in this connection is Article 33 which obliges the parties to any dispute to seek a solution by recognized peaceful methods of settlement; and Article 39 which gives jurisdiction to the Security Council to determine the existence of any threat to the peace, breach of the peace or act of aggression. The collective impact of these provisions would seem to make it almost certain that there is really a limited area in which coercive or forcible measures would not be prohibited by the Charter.[44] If this proposition be accepted, it may inevitably follow that the customary law as developed by the *Caroline Case* is no longer valid under the United Nations Charter,[45] for consistently with paragraph 3 of Article 2 such measures endanger "international peace and security, and justice."[46]

[42] Cf. D. W. Bowett, *op. cit.*, pp. 188–189.

[43] P. C. Jessup, *A Modern Law of Nations*, 162–193 (1947).

[44] J. Stone, *op. cit.*, pp. 286–287. Moreover, it should be noted that in this context there seems to be a contradiction between these last provisions of the Charter and Article 51, unless it is frankly admitted that Article 51 is equally restrictive in that self-defense becomes operative only when an armed attack unequivocally exists.

[45] See Q. Wright, "United States Intervention in the Lebanon," *Am. J. Int. L.*, Vol. 53, pp. 112, 115 (1959).

[46] Article 2, paragraph 3, of the Charter says: "All Members shall settle their inter-

The inevitable result of these provisions is to suggest that now a member of the United Nations is substantially restricted in the resort to the use of force in any form. Certainly, self-defense against armed bands would not seem to be included within the permitted area.

The cogency and validity of these observations can strikingly be illustrated by the *Corfu Channel Case*[47] recently decided by the International Court of Justice. Rejecting the United Kingdom's claim that under the right of self-preservation she had a right to send her navy into Albanian territorial waters for the purpose of effecting a minesweeping operation, the Court unmistakably declared that the action of the British Navy constituted a violation of Albanian sovereignty. That the Court rejected the right of a state to enter the territory of another allegedly on grounds of self-defense can be seen by the part of the opinion which says:

> The Court can only regard the alleged right of intervention as the manifestation of a policy of force, such as has, in the past, given rise to most serious abuses and such as cannot, whatever be the present defects in international organization, find a place in international law. Intervention is perhaps still less admissible in the particular form it would take here; for, from the nature of things, it would be reserved for the most powerful states, and might easily lead to perverting the administration of international justice itself.[48]

It is therefore submitted that incursions into a state's territory for the purpose of suppressing the activities of armed bands is probably no longer admissible under international law. There can of course be no doubt that allowing the formation of irregular bands would justify resort to the Security Council, though resort to self-defense would clearly be unlawful. In solving their disputes, states must resort to orderly and amicable methods, for self-defense is likely to cause injustice and anarchy in their relations.

ARMED BANDS AND THE RIGHT OF HOT PURSUIT

Hot pursuit is a well known operation of the law of the sea according to which a ship of a state can pursue into the high sea any foreign

national disputes by peaceful means in such a manner that international peace and security, and justice, are not endangered."

[47] *I.C.J., Reports*, 1949, p. 1.

[48] *Ibid.*, p. 35. Judge Hersch Lauterpacht, however, believes that this part of the opinion may be limited to this particular case. See H. Lauterpacht, *The Development of International Law by the International Court*, p. 317 (1958).

vessel that has violated the law while in its territorial waters.[49] An attempt has been made to justify the same doctrine in respect to bands that invade the territory. Hot pursuit thus applied implies the right of the invaded state to pursue the bands back into the territory from which they came for the purpose of administering punishment. It is further alleged that this right is nothing more than a corollary of the exercise of the right of self-defense. The United States' relations with Mexico are filled with measures of this kind and offer instructive illustrations of hot pursuit on land. Thus, when a company of Texas rangers pursued into Mexico a band of Mexican Indians who had previously made an incursion into Texas, Secretary of State Marcy stated that "If Mexican Indians whom Mexico is bound to restrain are permitted to cross its border and commit depredations in the United States, they may be chased across the border and then punished."[50] It must be noted that the Secretary of State acknowledged a similar right on the part of Mexico, should American Indians make incursions into Mexican territory. The Secretary of State thus said: "If Indians whom the United States are bound to restrain shall, under the same circumstances, make a hostile incursion into Mexico, this Government will not complain if the Mexican forces who may be sent to repel them shall cross to this side of the line for that purpose, provided that in so doing they abstain from injuring the persons and property of citizens of the United States."[51] That the United States Government based the right of hot pursuit squarely on the right of self-defense can scarcely be denied, for in an earlier communication the Secretary of State declared:

> You will find no difficulty in showing to the Mexican Government that it rests upon principles of the law of nations, entirely distinct from those on which war is justified – upon the immutable principles of self-defense – upon the principles which justify decisive measures of precaution to prevent irreparable evil to our own or to a neighboring people.[52]

The United States has adhered to this position with striking consistency, for it was subsequently reiterated by the commission appointed by the Secretary of War on August 30, 1912, to investigate

[49] See P. C. Jessup, *The Law of Territorial Waters and Maritime Jurisdiction*, pp. 106–110 (1927); H. A. Smith, *The Law and Custom of the Sea*, pp. 55–56 (2d ed., 1950).

[50] J. B. Moore, *op. cit.*, Vol. 2, p. 421. Note of Secretary of State Marcy to the Mexican Minister Almonte, February 4, 1856.

[51] *Ibid.*

[52] Note of Secretary of State Forsyth to the American Minister to Mexico, December 10, 1836, J. B. Moore, *op. cit.*, Vol. 2, p. 420.

the claims of American citizens for damages suffered within American territory and growing out of insurrections in Mexico. The pertinent part of the report said:

> ...When a state in the exercise of its sovereign right of self-defense has been compelled to inflict injuries as incidental thereto upon a neighboring and friendly power, prompt expressions of regret and prompt atonement in so far as money indemnity can atone are to be expected... *The ground upon which this position rests is simply that the right of self-defense rose superior in the particular instances to the right of territorial inviolability.*[53]

Other instances can be adduced where the United States resorted to the right of hot pursuit to chase bands into foreign territory. Mention should be made of the celebrated punitive expedition against Villa in 1916 which was supported on similar grounds.[54] But the exercise of the right of hot pursuit in this manner is not limited to the practice of the United States. It is interesting to note that the British practice also shows that as late as 1915 British forces pursued tribesmen into Afghanistan territory for their incursions into the Northwest Frontier Provinces of India.[55] And recently French forces in Algeria pursued rebels into the Tunisian frontier.[56]

This body of state practice suggests a few comments. It is clear that these are instances of the pursuit of persons in which the government thus acting does not count upon either the support or the assent of the government whose territory is invaded.[57] But it is to be noted that the pursuit of bands for the purpose of punishment is presumably on the theory that the invaded state is not able to exert measures of prevention.[58] But even if this be so, to base hot pursuit on an alleged right of self-defense is a wholly indefensible position, for as soon as the right of self-defense is invoked, there is introduced into the issue the idea of preventive action making it a somewhat curious paradox to talk of self-defense in the presence of a wrongful *fait accompli*.[59] By its very nature self-defense implies advanced action against a threat to the

[53] H. Doc. 1168, 62nd Cong., 3d sess., p. 14, G. H. Hackworth, *Digest of International Law*, Vol. 2, p. 289 (1941). Italics supplied.

[54] For the record of this expedition, see G. H. Hackworth, *op. cit.*, Vol. 2, pp. 291–299.

[55] Cited by D. W. Bowett, *op. cit.*, p. 39 n. 1.

[56] Cited by I. Brownlie, *op. cit.*, p. 712.

[57] D. W. Bowett, *op. cit.*, p. 39.

[58] Thus, President Wilson justified the expedition against Villa on the ground that "there were no military forces in Mexico that could protect our border from hostile attack and our people from violence..." Address delivered at Long Branch, September 2, 1916. Cited by C. C. Hyde, *op. cit.*, Vol. 1, p. 244 n. 21.

[59] B. Cheng, *General Principles of Law as Applied by International Courts and Tribunals*, p. 97 (1953).

security of the state; yet, the right of hot pursuit as a measure of self-defense contemplates action after bands have invaded the territory of the state and have returned to the territory from which they originally came. This observation merely calls attention to the punitive character of the right of hot pursuit and the correspondent absence of the necessities of self-defense *stricto sensu*. It is thus clear at this point that while the *Caroline Affair* was a measure of self-defense in that it was anticipatory of an imminent incursion, the cases of hot pursuit here discussed fall outside of this description. It may therefore be suggested that the right of hot pursuit can be more accurately described as a form of reprisal.[60] But reprisals to rectify wrongs, while permissible by customary international law before World War I, have been forbidden by international instruments.[61] Particularly applicable are the League of Nations Covenant, the Kellogg-Briand Pact and the United Nations Charter. It has been seen that Article 2, paragraph 3, of the Charter obliges Members of the United Nations "to settle their international disputes by peaceful means in such a manner that international peace and security, and justice, are not endangered." Restricting even more the scope of reprisals is Article 2, paragraph 4, which binds the Members to refrain from the "threat or use of force against the territorial integrity or political independence of any state, or in any other manner inconsistent with the Purposes of the United Nations." These provisions show remarkably well that the resort to coercive or punitive measures by a state against another, even to remedy illegal actions, are no longer permissible methods of settling international disputes.

Finally, to assimilate the right of hot pursuit on land to that on the high seas is a wholly untenable analogy, for while the latter must cease the moment the vessel being pursued enters the territorial waters of another state so as not to violate that state's territory, the right of hot pursuit on land is predicated precisely on this violation.[62]

It may, however, be suggested that the exercise of the right of hot pursuit is not as anarchical as the preceding observations intimate. For there are certain self-imposed limitations designed to keep it within measurable bounds. First, it is maintained that the pursuing forces must abstain from injuring persons or property of the state into whose territory hot pursuit is made. This condition was recognized by the United States when conceding to Mexico the right of hot pursuit

[60] Cf. E. S. Colbert, *Retaliation in International Law* (1948).
[61] J. Stone, *op. cit.*, p. 290.
[62] D. W. Bowett, *op. cit.*, p. 40.

into American territory should the United States fail to restrain incursions of American Indians into Mexico. The United States would not complain "if the Mexican forces who may be sent to repel them shall cross to this side of the line for that purpose, provided that in so doing they abstain from injuring the persons and property of citizens of the United States."[63] Secondly, there must be an absence of intention on the part of the pursuing government to occupy militarily part of the territory of the state into which hot pursuit is made. This condition follows not unnaturally, for hot pursuit accompanied by an intention to establish a possession in foreign territory is not only a challenge to sovereignty and territorial integrity but also the disguised exercise of an alleged right under international law. It is highly significant in this connection that the incursions of American forces into Mexican territory in hot pursuit of Indians and bandits were accompanied by disclaimers on the part of the United States of any hostile feeling or intention to establish a possession or claim in Mexican territory. Particularly instructive in this regard is the communication of the State Department of May 3, 1836, in which it said:

> The just and friendly purpose for which [General Gaines] does occupy it (if he should do so), being beforehand explained to Mexico, it is expected will prevent either belief or suspicion of any hostile or equivocal design on his part. It is not intended to be the assertion of a right of property or possession.[64]

Despite these limitations, which are obviously designed to keep hot pursuit within lawful bounds, it nevertheless remains true that the right of hot pursuit cannot be justified in the light of the standards laid down by the *Caroline Case*. Consequently, the right of hot pursuit cannot adequately be described as a corollary of self-defense. Even if that could be done, it still remains an unlawful means of settling disputes which, along with the right of self-defense, would be contrary to the United Nations Charter.

ARMED BANDS BEFORE THE UNITED NATIONS

The arguments adduced in the preceding pages seem to find powerful support in the cases that have come before the United Nations involving the activities of armed bands. The experience of the United

[63] Note of Secretary of State Marcy to the Mexican Minister Almonte, February 4, 1856, J. B. Moore, *op. cit.*, Vol. 2, p. 421.

[64] Memorandum of Secretary of State Forsyth to the Mexican Minister Gorostiza, May 3, 1836, J. B. Moore, *op. cit.*, Vol. 2, p. 419.

Nations in this regard clearly reveals that the incursion of armed bands into foreign territory is an unlawful activity which seriously endangers international peace and security. The earliest of these cases concerns the complaint of the Greek Government in respect to threats to its political independence and territorial integrity, which first reached the Security Council on December 3, 1946,[65] and was subsequently transferred to the General Assembly on September 15, 1947.[66] The Greek Government substantially maintained that its northern neighbors, Albania, Bulgaria and Yugoslavia, were aiding bands whose purpose was to overthrow the government. While it appears that the discussion of the case largely turned on questions of evidence,[67] what is perhaps more significant is the almost unanimous agreement existing among the representatives to the First Committee of the General Assembly that aid to armed bands is unlawful and, hence, contrary to the principles of the United Nations Charter. Thus, the representative of the Union of South Africa quite emphatically stated that the "intervention by Greece's northern neighbors was a threat to peace."[68] Similarly, the American representative declared that "... Albania, Bulgaria and Yugoslavia had violated the principle of international law according to which a state should not assist bands which were in rebellion against the legal Government of their country."[69] In almost identical terms the Chinese representative said that "it was a well established principle of international law that no state should give assistance to subversive groups among its neighbors."[70] Elsewhere the Paraguayan representative regarded the matter as an "act contrary to the purposes and principles laid down in the Charter."[71] And the Greek representative considered the activities of his northern neighbors as "acts of aggression in violation of international law and the obligations of the Charter."[72] Subsequently, he referred to the London Convention of 1933 which included support of armed bands as an act of aggression.[73]

[65] See *Report of the United Nations Special Committee on the Balkans*, U.N. General Assembly, Official Records, Sixth Session, Supplement No. 11 (A/1857), p. 1 (1951).

[66] U.N. General Assembly, Official Records, Second Session, First Committee, 60th Meeting, p. 9 (1947).

[67] I. Brownlie, *op. cit.*, p. 726.

[68] U.N. General Assembly, Official Records, Third Session, First Committee, 174th Meeting, p. 293 (1948).

[69] U.N. General Assembly, Official Records, Second Session, First Committee, 60th Meeting, p. 14 (1947).

[70] *Ibid.*, 66th Meeting, p. 58 (1947).

[71] *Ibid.*, 67th Meeting, p. 71 (1947).

[72] *Ibid.*, 63rd Meeting, p. 34 (1947).

[73] U.N. General Assembly, Official Records, Third Session, First Committee, 176th Meeting, p. 314 (1948).

It seems clear that aid to armed bands by a state constitutes a threat to peace, thus falling squarely within the investigatory powers of the United Nations.[74] In so far as there could be any doubt as to the true legal nature of the activities of armed bands, the fact that most of the representatives to the First Committee of the General Assembly characterized the situation as an act of aggression is the strongest available evidence supporting the conclusion that Article 51 of the Charter was clearly not applicable. For this evidential purpose it is highly immaterial that the American representative to the Security Council at one time declared that if the Security Council did not find a solution to the Greek question he was prepared to invoke Article 51 of the Charter,[75] for certainly the liberty of governments to resort to measures of self-defense under that article is not at all dependent upon the success or failure of the Security Council to find a solution to a situation or to undertake coercive measures.[76] It should be observed in this connection that the Greek delegate himself never regarded the situation as an armed attack but rather as an act of aggression thereby unmistakably barring the possibility of applying Article 51 of the Charter.[77] Even the resolution formally adopted by the First Committee, though acknowledging that Albania, Bulgaria and Yugoslavia had given assistance and support to the guerrillas fighting against the Greek Government, did not refer to this support as an armed attack, but instead called upon all the parties involved to settle their disputes by peaceful means, and at the same time set up a special committee to observe compliance with the terms of the resolution.[78] In these circumstances, the application of Article 51 of the Charter would be open to serious doubts.

[74] More properly, the investigatory powers of the Security Council, as it is this body that has the primary responsibility for the maintenance of international peace and security. See *U.N. Charter*, article 34.

[75] U.N. General Assembly, Official Records, Second Session, First Committee, 62nd Meeting, p. 27 (1947).

[76] Cf. J. Stone, *op. cit.*, p. 235.

[77] This characterization of the situation runs through his arguments at different times. At one time he said that "Greece was the victim of acts of aggression, and it asked for the protection to which a Member of the United Nations was entitled." U.N. General Assembly, Official Records, Second Session, First Committe, 68th Meeting, p. 81 (1947). Elsewhere, however, in the complaint of the Iron Curtain countries against the United States in respect to appropriations of the Mutual Security Act of 1951, the Greek representative then referred to the Greek question as an "armed aggression against Greece." U.N. General Assembly, Official Records, Sixth Session, First Committee, 475th Meeting, p. 115 (1951).

[78] This resolution was proposed by the United States delegate and was adopted by a vote of 36 to 6, with 10 abstentions. For text, see U.N. General Assembly, Official Records, Second Session, First Committee, 72nd Meeting, pp. 114–116 (1947).

That conclusion must now be examined in reference to other cases of a comparable nature. The complaint raised by the Iron Curtain countries against the United States on account of Section 101 (a) of the Mutual Security Act enacted by Congress in 1951[79] is another case in point. Section 101 (a) of the Act appropriates $ 100,000,000 to finance the incorporation of escapees from Communist dominated countries into the military forces of the North Atlantic Treaty Organization or for any other purpose which, in the opinion of the President, would contribute to the defense of the North Atlantic Area and to the security of the United States.[80] The Soviet representative to the First Committee specifically requested the General Assembly to condemn the Act as "an aggressive act and as intervention in the internal affairs of the other Members of the United Nations which was incompatible with the United Nations Charter and with international law."[81] It is significant that the Polish representative made special reference to the London Convention of 1933 which included, *inter alia*, the support of armed bands invading the territory of another state in the definition of aggression.[82] Wholly apart from the fact that the majority of the delegates regarded this complaint as groundless and emotionally charged, the significant observation must be made that the American representative nowhere questioned the statement of the law as given by the complaining nations but vigorously dissented from the interpretation attached to the Mutual Security Act.[83] The United States Government therefore in principle agreed that state support of armed bands undoubtedly constitutes aggression. It is therefore apparent that in dealing with its own case, the United States remained faithful to the position it had adopted in respect to the Greek question previously discussed.

Parallel with all these cases is the complaint of the Union of Burma regarding aggression against it by the Chinese Government of Formosa.[84] The Burmese complaint specifically alleged that Chinese bands

[79] Public Law 165, 82nd Cong., 1st Sess. (H.R. 5113), 65 Stat. 373.

[80] Dr. Charles G. Fenwick is of the opinion that this provision is violative of Article 2, paragraph 5 of the Draft Code of Offenses Against the Peace and Security of Mankind in that it undertakes and encourages activities calculated to foment civil strife in another state. See C. G. Fenwick, "Draft Code of Offenses Against the Peace and Security of Mankind," *Am. J. Int. L.*, Vol. 46, pp. 98, 99 (1952).

[81] U.N. General Assembly, Official Records, Sixth Session, First Committee, 472nd Meeting, p. 103 (1951).

[82] *Ibid.*, 473rd Meeting, p. 107 (1951).

[83] *Ibid.*, 472nd Meeting, p. 103 (1951). Cf. I. Brownlie, *op. cit.*, p. 727.

[84] U.N. General Assembly, Official Records, Seventh Session, First Committee, 605th Meeting, p. 653 (1953).

had invaded Burmese territory and had set up a reign of terror in the areas they controlled, engaging in looting and murder, all of which was allegedly accomplished with the support of the Formosan Government.[85] Like the previous cases, the Burmese Government considered such activities as a flagrant violation of its sovereignty and, therefore, as an act of aggression. A large number of representatives substantially supported the Burmese position. Thus, the representative of Yemen regarded the Chinese bands as an interference in the internal affairs of a state, which is clearly prohibited by the United Nations Charter.[86] Similarly, the American representative considered the presence of Chinese armed bands in Burma as a challenge to its sovereignty.[87] The delegate of New Zealand regarded the situation as likely to endanger international peace and security.[88] And in significant terms, the representative of Israel referred to such activities as "camouflaged aggression."[89]

The foregoing experience of the United Nations is powerfully reinforced by a similar experience of the Inter-American System, which has been much troubled by activities of armed bands. Of particular importance in this connection is the complaint which the Costa Rican Government took to the Council of the Organization of American States on December 11, 1948, alleging that armed bands formed in Nicaragua had invaded Costa Rican territory.[90] Though the Inter-American Treaty of Reciprocal Assistance, generally known as the Río Treaty,[91] provides for the right of self-defense in the presence of an armed attack in Article 3, it is of cardinal importance that the Costa Rican Government invoked Article 6 of the Treaty, which deals with an aggression which is not an armed attack.[92] While under Article 3 a state attacked may resort to measures of self-defense in the manner

[85] *Ibid.*, 606th Meeting, p. 661 (1953).
[86] *Ibid.*, 607th Meeting, p. 663 (1953).
[87] *Ibid.*, 609th Meeting, p. 673 (1953).
[88] *Ibid.*, 607th Meeting, p. 664 (1953).
[89] *Ibid.*, 608th Meeting, p. 669 (1953).
[90] All the documents of this controversy were published by the Pan American Union in a voluminous mimeographed book and an equally voluminous supplement under the title of *Documentos Relativos a la Situación Entre Costa Rica y Nicaragua* (1949).
[91] For text of the Río Treaty, see *Am. J. Int. L. Supp.*, Vol. 43, p. 53 (1949).
[92] Article 6 says: "If the inviolability or the integrity of the territory or the sovereignty or political independence of any American state should be affected by an aggression which is not an armed attack or by an intra-continental or extra-continental conflict, or by any other fact or situation that might endanger the peace of America, the organ of consultation shall meet immediately in order to agree on the measures which must be taken in case of aggression to assist the victim of the aggression or, in any case, the measures which should be taken for the common defense and for the maintenance of the peace and security of the continent."

prescribed by Article 51 of the United Nations Charter, on the other hand, under Article 6 such measures are unlawful in the presence of an aggression which is not an armed attack and the obligations of the American Republics is to meet in consultation to agree upon collective measures to help the victim of the aggression. The case was finally settled after a commission of inquiry had gone to the scene of the conflict and reported that both countries were negligent for not having taken adequate measures to prevent the organization in their territories of movements tending to overthrow the Government of Costa Rica on the one hand, and to conspire against the territory of Nicaragua and other American Republics on the other. Special reference was made to the Caribbean Legion, which was an organization of private persons and which allegedly received moral and material support from the Costa Rican Government to overthrow certain regimes, particularly that of Nicaragua. On the basis of these findings, the Council ordered both governments to abstain from further hostilities in the name of the principles of non-intervention and continental solidarity.

One could of course cite other cases involving armed bands where substantially similar conclusions have been reached. The few cases here discussed are important because certain significant precedents of an interpretative nature have been established for the future. Whether invasion by armed bands is referred to as an aggression, a violation of the territorial integrity and political independence of the state, or as a situation likely to endanger international peace and security, the point that is particularly striking is the almost total absence of a conviction among governments that the activities of armed bands constitute an armed attack, thus justifying measures of self-defense under Article 51 of the United Nations Charter. While the matter may not yet be free from doubts, the cases here discussed would seem to make it almost certain that support to armed bands by a state is tantamount to complicity in the act, and, as such, constitutes a serious breach of the duty which states owe each other at all times. Such a violation not only justifies vigorous protests on the part of the invaded state but also the application of preventive or enforcement measures on the part of the United Nations. To say this is to recognize that since coercive measures can be applied by the United Nations, individual resort to such measures has no longer any conceivable legal basis. This conclusion certainly goes a long way toward both mitigating the anarchical elements existing in the world community and helping to implant law and justice as the basis of the relations between states.

CONCLUSION

Prohibition of the use of force by a state against armed bands rests on the assumption that the use of force in any form may create a situation likely to endanger international peace and security clearly out of proportion to the evil intended to suppress.[93] Since the exercise of the right of self-defense is fraught with explosive possibilities, states must resort to other measures in an effort to control adequately irregular bands formed within their jurisdiction.

The body of evidence gathered in this chapter clearly suggests that the activities of armed bands directed against other states constitute an unlawful behavior under existing international instruments. It has also been abundantly shown that toleration by the state in whose jurisdiction they are formed amounts to an international wrong prohibited by modern principles of international law. The right of a state to independence and the corresponding duty of non-intervention on the part of other states relevantly come into play. But over and above these structural frameworks of international law, it must frankly be recognized that activities of armed bands present a situation likely to disturb the peace and security of mankind. It is precisely for this reason that under overriding principles of the United Nations Charter, the invaded state cannot proceed under measures of self-defense as though it is alone affected; this is a situation falling squarely within the coercive powers of the world organization. It follows, therefore, that any unilateral coercive measure is probably illegal under the Charter.

[93] I. Brownlie, *op. cit.*, p. 730.

CHAPTER VIII

COUNTERFEITING OF FOREIGN CURRENCY

The uncertainties and difficulties attending the punishment of the actions of private persons discussed in the preceding chapters would seem to be partially ameliorated in respect to counterfeiting the currency of foreign states. While states usually assert a right to exercise jurisdiction and to punish the falsification of their currency and securities wheresoever and by whomsoever committed,[1] it is equally true that it is in this area where the territorial state is less hesitant to enact legislation punishing counterfeiters of foreign currency, thus attaining a greater measure of international cooperation.[2] This does not imply that under the present law states owe each other a general duty to protect their monetary system;[3] what it does imply is that on one specific duty there is general agreement, namely, that of preventing and punishing the counterfeiting of a foreign state's currency. The present chapter has been added precisely to show how that duty has entered the common law of nations and to suggest that perhaps similar steps can be taken in respect to the other offenses previously discussed.

GENERAL CONSIDERATIONS

Unlike other hostile private acts against foreign states, the falsification of a state's currency and securities is generally regarded as highly reprehensible, so that every nation is vitally interested in seeing criminal punishment meted out to those who have attempted to undermine another's financial stability. The potential danger of counterfeiting to the credit of a nation has underlain its non-political aspect so that it is almost uniformly classed as a common crime.[4]

[1] Research in International Law Under the Auspices of the Harvard Law School, "Jurisdiction with Respect to Crime," *Am. J. Int. L. Supp.* Vol. 29, p. 561 (1935).

[2] P. C. Jessup, *A Modern Law of Nations*, p. 178 (1947).

[3] F. A. Mann, "Money in Public International Law," *Brit. Y.B. Int. L.*, 1949, Vol. 26, pp. 259, 271 (1949).

[4] Professor Vespasian V. Pella maintains that the falsification of currency may be a common crime, a political offense, and an offense between the states. See V. V. Pella,

While this does not necessarily mean that a situation may not be found where the falsification of a foreign currency is due to a most noble political motive,[5] it does invite the states to use greater diligence in its suppression. The common nature of this offense had already been perceived by Emerich de Vattel who said:

> From the principle we have just laid down, it is easy to draw the conclusion that if one Nation counterfeits the money of another, or if it permits counterfeiters to do so, and protects them, it does a wrong to that Nation... There is another custom of more recent date and of no less advantage to commerce than the use of money. It consists in *exchange*, or the business of banking, by means of which a merchant can remit from one end of the world to another immense sums of money almost without expense and, if he wishes, without risk. For the same reasons that sovereigns ought to protect commerce, they are obliged to maintain this custom by good laws which shall secure the interests of all merchants, whether foreigners or citizens. In general, it is equally the interest and the duty of every Nation to establish wise and just commercial laws.[6]

Essentially, therefore, it is to the advantage of every nation that the falsification or counterfeiting of the currency of another state be everywhere suppressed and that the duty in this regard be scrupulously observed.[7] It should be of some significance to add that because all nations have an equal interest in the apprehension and punishment of these offenders, it has been strongly suggested that the crime of counterfeiting be regarded as falling within the category of *delicta juris gentium*, thus being assimilated to acts of piracy and treated in similar fashion.[8] In fact, the learned literature on this subject seems to proceed from this point of departure. Thus, the Harvard Research in International Law concludes that "Crimes of counterfeiting now belong clearly to the category of offenses which are coming more and more to be regarded as of the nature of *delicta juris gentium*," and it classifies counterfeiting in the same category as piracy, slave trade, and others.[9] Reasoning from the same premise, Professor Philip C. Jessup suggests that the counterfeiting of foreign currency is of sufficient international concern to warrant its assimilation "to acts of piracy or treated in the

La Coopération des États dans la Lutte contre le Faux Monnayage, pp. 11–14 (1928). For the discussion of the political aspect of the offense, see pp. 101–105.

[5] This was contended in the celebrated case The Emperor of Austria v. Day and Kossuth, Great Britain, High Court of Chancery, 2 Giffard 628 (1861).

[6] E. de Vattel, *Le Droit des Gens*, bk. I, c. 10, secs. 108, 109 (Transl. by C. G. Fenwick, 1916). (Italics are those of Vattel). Professor Arthur Nussbaum abundantly illustrates the severity with which counterfeiting was punished. These penalties, however, applied only to the counterfeiting of domestic currency. See A. Nussbaum, *Money in the Law: National and International*, pp. 40–44 (Rev. ed. 1950).

[7] J. W. Garner, "International Convention for the Repression of Counterfeiting," *Am. J. Int. L.*, Vol. 24, p. 135 (1930).

[8] V. V. Pella, *op. cit.*, pp. 7–16, 106.

[9] For text, *Am. J. Int. L. Supp.*, Vol. 29, pp. 478, 479, 563.

same way."[10] Though this approach to the matter is manifestly desirable, the analogy between *delicta juris gentium* and counterfeiting is, on the whole, fanciful and misleading on two counts. First, the offense of falsification or counterfeiting is not strictly speaking an offense against international law, but only against a state's municipal law, which international law clearly permits a state to punish.[11] Even in the Convention for the Suppression of Counterfeiting Currency of 1929, counterfeiting remains a crime under the municipal law of the states that make it punishable. Crimes *juris gentium*, on the other hand, are offenses against the law of nations, thus making the individual involved a subject of an international obligation.[12] Secondly, while crimes *juris gentium* may be tried and punished in the courts of justice of any nation, for in relation to these crimes the territoriality of criminal jurisdiction is held not to apply,[13] on the other hand, since counterfeiting is an offense created by municipal law, it can only be tried by the state in whose jurisdiction the offense was committed.[14] The most that international law permits is the exercise of protective jurisdiction by the aggrieved government when counterfeiting takes place in the jurisdiction of another state.

To recognize these differences, however, is not to deny the general duty of the state to suppress and punish the counterfeiting within its territory of another nation's currency. The activities of private individuals in counterfeiting foreign currency is one of those acts which the territorial state has a clear duty to suppress; the affected community having a corresponding right to redress.[15] A more precise way

[10] P. C. Jessup, *op. cit.*, p. 178.

[11] Thus, the state courts are merely acting as organs of the state, not of international law. See on this H. Lauterpacht, *The Development of International Law by the International Court*, p. 20 (1958).

[12] H. Kelsen, *Principles of International Law*, pp. 124–126 (1952); O. Svarlien, *An Introduction to the Law of Nations*. pp. 92–93 (1955).

[13] H. Wheaton, *Elements of International Law*, p. 164 (R. H. Dana ed. 1866). It is also interesting to note that some states refer to piracy as established by international law. Thus, the Law of the United States punishes those who "commit the crime of piracy as defined by the law of nations." 18 U.S.C.A., sec. 481 (Criminal Code, section 290). See also C. C. Hyde, *International Law Chiefly as Interpreted and Applied by the United States*, Vol. 1, p. 769 (2d ed. 1945). Cf. C. Parry, "Some Considerations upon the Content of a Draft Code of Offenses Against the Peace and Security of Mankind," *Int. L. Q.*, Vol. 3, pp. 208, 211 (1950).

[14] It should be noted that even in respect to piracy there are certain acts which are only piratical under the law of a particular state, though not so under international law. Professor James L. Brierly cites as an example that in English criminal law it is piracy to engage in slave-trade. See J. L. Brierly, *The Law of Nations*, pp. 240–241 (5th ed. 1955).

[15] While the duty to protect foreign monetary systems in general is denied, the duty to punish counterfeiting of foreign currency is generally conceded. See A. Nussbaum, *op. cit.*, pp. 322–323; also F. A. Mann, *op. cit.*, pp. 259, 271.

of stating this legal position is to say that under the law of nations every government is required to use "due diligence" to prevent a wrong being done within its dominions to another nation with which it is on friendly terms, and it is within this general obligation that the particular duty to punish counterfeiting is included. It should therefore be clear that the latter obligation is only a phase of the general duty of the state, seen throughout this book, to prevent the commission of injurious acts against friendly foreign nations.

There can be no doubt that the recognition of the foregoing obligation is an important expression of the sense of world community, for it is the concern of the international community to suppress offenses which seriously impair the monetary security of the states.[16] This not only results in undermining the security of the national currency involved, but may have serious repercussions in the public confidence placed in money as a medium of international exchange.[17] If there are interests common to all nations, the monetary stability of each state would seem to hold a prominent place.

Though the above observations are compelling and seem unquestioned in the contemporary world, a glance at history will immediately reveal that they failed to gain recognition by states. Reasons of national sovereignty, diverse conceptions of criminal law and the stubborn disposition of some countries to regard counterfeiting as political in character uniformly militated against the attainment of some sort of international cooperation.[18] This situation prevailed throughout the nineteenth and early twentieth century, and is really a sad reflection that the notion of one community of civilized nations for the repression of crime had not emerged. The shift away from such a situation is a result not so much of any recognition of a society of nations but of the general conviction that the counterfeiting of foreign currency was an offense which clearly needed concerted action in its suppression. This purely pragmatic consideration brought about basic changes in the reciprocal obligation of the states and a corresponding change in the relations of the state with individuals. And these changes supplied a

[16] For this reason, counterfeiting of currency has been used as a means of warfare to destroy the enemy's monetary system. Doubts exist as to whether this is a legitimate means of warfare. See F. A. Mann, *The Legal Aspects of Money*, p. 437 (2d ed. 1953). It is generally known that the Nazi Government engaged extensively in counterfeiting foreign currency some of which was to be used to upset the British financial system. See L. A. Mander, *Foundations of Modern World Society*, pp. 272–273 (Rev. ed. 1947).

[17] E. Fitz-Maurice, "Convention for the Suppression of Counterfeiting Currency," *Am. J. Int. L.*, Vol. 26, pp. 533–534 (1932).

[18] J. W. Garner, *op. cit.*, p. 136.

powerful support to the emergence of international organization with its emphasis upon limitations of state sovereignty and the recognition of the values of the world community.

THE LAW OF THE VARIOUS COUNTRIES

Despite the preceding tendency, a generally accepted practice punishing counterfeiting of foreign currency cannot even today be postulated with confidence. For even the twentieth century domestic legislation of the various countries lends slender support to the proposition that the counterfeiting of foreign currency and documents has been universally regarded as a criminal offense. Admittedly, on occasions governments have made reference to the existence of a duty in this connection, but the limited action taken in its enforcement can scarcely rank as a recognition of a legal duty. It is precisely this absence of state action that led to the adoption of the Convention for the Suppression of Counterfeiting Currency in 1929.[19] As this Convention will be subsequently discussed, for present purposes it suffices to know that apparently the legislation of a limited number of states provide for the punishment of counterfeiting foreign currency on equal footing with domestic currency. It seems that included in this selected category are the United States, Great Britain, Italy and a number of Latin American states.

As regards the United States there is ample support in authoritative practice for the assertion that in American statutory and case law a duty under international law to punish counterfeiters of foreign currency and documents has been decisively accepted. Thus, the United States Criminal Code provides:

> Whoever, within the United States, with intent to defraud, falsely makes, alters, forges, or counterfeits any bond, certificate, obligation, or other security of any foreign government, purporting to be or in imitation of any such security issued under the authority of such foreign government, or any treasury note, bill, or promise to pay, lawfully issued by such foreign government and intended to circulate as money, shall be fined not more than $ 5,000 or imprisoned not more than five years, or both.[20]

The Criminal Code similarly punishes the counterfeiting of coins,[21]

[19] For text, see M. O. Hudson, *International Legislation*, Vol. 4, p. 2692 (1931).
[20] 18 U.S.C. sec. 478.
[21] 18 U.S.C. sec. 486. Punishment is not more than $ 3,000 or imprisonment not more than five years or both.

bank notes or bills issued by a bank or corporation of a foreign country,[22] and postage stamps of foreign governments.[23]

The foregoing provisions have not remained without practical effect, for they have come before the courts. The leading case in this connection is *United States v. Arjona,*[24] involving the counterfeiting within the United States of currency issued by the Colombian Government. The Court, in upholding the pertinent provision of the statute on the basis of the power of Congress "to define and punish... Offenses against the Law of Nations,"[25] succinctly said:

> The law of nations requires every national government to use 'due diligence' to prevent a wrong being done within its own dominion to another nation with which it is at peace, or to the people thereof; and because of this the obligation of one nation to punish those who, within its own jurisdiction, counterfeit the money of another nation has long been recognized.[26]

It is to be immediately observed that in this decision the statute punishing the counterfeiting of foreign currency was viewed in the light of its *raison d'être,* namely, the international obligation of the United States to punish those who within its jurisdiction commit an injurious act against a foreign government. It is precisely for this last proposition that the opinion in the *Arjona Case* can be said to be an undisputable authority. It is also to be added that the rationale of this opinion found powerful endorsement in Article 1, section 8, paragraph 10 of the Constitution, which expressly grants to Congress the power to "define and punish... Offenses against the Law of Nations." Other cases may be cited which underscore the broad terms of the statute. It has thus become well established that both the possession of counterfeit obligations and the printing of counterfeit notes of foreign governments are offenses included within the reach of the statute.[27] From the standpoint of constitutional law, it is of some significance to observe that the counterfeiting of notes at different times, although apparently of the same series and printed from the same plate, constitutes distinct offenses so that conviction for one is no bar to prosecution for the others.[28]

[22] 18 U.S.C. sec. 482. Punishment is not more than $ 2,000 or imprisonment not more than two years or both.

[23] 18 U.S.C. sec. 349.

[24] 120 U.S. 479 (1887).

[25] U.S. Const. art. 1, sec. 8, paragraph 10.

[26] United States v. Arjona, 120 U.S. 479, 499 (1887).

[27] Forlini v. United States, 12 F2d 631 (CCA N.Y., 1926); United States v. White 25 F2d 716 (D.C. Tex., 1885).

[28] Bliss v. United States, 105 F2d 508 (CCA Mass., 1901). Double jeopardy is, therefore, not a constitutional defense. See, U.S. Const. Amend. V.

It is intensely relevant to add that the communications of the State Department to foreign governments have similarly regarded the punishment of counterfeiting of foreign currency as the performance of an international duty. Thus, when the Brazilian Government approached the Government of the United States with a proposal to enter into an agreement to punish counterfeiters of each other's currency, the State Department succinctly answered that no such agreement was necessary, explicitly suggesting that the laws of the United States have made provision for the prosecution and punishment of any person who "within the United States or any place subject to the jurisdiction thereof, with intent to defraud," counterfeits currency, bonds and other papers of any foreign government.[29] Many more pronouncements can be adduced where similar views have been expressed.[30] It may be concluded, therefore, that in both principle and practice the United States offers adequate protection to foreign governments in respect to the integrity of their currency and other documents. This being the case, it would seem incontestable that fairness demands reciprocity between other states and the United States. It also follows that such reciprocity has both a legal foundation and a basis in reason and international policy. It is precisely on these grounds that the United States has complained to foreign governments on several occasions to the effect that advertisements were being circulated on which was imprinted a facsimile reproduction of American dollar certificates.[31] Though the available evidence shows that in a number of cases the foreign government in question was unable to punish counterfeiters of American currency because of the absence of legislation on the subject,[32] it seems that on the whole the protests of the United States Government were adequately satisfied.[33] Particularly instructive in this connection is the attitude of the Colombian Government when confronted with American protests that silver dollar certificates were printed and circulated in Bogotá for advertising purposes. The Colombian Ministry replied that though the printing and distribution of facsimiles of foreign currency for advertising purposes was not an offense under Colombian law, it nevertheless gave notice to the store which was using

[29] See Note of Counselor Moore of the State Department to Ambassador da Gama of Brazil, November 8, 1913, G. H. Hackworth, *Digest of International Law*, Vol. 2, pp. 350–351 (1941).

[30] For such communications, *Ibid.*, pp. 350–354.

[31] *Ibid.*, pp. 351–353.

[32] Note of the American Minister to Belgium to the Secretary of State, March 30, 1888. J. B. Moore, *A Digest of International Law*, Vol. 2, pp. 450–451 (1906).

[33] G. H. Hackworth, *op. cit.*, Vol. 2, p. 353.

them as advertisement to refrain from such a practice "for reasons of international courtesy."[34]

The preceding survey would seem to leave no room for doubt that underlying American law two principles can be found which have been articulated by the courts. On the one hand, the United States unmistakably recognizes the right of the nation whose currency has been forged to call on the government concerned to provide punishment for the offense. Concurrent with this is the recognition of the duty of the nation in whose jurisdiction the offense was committed to afford protection as circumstances reasonably permit. Indissolubly linked with this right-duty dichotomy is that harmony between nations which each is bound to promote and cultivate.

The principles enunciated in the above passages have largely guided British law and practice in these matters. Indeed, considerations of international nature have played a prominent role in statutory enactments. Thus, the Coinage Offenses Act of 1861, provides:

> Whoever shall make or counterfeit any Kind of Coin not being the Queen's current Gold or Silver Coin, but resembling or apparently intended to resemble or pass for any Gold or Silver Coin of any Foreign Prince, State, or Country, shall in England and Ireland, be guilty of Felony, and in Scotland of a high Crime and Offense, and being convicted therefore shall be liable, at the Discretion of the Court, to be kept in Penal Servitude for any Term not exceeding Seven Years and not less than Three Years, or to be imprisoned for any Term not exceeding Two Years, with or without Hard Labour, and with or without Solitary Confinement.[35]

It must also be added that the Act of 1935[36] was specifically enacted to give effect to the International Convention for the Suppression of Counterfeiting Currency of 1929 by applying to foreign currency and documents the protections already existing in respect to British currency.[37]

An early authoritative statement of the conditions under which the statute of 1861 would apply is that contained in the judgment of the High Court of Chancery in the celebrated case *The Emperor of Austria v. Day and Kossuth*,[38] involving an injunction brought by the Emperor

[34] *Ibid.*

[35] The Coinage Offenses Act of August 6, 1861, 24 & 25 Vic., chap. 99.

[36] Act of 1935, 25 & 26 Geo. V c. 25.

[37] This is particularly significant, for Great Britain did not ratify the Convention, yet she incorporated the principles of the Convention into her domestic law. The following acts were amended: The Coinage Offenses Act of 1861, 24 & 25 Vic. c. 99; the Forgery Act of 1913, 3 & 4 Geo. V. c. 27; the Counterfeit Medal Act of 1883, 46 & 47 Vic. c. 45; and the Extradition Act of 1870, 33 & 34 Vic. c. 52.

[38] Great Britain, High Court of Chancery, 2 Giffard 628 (1861).

of Austria to restrain defendants from manufacturing printed papers to serve as the public money of the Kingdom of Hungary. The Emperor of Austria alleged an infringement of his property rights, and the court agreed with his contention. The mere statement of this factual situation will immediately indicate that while in the *Arjona Case* the United States itself was the real party interested in protecting the currency of the Colombian Government, in the present case the Emperor of Austria directly resorted to the British courts in an effort to protect alleged property rights. It is perhaps for this reason that the critical issue of the case turned upon the jurisdiction of the court to grant injunctive relief to a foreign sovereign to enforce its rights in the regulation of currency. Recognizing that the issuance of money is not only a prerogative of each sovereign state but also a public right protected by the law of nations, the court granted the injunction adding that the law of nations was a part of the common law of England, and that, money being the medium of commerce, a foreign sovereign at peace with the Crown of England might, by suit in the Court of Chancery, protect his prerogative right of issuing coin or paper money. As regards the purpose of the statute, the court declared:

> This statute is a legislative recognition of the general right of the sovereign authority in foreign states to the assistance of the laws of this country, to protect their rights as to the regulation of paper money as well as their coin, and to punish, by the law of England, offenses against that power.[39]

It can hardly be denied that this opinion, like the American corresponding cases, regards the duty to punish counterfeiters of foreign currency as stemming from accepted principles of international law. So clearly indeed have these principles become the basis of Anglo-American law that the statutes and cases here outlined reveal the commendable tendency to treat foreign currency on an equal footing with domestic currency for the purpose of protection. To a large extent, the same principles have been closely followed by Italy[40] and some Latin American countries[41] in their respective penal legislation. It may therefore be concluded that the law of these countries has established a fairly uniform pattern in these matters and, what is vastly more important, has proceeded upon a consistent theory as to the existence of common interests upon which rights and obligations under the law

[39] *Ibid.*

[40] See *Italian Penal Code, 1930,* article 256.

[41] See in this connection, *Venezuelan Penal Code,* art. 281; *Penal Code of Panama,* 1922, art. 216(a).

of nations are founded. This undoubtedly constitutes an important break with the nineteenth century practice of nations in that counterfeiting of foreign currency largely went unpunished.

It may be added that the duty to punish counterfeiters of foreign currency is in reality one to be discharged in derogation of territorial sovereignty. While the injured nation's right to protection must be conceded, the duty of the territorial state may not be operative at all as long as concrete legislation to that end has not been enacted. To admit this, however, is not to say that the right of the injured nation is to be determined solely by the interests of the territorial state. This is not a duty to be discharged according to considerations of expediency, nor is it a purely theoretical obligation. It is a duty imposed by international law embracing the hopes and aspirations of mankind that interests of property be adequately protected. A better way of stating this position is simply to suggest that measures to protect foreign currency are, in the first instance, measures of municipal law, but these municipal measures operate within the framework of a duty imposed by international law on each individual state. On this view, it may not be an entire novelty to submit that, given the requisite jurisdiction of the International Court of Justice, there is no compelling reason why it should not be invoked by a state whose currency has been forged in the form of a claim for damages should another state have refused to extend protection in its jurisdiction to the former's currency.[42] To deny all this is tantamount to a total denial of world community and law, for these conceptions lose their useful meaning if states do not regard themselves bound by reciprocal obligations enforced by a superior legal order.[43]

Despite the cogency of the foregoing observations, and even though their soundness can scarcely be denied, it nevertheless remains true that concrete domestic legislation punishing counterfeiters of foreign currency on equal grounds with counterfeiters of domestic currency has apparently been limited to the countries above discussed. A study made by Professor Vespasian V. Pella in 1928 interestingly revealed that most legislations on the subject have fundamentally limited their operation in that greater protection is afforded to domestic currency.[44]

[42] There is no reason why this claim would not adequately fall within Article 36, paragraph 2(c) of the Statute of the International Court of Justice, which extends the jurisdiction of the Court, *inter alia*, to "the existence of any fact which, if established, would constitute a breach of an international obligation."

[43] Cf. P. E. Corbett, *Law and Society in the Relations of States*, p. 76 (1951).

[44] V. V. Pella, *op. cit.*, pp. 32–35. Also A. Nussbaum, *op. cit.*, p. 508, n. 28. Here are included the penal codes of France and Belgium. Specifically, the French Penal Code

The distinction between domestic and foreign currency for the purpose of protection may conceivably have had some rational basis when counterfeiting was regarded as an offense against the sovereignty of the state and, thus, political. Today, however, when money has assumed an international character this distinction has no justifiable basis, for individual property rights may be predicated upon money as a means of exchange, and when the character of this money has been fraudulently altered, this action appears squarely as a wrong against the person. It is therefore submitted that since counterfeiting is a crime which in reality transcends political boundaries, it not only affects the particular state involved but may also defraud legitimate individual expectations.

THE CONVENTION FOR THE SUPPRESSION OF COUNTERFEITING CURRENCY

It was precisely in response to the foregoing considerations that under the auspices of the League of Nations the Convention for the Suppression of Counterfeiting Currency was adopted on April 20, 1929.[45] It is unfortunate to observe that the Convention has been ratified only by 25 states, including Germany, Italy, the Netherlands, Poland and the Soviet Union. The United States, Great Britain and France are conspicuously absent from this list.[46] The gap is even wider today with the enlarged membership of the world community and the corresponding greater opportunity for the commission of this crime. Since, in any event, the Convention has substantially become part of the law of many states and it represents a decided step in the effort to lay the foundations of international cooperation in the suppression of this offense, it may be beneficial to discuss it at some length.

It must be said from the outset that despite proposals to the contrary, the Convention is exclusively limited to the suppression of counterfeiting currency and does not embrace such other matters as bank checks, bonds and other securities.[47] The Convention contains some

penalizes the counterfeiting of domestic currency more severely than that of foreign currency. In this connection, compare Article 132 dealing with domestic currency with Article 133 dealing with foreign currency.

[45] For text, see M. O. Hudson, *International Legislation*, Vol. 4, p. 2692 (1931).

[46] A. Nussbaum, *op. cit.*, p. 323. It has been seen, however, that the law of the United States and Great Britain is far ahead of international requirements.

[47] However, according to Article 2 of the Convention, "the word 'currency' is understood to mean paper money (including banknotes) and metallic money, the circulation of which is legally authorized." In May, 1937, the League of Nations set up a Com-

28 articles; it is believed, however, that the obligations undertaken by the signatory states may be classified in three major categories.

The first major obligation is contained in Article 3, which says:

> The following should be punishable as ordinary crimes:
> (1) Any fraudulent making or altering of currency, whatever means employed;
> (2) The fraudulent uttering of counterfeit currency;
> (3) The introduction into a country of or the receiving of or obtaining counterfeit currency with a view to uttering the same and with knowledge that it is counterfeit;
> (4) Attempts to commit, and any international participation in, the foregoing acts;
> (5) The fraudulent making, receiving or obtaining of instruments or other articles peculiarly adapted for the counterfeiting or altering of currency.

This is by far the most important part of the Convention. Embedded in this provision there are three obligations which must particularly be discussed. First, it should be clear that this provision not only gives an exhaustive enumeration of the offenses which fall under the heading of counterfeiting, but makes it fairly plain that all of these acts are distinct offenses which must separately be punished. In fact, such an interpretation is powerfully reinforced by Article 4 which says that "Each of the acts mentioned in Article 3, if they are committed in different countries, should be considered as a distinct offense." Secondly, while it has been maintained that this provision does not require the signatory states to alter their domestic law,[48] a contrary assertion would seem to be more accurate for the provision unmistakably provides that such acts must be punished as ordinary crimes. Thus, the states which up to that time did not have provision in their domestic law for the punishment of counterfeiting, thereby allowing impunity to guilty offenders, by the adoption of the Convention may no longer do so. The Article leaves no room for doubt that all the parties to the Convention have adopted the specific obligation to punish counterfeiting as an ordinary crime. What is still left to the individual action of states is the exact definition, prosecution and punishment of counterfeiting. Therefore, the freedom of the parties is substantially restricted to imposing such punishment as they consider adequate and fair. Article 18 of the Convention amply supports this interpretation, for it provides that "The present Convention does not affect the principle that the offenses referred to in Article 3 should in each country, without

mittee of Jurists to prepare a draft additional protocol to the 1929 Convention "the object of which was to extend to the suppression of the falsification of documents of value the provisions of this Convention." See L. A. Mander, *op. cit.*, p. 272.

[48] J. W. Garner, *op. cit.*, p. 137.

ever being allowed impunity, be defined, prosecuted and punished in conformity with the general rules of its domestic law." This freedom of the parties in respect to the manner of punishment is similarly expressed in the protocol signed simultaneously with the Convention, for its pertinent provision says that "The Convention does not affect the right of the High Contracting Parties freely to regulate, according to their domestic law, the principles on which a lighter sentence or no sentence may be imposed, the prerogative of pardon or mercy and the right to amnesty."[49] Finally, the most important feature of Article 3 lies in that it recognizes that counterfeiting "should be punishable as an ordinary crime." The underlying assumptions of policy embodied in this principle have been subjected to varying and, sometimes, conflicting, interpretations. While it should be quite obvious that Article 3 does not say that counterfeiting can never be considered as a political offense,[50] it does incorporate an injunction to the states that, as far as it is possible, counterfeiting should not be given the privileges generally established in favor of political offenses.[51] Article 10 of the Convention and the Optional Protocol may shed additional light upon this problem. Article 10 provides that "The offenses referred to in Article 3 shall be deemed to be included as extradition crimes in any extradition treaty which has been or may hereafter be concluded between any of the High Contracting Parties. The High Contracting Parties who do not make extradition conditional on the existence of a treaty or reciprocity, henceforward recognize the offenses referred to in Article 3 as cases of extradition as between themselves." And the pertinent provision of the Optional Protocol says that "Recognizing the important progress regarding the suppression of counterfeiting currency which has been realized by the Convention for the Suppression of Counterfeiting Currency bearing this day's date, the High Contracting Parties signatory to this Protocol, subject to ratification, undertake, in their mutual relations, to consider, as regards extradition, the acts referred to in Article 3 of the said Convention as ordinary offenses." These provisions still afford no foundation for the assertion that under the Convention

[49] For text, see M. O. Hudson, *International Legislation*, Vol. 4, p. 2705 (1931).

[50] There is general agreement on this. See J. W. Garner, *op. cit.*, p. 138; E. Fitz-Maurice, *op. cit.*, p. 545. This provision should be compared with Article 7 of the Convention on the Prevention and Punishment of the Crime of Genocide of December 9, 1948, which says that "Genocide and the other acts enumerated in Article III shall not be considered as political crimes for the purpose of extradition." For text, see *Am. J. Int. L. Supp.*, Vol. 45, p. 7 (1951). Thus, unlike counterfeiting, genocide shall never be considered as a political offense.

[51] For an extensive discussion of political offenses, see M. R. García-Mora, *International Law and Asylum as a Human Right*, c. 6 (1956).

counterfeiting is never a political offense.[52] What the Convention has denied is an inherent political character to counterfeiting, but at the same time leaves to the states sufficient discretion to determine in the presence of each particular case whether the offender was motivated by political ends, thus entitling him to asylum. It is, therefore, legally possible for a state to regard a particular case as falling squarely within the category of a political offense.

It is also of some significance to add that under Article 10 of the Convention not all the signatory states have to recognize the offenses of Article 3 as extraditable, for it specifically exempts from its provision the states that make extradition conditional on the existence of a treaty or on the basis of reciprocity.[53] It may be readily perceived that in the countries adhering to such principles the surrender of counterfeiters largely depends upon discretion. Since the United States and Great Britain recognize the principle of no extradition apart from treaty,[54] it follows logically that under the Convention they are not legally obliged to extradite counterfeiters unless an extradition treaty exists between these countries and the demanding state. It is, however, clear that assuming the existence of a treaty, counterfeiting will be regarded as extraditable even though it may not have been origi-

[52] It is interesting to observe that counterfeiting was not included by the International Law Commission of the United Nations in its Draft Code of Offenses Against the Peace and Security of Mankind because it was not believed to contain "a political element... which endangers or disturbs the maintenance of international peace and security." See Report of the International Law Commission Covering the work of its Third Session, 16 May–27 July, 1951, U.N. General Assembly, Official Records, Sixth Session, Supplement No. 9 (A/1858, p. 11 (1951).

[53] Article 10 says: "The offenses referred to in Article 3 shall be deemed to be included as extradition crimes in any extradition treaty which has been or may hereafter be concluded between any of the High Contracting Parties. The High Contracting Parties who do not make extradition conditional on the existence of a treaty or reciprocity, henceforward recognize the offenses referred to in Article 3 as cases of extradition as between themselves."

[54] A classical statement of this doctrine was neatly expressed by the Supreme Court of the United States in Factor v. Laubenheimer, 290 U.S. 276 (1933). In this case, the Court said: "The principles of international law recognize no right to extradition apart from treaty." *Ibid.*, p. 287. A more recent statement of the doctrine was expressed by the Department of State on January 20, 1947, when it refused to extradite a former employee of the Soviet Embassy in Mexico who was accused of embezzlement and who had taken refuge in the United States. At this time, the State Department said: "It is a well-established principle of international law that no right to extradition exists apart from treaty. No extradition treaty exists between the United States and the Soviet Union." *Dept. State Bull.*, Vol. 16, p. 212 (1947). It is worth noting that the Constitution of Honduras provides in Article 20 that "extradition may only be granted by virtue of a law or by treaty..." For text, see R. H. Fitzgibbon, *The Constitutions of the Americas* p. 468 (1948); T. A. Taracouzio says that the Soviet Government extradites criminals only on the basis of extradition treaties, but in the absence of treaties, upon "special consent granted for each individual case." T. A. Taracouzio, *The Soviet Union and International Law*, pp. 145–146 (1935).

nally included in the list of extraditable offenses. Similar observations may be made in respect to reciprocity, for even though the Continental European and Latin American countries grant extradition in the absence of a treaty, such surrender is conditioned upon the principle of reciprocity,[55] which would seem to suggest that even in these countries the extradition of counterfeiters cannot confidently be asserted. It may thus be concluded that as regards extradition the weakness of the Convention is glaringly obvious and that, on such bases, it can scarcely be expected to achieve satisfactory results.

The second major obligation of the Convention is found in Article 5 which provides:

> No distinction should be made in the scale of punishments for offenses referred to in Article 3 between acts relating to domestic currency on the one hand and to foreign currency on the other; this provision may not be made subject to any condition of reciprocal treatment by law or by treaty.

One needs no great effort to realize that the significance of this provision lies in that it incorporates the principle of equality of treatment between domestic and foreign currency, which was clearly seen in the penal legislation of some countries. It is also to be noted that the incorporation of equality of treatment is a commendable recognition that counterfeiting is an offense of international concern. But since this offense is to be punished by municipal courts, the interesting question has arisen as to the habitual criminality of an offender from an international standpoint. The problem in its simplest terms is the weight which a municipal court should give to previous convictions in other countries for the purpose of establishing habitual criminality. While it may be readily perceived that this problem touches serious matters concerning the purely territorial character of penal sentences,[56] the Convention has clearly adopted an intermediate position, thus striking a proper balance between the demands of state sovereignty and the international aspect of the crime. Article 6 says in this connection that

[55] A typical formulation of the doctrine of reciprocity is well illustrated by Article 646 of the Argentine Code of Criminal Procedure, which provides as follows: "Extradition of criminals, whether requested by the Republic or granted by it at the request of another State, shall only take place: (1) In the cases provided for by existing treaties; and (2) In the absence of treaties, in the cases in which extradition is proper according to the principle of reciprocity or the uniform practice of States." Cited by the Harvard Research in International Law, Extradition, *Am. J. Int. L. Supp.*, Vol. 29, p. 360 (1935). The Argentine Extradition Law of 1885 contained an identical provision. For text, see *U.S. Foreign Rel.* 1886, p. 4 (1887).

[56] E. Fitz-Maurice, *op. cit.*, p. 541.

In countries where the principle of the international recognition of previous convictions is recognized, foreign convictions for the offenses referred to in Article 3 should, within the conditions prescribed by domestic law, be recognized for the purpose of establishing habitual criminality.

It must be observed that this formulation, even if accepted as a desirable compromise between the demands of sovereignty and those of the world community, still leaves the requirements of sovereignty singularly free, for the provision is only applicable in jurisdictions where "the principle of the international recognition of previous convictions is recognized." It follows *a fortiori* that this provision remains wholly inoperative in the countries which clearly do not recognize previous convictions in other jurisdictions for the purpose of establishing habitual criminality. The net result of this situation may well be a benefit to the professional criminal, who is likely to receive a lighter sentence in countries not recognizing international criminality while in reality one or more convictions for the same offense would seem to demand a more severe punishment. It is in this connection that the Convention may give rise to highly unjust decisions. It does not at all meet the argument to say that penal sentences ought to be a matter of territorial competence and thus, should not be given extraterritorial effect. For this argument breaks down altogether and loses all its force when remembering that counterfeiting has been regarded as a crime of international concern, and it is precisely because of the possible existence of organized criminals on a world-wide level that domestic legislation alone is not sufficient to suppress it.[57] This argument is even more persuasive when considering that it is the professional counterfeiter who more effectively evades the application of domestic law. It may be pertinent to add that the conception of one world community and the requirements of justice would seem to militate strongly in favor of considering previous convictions in other countries in order to determine the habitual criminality of the offender. To leave this matter entirely to the unfettered discretion of the states not only strikes a serious blow to the need for uniformity on the subject but is also a sad reflection that a cohesive world community, even in this matter, has not yet been attained. It would seem that if counterfeiting is to be regarded as an international crime, previous convictions in other jurisdictions must be considered in establishing habitual crimi-

[57] J. Paoli, "Contribution à L'étude des crimes de Guerre et des crimes contre l'Humanité en Droit Penal International," *Rev. Gén. de Droit Int. Public.* Vol. 39, p. 147 (France, 1941–1945).

nality. This conclusion would seem to follow naturally not only from the nature of the crime involved but also from the international character of the Convention itself.

Finally, the third major obligation of the Convention is contained in Article 8, which says:

> In countries where the principle of extradition of nationals is not recognized, nationals who have returned to the territory of their own country after the commission abroad of an offense referred to in Article 3 should be punishable in the same manner as if the offense had been committed in their own territory, even in a case where the offender has acquired his nationality after the commission of the offense.

This is a far-reaching provision indeed, for in principle it aims at insuring that an offender will not escape punishment merely because he happens to return to his country of origin and the latter provides for the non-extradition of its nationals.[58] It is, however, in this respect that the Convention clearly commands the countries which do not extradite their own nationals to punish the offenders as if the offense had been committed within their jurisdiction. But in so doing difficulties of a purely penal order are likely to arise, for though international law allows a state to exercise jurisdiction over nationals for crimes committed abroad,[59] this jurisdiction is limited to violations of the national law. A different problem presents itself in dealing with the prosecution of a national for the crime of counterfeiting committed against the law of another country in the latter's jurisdiction. Since the offender has not violated his national law but that of another country, it is difficult to see the basis on which his own state can exercise jurisdiction. It would seem that confronted with this situation, the extradition of the offender is the only desirable course of action. It is exactly in this connection that the Convention clearly requires a substantial change in the practice of extradition, for there can be no reasonable doubt that the principle of non-extradition of nationals ultimately allows offenders to escape punishment. While undoubtedly drastic changes will have to be made in the law of Continental countries, no change is required in the case of the United States and Great Britain, for these countries have consistently adhered to the principle of extradition of their own nationals.[60]

[58] This seems to be the general practice of the countries whose system of law is based on Roman Law. See, C. C. Hyde, *International Law Chiefly as Interpreted and Applied by the United States*, Vol. 2, pp. 1027–1029 (2d ed. 1945).

[59] See in this connection Article 5 of the Harvard Research, "Jurisdiction with Respect to Crime," *Am. J. Int. L. Supp.*, Vol. 29, pp. 519–535 (1935).

[60] See C. C. Hyde, *op. cit.*, Vol. 2, pp. 1027–1029. For the British view, see L. Oppenheim, *International Law*, Vol. 1, pp. 699–700 (8th ed. by H. Lauterpacht, 1955).

It is believed to be important for an accurate consideration of this problem to distinguish the provision of Article 8 from that of Article 9, which says:

> Foreigners who have committed abroad any offense referred to in Article 3, and who are in the territory of a country whose internal legislation recognizes as a general rule the principle of the prosecution of offenses committed abroad, should be punishable in the same way as if the offense had been committed in the territory of that country... The obligation to take proceedings is subject to the condition that extradition has been requested and that the country to which the application is made cannot hand over the person accused for some reason which has no connection with the offense.

The principle incorporated in the above provision expressly recognizes the exercise of jurisdiction for counterfeiting committed by foreigners in another country's territory. It will shortly be seen that this type of jurisdiction is justified on the basis of protection and, though its exercise in respect to political offenses of foreigners abroad is cast into the gravest doubts, in respect to counterfeiting protective jurisdiction seems to be generally accepted.[61] The obligation of Article 9 in respect to foreigners is quite similar to that of Article 8 in respect to nationals, for Article 9 imposes upon states that exercise protective jurisdiction the obligation to punish offenses committed abroad, subject to the condition that extradition had been requested but could not be granted for some reason unconnected with the offense.

The exercise of protective jurisdiction is so general, and so explicit are international conventions recognizing it, that it has been generally regarded as a clear indication of a marked tendency towards universal competence.[62] Underlying this assertion there is concealed the supposition that this universal competence is somewhat similar to that exercised by a state as regards piracy or slave trade. This assumption is indefensible on all accounts, for Article 9 of the Convention merely recognizes the competence of the state in respect to the counterfeiting of its own currency committed by foreigners abroad. It cannot reasonably be inferred from the Convention that a state has competence to punish foreigners who counterfeit the currency of a third state upon foreign territory. Admittedly, there are powerful reasons of a criminal law nature which militate against the adoption of this radical position.[63]

[61] See Chapter IX, *infra*.

[62] E. Fitz-Maurice, *op. cit.*, p. 543.

[63] Thus, when the Brazilian Government requested the American Government to punish persons who in Brazil counterfeited Brazilian currency and came to the United States, the State Department answered that "As the territorial theory of crime obtains

What the Convention does in this situation is to impose upon the state wherein the offender has taken refuge the obligation to deliver the offender to the government that is asking for his extradition.[64] It is in this respect that the Convention falls short of reasonable expectations, for it has failed to assimilate counterfeiting to *delicta juris gentium*, thereby making it possible for states to exercise universal competence over counterfeiters of other nation's currency who happen to come to their jurisdiction.[65] The Convention has merely established a system of national competences, and does not contemplate international jurisdiction even as a remote alternative. It is thus submitted that progress in this area would be significantly limited unless counterfeiting is finally recognized as an offense against the world community, for it seriously impairs international monetary order and, consequently, the peace and well-being of mankind.[66] On this view, counterfeiting becomes an offense against the law of nations, which states have the legal obligation to suppress and punish regardless of the *locus* of the offense and the particular currency involved. Disregard of this obligation substantially engages the international responsibility of the state, thus amounting to an international delinquency.[67]

CONCLUSION

Underlying the preceding observations is the idea that in the presence of a crime of international dimensions, every state should be under an explicit legal obligation to punish it. This is so not only because of the

in the United States, it would not be practicable for this Government to enter into a treaty arrangement with the Brazilian Government providing for the prosecution of persons for committing in Brazil the crimes of counterfeiting Brazilian money, securities, etc." See Note of Counselor Moore to Ambassador da Gama, November 8, 1913, G. H. Hackworth, *op. cit.*, Vol. 2 p. 351.

[64] Thus, Article 10 of the Convention says: "The offenses referred to in Article 3 shall be deemed to be included as extradition crimes in any extradition treaty which has been or may hereafter be concluded between any of the High Contracting Parties. The High Contracting Parties who do not make extradition conditional on the existence of a treaty or reciprocity, henceforward recognize the offenses referred to in Article 3 as cases of extradition as between themselves."

[65] It should be obvious that in respect to piracy or slave trade there is universal competence because the crime is one against the law of nations. The state that happens to capture a pirate or one engaged in the slave trade will have competence to punish him. In respect to counterfeiting, however, only the state whose law has been violated has competence to punish an offender.

[66] Professor Vespasian V. Pella regarded counterfeiting as an offense against the peace and security of mankind sometime ago. See V. V. Pella, *op. cit.*, p. 106.

[67] *Ibid.*, pp. 106–107. This responsibility of course depends upon the measures of exertion discussed previously.

interdependent nature of this crime but also because of the duty of every nation to protect legitimate expectations of individuals everywhere. It is precisely for these reasons that counterfeiting should be established as an offense against the law of nations, which implicitly assumes that individuals themselves are bound by its provisions. Attainment of this goal of necessity requires a critical reappraisal of the role of domestic penal legislation in relation to international standards. Though the Convention for the Suppression of Counterfeiting Currency is undoubtedly a step in that direction, no additional progress has been made since its adoption. It has been seen that the Convention itself falls short even of its own aspirations. For while it was intended "to formalize the broad principles of modern international law on this point,"[68] the Convention regrettably remains unratified by a substantial number of states. Complete protection of foreign currency may thus be frustrated in part by the unwillingness of many nations to conform to its provisions. It has also been seen that as to the range of its provisions, the draftsmen left many matters of importance to the discretion of the states. It must be readily conceded, however, that these shortcomings were dictated by the demands of compromise necessary to secure acceptance by all the participant states, and it would be highly unfair not to recognize that despite them, the Convention is a considerable advance. It represents a fairly successful attempt to regulate by the concerted action of the states an offense committed by private persons, which seriously affects the well-being of other nations.

[68] F. A. Mann, "Money in Public International Law," *Brit. Y.B. Int. L.* 1949, Vol. 26, p. 272 (1949).

PART THREE

JURISDICTION FOR THE PUNISHMENT OF PRIVATE PERSONS

CHAPTER IX

SO-CALLED PROTECTIVE JURISDICTION OF THE THREATENED COMMUNITY

It has long been an unquestioned postulate of legal theory that criminal jurisdiction is essentially territorial and that a state has very wide powers to exercise jurisdiction over nationals and aliens for unlawful acts committed in whole or in part within its territory.[1] There is, however, an almost universal municipal legal practice which is somewhat difficult to reconcile with the exclusive territorial theory of penal competence and which relates to the exercise of jurisdiction over offenses entirely committed by foreigners in a foreign land.[2] While there may be a number of acts which fall within the exercise of this type of jurisdiction,[3] the least discussed and not always well observed is the application of a state's laws to punish politically hostile acts committed by foreigners within the jurisdiction of another state. This is the manner in which states cope with the offenses of private persons here discussed. As an exception to the territorial principle, the legal basis of this principle is largely a matter of controversy and doubt.[4] Since this is an area singularly free of any authoritative guidance, speculative implications may be sought in the legal practice of the countries which have had considerable experience on the subject.

[1] A. Levitt, "Jurisdiction over Crimes," *J. Crim. L. & Criminology*, Vol. 16, pp. 316, 324 (1925); W. Berge, "Criminal Jurisdiction and the Territorial Principle," *Mich. L. R.*, Vol. 30, p. 233 (1931). The territorial principle is generally considered as an established rule of international law. See E. G. Schuck, "Concurrent Jurisdiction Under NATO Status Forces Agreement," *Colum. L. R.*, Vol. 57, pp. 355, 359 (1957).

[2] Research in International Law Under the Auspices of the Harvard Law School, "Jurisdiction With Respect to Crime," *Am. J. Int. L. Supp.*, Vol. 29, p. 543 (1935).

[3] See for instance, W. W. Cook, "The Application of the Criminal Law of a Country to Acts Committed by Foreigners Outside the Jurisdiction," *W. Va. L. Q.*, Vol. 40, p. 303, (1933–1934).

[4] There is evidence to the effect that the resort to this practice is on the increase. See P. C. Jessup, *Transnational Law*, p. 50 (1956). Perhaps Professor Edward D. Dickinson was a bit premature in asserting that the exercise of this type of jurisdiction was vanishing. His assertion was made before the numerous postwar cases arose. See E. D. Dickinson, "International Law – An Inventory," *Calif. L.R.*, Vol. 33, pp. 506, 523 (1945).

THE SO-CALLED PROTECTIVE THEORY OF JURISDICTION

Present international consensus unmistakably postulates that, in the absence of permissive rules of international customary or treaty law, a state has no legal power to exercise jurisdiction within the territorial domain of another state.[5] As a general legal proposition, this is undoubtedly correct. The international legal order, however, presents a disturbing picture of conflicting theory and reality, for, in respect to certain offenses committed by foreigners abroad and aimed at the security of the state, jurisdiction has been successfully exercised on the basis of what is generally termed the protective principle. Introduced into the law long before the emergence of the national state,[6] this mischievous principle subsequently became a verbal formula invoked to demand a wider measure of freedom for the states to maintain their own security against threats coming from external sources. Its present underlying postulates are, however, clear enough. On the one hand, it is vigorously asserted that a state has a right to the free development of its political institutions and that this right is guaranteed by international law.[7] On the other hand, it is recognized as implicit in this very statement that in the absence of a centralized authority capable of protecting its security, the state has the competence to punish those who from foreign territory frustrate the possibility of internal peace.[8] These postulates, whose precise implications vary in many concrete situations, are also cut across by the survival in some measure of theories of absolute sovereignty which imperatively demand that every state be free to determine the scope and operation of its penal law.[9] At the base of all these postulates is the denial of a community of interests existing in the world society and the belief that nations live in isolation concerned only with interests of their own. Though this conception may have had some sem-

[5] Justice J. Story said quite sometime ago: "... no State or nation can by its laws directly affect or bind property out of its own territory, or bind persons not resident therein, whether they are natural-born subjects or others." J. Story, *Commentaries on the Conflict of Laws*, sec. 18 (4th ed. 1852). More recently, the Permanent Court of International Justice said in the celebrated *Lotus* case: "... clearly a State may not exercise its power within another State's territory." The S.S. "Lotus," *P.C.I.J.*, Ser. A, No. 10, p. 18 (1927).

[6] D. H. De Vabres, *Les Principes Modernes du Droit Pénal International*, p. 87 (1928).

[7] H. Lauterpacht, "Revolutionary Activities by Private Persons Against Foreign States," *Am. J. Int. L.*, Vol. 22, p. 105 (1928).

[8] This is the reason why protective jurisdiction in Continental Europe is asserted on the basis of self-defense. See D. H. De Vabres, *op. cit.*, p. 87.

[9] C. De Visscher, *Theory and Reality in Public International Law*, p. 245 (Transl. by P. E. Corbett, 1957). See also M. Miele, *Principi di Diritto Internazionale*, p. 181 (1953).

blance of reality in the early development of international law, its continuous adherence is highly incompatible with the existence of a world community fundamentally grounded on the conception of the interdependence of states.

With this background in mind, it will at once be seen that, unlike other principles of jurisdiction which are founded upon either the locus of the crime or the nationality of the offender,[10] the protective principle exclusively relies upon fundamental interests of the state involving its security, territorial integrity and political independence. It will shortly be seen that the primacy of security interests exhibited in this field accounts in no small measure for the high degree of flexibility with which the protective principle has been practically applied. The attitude of the states in this regard instructively illustrates that, though differing in degree, there is a persistent adherence to the exercise of jurisdiction on these bases. Looking comprehensibly at the practice of the states, two different criteria immediately emerge, which forcibly suggest the classification of the states into two clearly defined categories. One group, which includes the United States and Great Britain, tenaciously adheres to the principle of territoriality of criminal jurisdiction, thereby declining to assume jurisdiction over hostile acts committed by foreigners abroad unless a bond of allegiance between the actor and the sovereign is unequivocally found. The existence of allegiance is, therefore, the controlling consideration, and acts resulting from the breach of it are generally regarded as treason. The other group, which includes the Continental European and Latin American states, though accepting the principle of territoriality, admits exceptions based on the principle of self-defense for acts directed against the security of the state.[11] Since the principle of self-defense is particularly free of legal regulation, the resulting jurisdiction asserted on this ground is rather broad and liberally applied. The merits of these two doctrines will be analyzed in dealing with the law of the various countries.

[10] H. W. Briggs, *The Law of Nations: Cases, Documents, Notes*, pp. 575–576 (2d ed. 1952).

[11] Thus, Professor Alf Ross, though adhering to what he calls "the maxim of territorial competence of jurisdiction," says that this maxim does not restrict the legislative competence of the state to attach legal consequences to facts which have taken place outside the territory. See A. Ross, *A Text-Book of International Law*, pp. 155–156 (1947).

THE DUTY OF ALLEGIANCE THEORY

The territorial principle of criminal jurisdiction was erected into a legal absolute by Anglo-American law.[12] Such a principle not only became a commonplace of Anglo-American legal theory, but has been applied with remarkable uniformity in concrete situations. Despite this substantial similarity existing between American and English laws, nevertheless, their respective historical developments show diverse characteristics, thus warranting separate treatments.

The British Law[13]

The Treason Act of 1351, which is the oldest legislation on the subject still in force, includes among breaches of allegiance the act of "adhering to the King's enemies in his realm by giving them aid and comfort in the realm or elsewhere."[14] But whether or not the act of aiding and comforting the King's enemies *outside the realm* falls within the provisions of the Treason Act entirely depends upon the relation in which the offender stood to the King at the time of the commission of the act.[15] The issue of law and fact thus posed is whether at the time of the commission of the offense the alien in question owed allegiance to the King. Conceived in these terms, the test of allegiance is most certainly decisive and the courts have managed to apply it without serious difficulty. The duty of allegiance is, however, in turn wholly dependent upon the existence of the King's protection, for the British law has consistently adhered to the principle *protectio trahit subjectionem et subjectio protectionem.*[16] It should be observed, however, that the early law found a duty of allegiance only when the alien was residing within the realm, precisely because the King's protection could not possibly extend beyond his territorial domains. This principle became firmly established in the *Calvin's Case* where the House of Lords most explicitly said:

[12] In this connection, Secretary of State Calhoun said: "We hold that the criminal jurisdiction of a nation is limited to its own dominions and to vessels under its flag on the high seas, and that it cannot extend to acts committed within the dominions of another without violating its sovereignty and independence." J. B. Moore, *A Digest of International Law*, Vol. 2, p. 255 (1906).

[13] "British Law" embraces those of the countries members of the British Commonwealth of Nations, since for the purposes of allegiance they all stand on the same ground.

[14] 25 Edw. III, stat. 5, c. 2.

[15] See Joyce v. Director of Public Prosecutions, House of Lords, February 1. 1946 [1946] A.C. 347, 365.

[16] *Ibid.*, p. 366.

...When an alien that is in amity cometh into England, because as long as he is within England he is within the King's protection; therefore, so long as he is here, he oweth unto the King a local obedience or ligeance... But if an alien enemy come to invade this realm, and be taken in war, he cannot be indicted for treason... for he never was in the protection of the King.[17]

Blackstone confirmed these ideas in almost identical terms:

Local allegiance is such as is due from an alien, or stranger born, for so long a time as he continues within the King's dominion and protection; and it ceases, the instant such stranger transfers himself from his kingdom to another... as the prince affords his protection to an alien, only during his residence in this realm, the allegiance of an alien is confined (in point of time) to the duration of such his residence, and (in point of locality) to the dominions of the British Empire.[18]

Against the background of these authoritative pronouncements, the exercise of protective jurisdiction loses all of its controversial ring. For in logic the exercise of jurisdiction over foreigners residing within the realm presents itself as nothing more than the pure application of the territorial principle of jurisdiction which is sanctioned by international law. It is only when applied to foreigners for acts committed abroad that protective jurisdiction acquires the significance and controvery attributed to it, simply because the perplexing question then arises whether protection and, thus, a duty of allegiance is deemed to exist. While the determination of this matter, in the infinite variety of situations, is extremely complicated, it must nevertheless be observed that three contemporary decisions have laid down general patterns of statutory interpretation extending a foreigner's allegiance by rather subtle means.

The first of such cases is *Lodewyk Johannes de Jager v. The Attorney General of Natal*[19] involving an alien residing in Natal who, upon the subsequent occupation of the area by the Boer forces, joined the latter aiding and assisting them both as a commandant and as a commissioner and justice of the peace. The crucial issue in its simplest terms was whether by enemy occupation the accused lost the protection of the Crown, thus relieving him of the duty of allegiance and depriving his act of a treasonable character. The court succinctly disposed of the issue:

It is old law that an alien resident within the British territory owes allegiance to the Crown, and may be indicted for high treason, though not a subject... The protection of the State does not cease merely because the State forces, for

[17] [1608] 4 Co. Rep. 1, 10, 11 (1793).

[18] W. Blackstone, *Commentaries*, Vol. 1, pp. 370, 371 (E. Christian ed. 1818).

[19] [1907] A.C. 326.

strategical or other reasons, are temporarily withdrawn, so that the enemy for the time exercises the right of an army in occupation. On the contrary, when such territory reverts to the control of its rightful sovereign, wrongs done during the foreign occupation are cognizable by the ordinary courts. The protection of the Sovereign has not ceased. It is continuous, though the actual redress of what has been done amiss may be necessarily postponed until the enemy forces have been expelled.[20]

Tested by the requirements of the *Calvin's Case*, the preceding opinion would seem to go further in regarding allegiance still existing even though the protection of the King was temporarily suspended.[21] It would seem, therefore, that though the right of protection may be in suspense, the duty of allegiance still remains. It suffices if the alien once enjoyed the protection of the Crown, for while he remains within the realm under the circumstances of this case, this protection in principle continues, as it were, in suspended animation. It is precisely on this ground that the *Jager Case* presents itself as the first break away from the basic postulate of the concept of allegiance, for the decision is fundamentally based on a broader concept of protection substantially departing from the traditional view.

The second major landmark in the development of the British law is represented by the case *Rex v. Neumann*[22] where the theory of vicarious protection was given practical expression.[23] This case involved a German national by birth who, having emigrated to South Africa in 1940, enlisted in the South African Defense Forces taking an oath of allegiance to the Crown, but without becoming in any way a British subject. When subsequently captured by the Germans, he was seen serving the Axis forces in Italy. Upon returning to South Africa after the termination of the war, he was charged with the crime of high treason. The accused challenged the jurisdiction of the court on the ground that he owed no allegiance to the Crown at the time of the

[20] *Ibid.*, pp. 328, 329.

[21] It is pertinent to contrast this decision with what Hobbes said about those who are in the power of the enemy: "Where a man is captive, or in the power of the enemy (and he is then in the power of the enemy, when his person, or his means of living, is so), if it be without his own fault, the Obligation of the Law ceased; because he must obey the enemy, or die; and consequently such obedience is no Crime; for no man is obliged (when the protection of the law failed) not to protect himself, by the best means he can." T. Hobbes, *Leviathan*, pp. 231–232 (W. G. Smith ed. 1947). While this passage is not legally authoritative, it is a declaration of principle which must be taken into account in judging the rationality of the law.

[22] Union of South Africa, Special Criminal Court, Transvaal, October 16, 1956, *Annual Digest 1949*, p. 239 (H. Lauterpacht ed. 1955).

[23] This theory, however, was mentioned in the previous case, *Joyce v. Director of Public Prosecutions*, House of Lords, February 1, 1946, [1946] A.C. 347, 368, but was discarded.

commission of the offense. The reasoning of the court, however, was clear and unmistakable, for it squarely based allegiance on the rather novel theory that the protection of the King continues abroad if the alien leaves his family behind giving to his departure a purely temporary character. The court was most explicit:

> Without doubt allegiance is required of a resident alien while he himself is physically present in the country. The leaving of his family behind may *per se* involve a continuation in respect to his family and for his benefit, of the protection until then enjoyed by him for himself and his family... where it is clear that his departure is of a purely temporary character, accompanied by a definite intention to return for permanent residence, the protection previously acquired does not cease on departure. ...If on principle... it is the *protectio* which creates the obligation of allegiance, this court should... hold that when the accused left the country temporarily in consequence of his enlistment as a soldier in the Union Forces, his existing allegiance continued...[24]

The foregoing paragraph would seem to suggest that even if residence within the realm has ceased, a foreigner's allegiance to the King will unavoidably continue if a requisite connection with the Crown still exists. In logic it thus follows that a tie of a particular kind and sufficiently apparent must be found to continue the duty of allegiance formerly existing. In this context, the protection available to an alien previously residing within the realm and leaving his family behind does not come to an end but is clearly of a different nature so that a duty of allegiance cannot be successfully avoided. The *Neumann Case* significantly illustrates that protective jurisdiction is likely to be based on grounds rather novel in legal nature involving facts which the court regarded as vital and substantial.[25]

The third important case which significantly departed from the original standards of the *Calvin's Case* is *Joyce v. Director of Public Prosecutions*,[26] which has today become a *cause célèbre* in the history of treason. The facts here relevant are as follows. William Joyce, otherwise known as "Lord Haw Haw," was convicted of the crime of high treason by adhering to the King's enemies outside the realm. Specifically, the treasonable act consisted in broadcasting propaganda on behalf of Germany during World War II. The evidence was conclusive upon the fact that while traveling abroad, the accused was in

[24] *Rex v. Neumann, Annual Digest 1949*, pp. 239, 242–243 (1955).

[25] See also Rex v. Christian, Union of South Africa, Appellate Division, November 30, 1923, where it was held that an inhabitant of a Mandate under the administration of the Union of South Africa owed allegiance to the Crown and, therefore, could be guilty of the crime of high treason against the Union. *Annual Digest* 1923–1924, pp. 27, 31 (1933).

[26] House of Lords, February 1, 1946, [1946] A.C. 347.

possession of a valid passport issued by the British Government. In dealing with the issue whether William Joyce owed allegiance to the King outside the realm, the House of Lords successively reviewed the various doctrines of protection with no apparent success.[27] It found, however, powerful support in the somewhat spectacular doctrine that an alien's duty of allegiance does not cease if by the possession of a passport he continues to enjoy the protection of the King abroad. Possession of a passport was thus decisively controlling, for in reality it was considered of sufficient force for the alien to demand the protection of the King outside the realm. On this ground, the duty of allegiance could not possibly be avoided.[28] The continued protection thus acquired remained until and unless the alien unequivocally dissociated himself from any bond linking him with the protection of the King. This the accused could have done by the surrender of the passport, the duty of allegiance immediately ceasing as from the moment of surrender.[29] Despite possible inferences from some of the judicial language,[30] it seems clear that the "passport test" is not a substitute for the test of local residence but is simply an additional test to achieve substantially similar results. It is undoubtedly for this reason that the court was able to remain within the holding of the *Calvin's Case* without having to draw a line of distinction between these two cases.

In another aspect of the case the court uncompromisingly rejected the argument that protection could not exist because the passport was fraudulently obtained. It effectively met this argument by resorting to the admittedly unassailable assumption that protection existed until the fraud was disclosed.[31] Nor was it material that the accused never in fact invoked the protection of the King, for, the court reasoned, by holding a passport he claimed the continued protection of the Crown thereby maintaining an unbroken bond of allegiance to the King.[32] It is indeed in this connection that the most significant

[27] More particularly, the court set aside the doctrine of vicarious protection since the accused left no family behind. *Ibid.*, p. 368.

[28] For a discussion of the relation between the holder of a passport and the country granting it, see P. Weis, *Nationality and Statelessness in International Law*, pp. 219–229 (1956).

[29] Apparently, the court inferred that because Joyce never surrendered his passport, he intended to continue his allegiance. [1946] A.C. 347, 371.

[30] Particularly at pp. 370–371.

[31] It seems that Joyce obtained the passport by representing himself as a British subject, when in reality he was an American citizen and had never taken steps to become a British subject. *Ibid.*, p. 359.

[32] *Ibid.*, p. 371.

aspect of the decision lies, for this all-inclusive language gives foundation to the assertion that a foreigner's duty of allegiance to the Crown can be more generally derived from his right to protection and not only from his *de facto* enjoyment of it.[33] Such a result was emphatically laid down by the court in language which leaves no room for doubt:

> It is not, therefore, an answer to the Sovereign's claim to fidelity from an alien without the realm who holds a British passport that there cannot be extended to him the protection of the law... it appears that the Crown in issuing a passport is assuming an onerous burden, and the holder of the passport is acquiring substantial privileges... This rule [of protection] may be asserted by the holder of a passport which is for him the outward title of his rights.[34]

On such a basis, it will be immediately perceived that the holding in the *Joyce Case* opened up vast new fields to the doctrine of the protection of the King as a basis of allegiance. That doctrine is, as it were, refurbished for use against an alien who at one time or another found himself under the protection of the King. The court regarded the protection afforded by a passport as included in the original doctrine of allegiance regardless of whether actual protection was ever enjoyed.[35] The question in short, was no longer one of allegiance by residing within the realm. It became a more generalized inquiry into probabilities regardless of their factual support.

Against the background of the *Calvin's Case*, there can be little doubt that allegiance based on local residence has been extended beyond its original bounds. The new climate of policy reflected in the *Neumann* and *Joyce* cases is the more striking as it reveals an unmistakable tendency on the part of the British courts to prosecute foreigners for acts committed abroad on looser grounds and to make the test of requisite allegiance broader thereby enlarging the latitude of prosecutions.[36] Although this interpretation may be highly desirable in some cases, it is liable to abuse, for in practice it amounts to converting an act of a private person abroad into a treasonable offense merely because for some reason, however tenuous, the offender was found to have a right to the protection of the King.

[33] S. C. Biggs, "Treason and the Trial of William Joyce," *U. of Toronto L. J.*, Vol. 7, pp. 162, 181 (1947–1948).

[34] [1946] A.C. 347, 370–371.

[35] It should be mentioned that no passport was found in Joyce's actual physical possession, but the court went on the assumption that since one was issued, it must have been used. *Ibid.*, pp. 369, 372.

[36] This general tendency was already perceived by Professor Charles C. Hyde in 1945. See C. C. Hyde, *International Law Chiefly as Interpreted and Applied by the United States*, Vol. 1, p. 806 (2d ed. 1945).

The American Law

The American constitutional provision in regard to treason[37] is historically traceable to the English Treason Act of 1351 previously discussed. As applied to aliens, the law of treason is similarly grounded on the existence of allegiance to the United States. Thus, the United States Code provides that "Whoever, *owing allegiance to the United States*, levies war against them or adheres to their enemies, giving them aid and comfort within the United States or elsewhere, is guilty of treason..."[38] But in contrast with the English law, which has occasionally resorted to the exercise of protective jurisdiction in the manner indicated, the American law has thus far remained faithful to the conception of allegiance strictly based on local residence much in the manner of the *Calvin's Case*. Of particular significance in this connection is a report which Secretary of State Webster made to the President on December 23, 1851, relating to the celebrated *Thrasher's Case*. This case involved the prosecution on subversive grounds of an American citizen residing in Cuba. The pertinent parts of the report said:

> Every foreigner born residing in a country owes to that country allegiance and obedience to its laws so long as he remains in it, as a duty upon him by the mere fact of his residence... Independently of a residence with intention to continue such residence; independently of any domiciliation; independently of the taking of any oath of allegiance or of renouncing any former allegiance, it is well known that, by public law, an alien or a stranger born, for so long a time as he continues within the dominions of a foreign government, owes allegiance to the laws of that government, and *may be punished for treason* or other crimes as a nativeborn subject might be, unless his case is varied by some treaty stipulation.[39]

The doctrine enunciated in the above passage represents the standard treatment of the subject in American law. There can be no doubt that such a doctrine treats the conception of allegiance of a foreigner in a rather restrictive fashion, for it confines allegiance to residence within the jurisdiction. It is significant that this construction has been endorsed by the courts. Thus, in the early case *Hannuer v. Doane*, involving certain resident aliens who during the Civil War aided the Confederate forces, the court said:

[37] U.S. Const. art. III, sec. 3. See W. Hurst, "English Sources of the American Law of Treason," [1945] *Wis. L. Rev.*, p. 315.

[38] 18 U.S.C., sec. 2381. Italics supplied.

[39] See F. Wharton, *A Digest of International Law of the United States*, Vol. 2, secs. 190, 198, 203, 229, 230, 244, 357 (2d ed. 1887). Italics supplied.

> No crime is greater than treason. He who, being bound by his allegiance to a government, sells goods to the agent of an armed combination to overthrow that government, knowing that the purchaser buys them for that treasonable purpose, is himself guilty of treason or a misprision thereof. He voluntarily aids the treason. He cannot be permitted to stand on the nice metaphysical distinction that, although he knows that the purchaser buys the goods for the purpose of aiding the rebellion, he does not sell them for that purpose. The consequences of his acts are too serious and enormous to admit of such a plea.[40]

Another case of comparable nature is *Carlisle v. United States*, similarly involving resident aliens giving aid to the Confederate states. Mr Justice Field, who delivered the opinion of the court, was most explicit. After stating that "all strangers are under the protection of the sovereign while they are within his territories, and owe a temporary allegiance in return for that protection," significantly added:

> Such being the established doctrine, the claimants here were amenable to the laws of the United States prescribing punishment for treason and for giving aid and comfort to the rebellion. They were, as domiciled aliens in the country prior to the rebellion, under the obligation of fidelity and obedience to the government of the United States. They subsequently took their lot with the insurgents, and would be subject like them to punishment under the laws they violated but for the proclamation of the President of December 25th, 1868.[41]

The consistent adherence to this rigid test of local residence as an element of allegiance greatly accounts for the well known fact that there appears to be no case where a foreigner has been prosecuted for treason against the United States committed in foreign territory.[42] It seems clear that, in the absence of protection strictly confined to residence within the jurisdiction, allegiance cannot be found and, hence, one of the elements of treason would accordingly be lacking. This conclusion is well supported by the number of treason cases which came before the courts in the postwar period. These cases conclusively show that as to acts taking place abroad, the treason law is only available against those owing allegiance to the United States on grounds of nationality or citizenship. Of contemporary importance is *Kawakita v. United States*[43] where the accused was convicted of treason for having worked for the Japanese Government during the war and for maltreating American prisoners of war. Against the court's jurisdiction, the defendant pleaded the existence of dual nationality and, concurrently with this, that certain of his acts clearly showed his intention to retain

[40] 12 Wall. 342, 347 (U.S. 1870).
[41] 16 Wall. 147, 154, 156 (U.S. 1872).
[42] G. H. Hackworth, *Digest of International Law*, Vol. 2, pp. 202–203 (1941).
[43] 343 U.S. 717 (1951), rehearing denied, 344 U.S. 850 (1952).

the Japanese citizenship. Though the evidence was conclusive upon the issue of dual nationality, the court nevertheless affirmed his conviction on the ground that his allegiance to the United States remained in the absence of a clear showing of expatriation under American law.[44] The requisite allegiance having been found, the defendant's acts inescapably fell within the provision of the United States Code. Even if this decision does not directly bear upon the matter under consideration, it is at least significant in showing that if the accused had not been found to be a citizen, his conviction could not have been sustained.[45] This idea runs through the court's opinion and implicitly confirms the proposition that treason by a foreigner under American law can only exist if allegiance is unmistakably drawn from local residence.

On the basis of the foregoing consideration, whether the United States would prosecute a foreigner for treasonable acts committed abroad would seem, on the evidence, to be answered in the negative.[46] One may well wonder, however, whether the attitude of the United States would profoundly change were it threatened by actions of aliens against its security in the manner experienced by the European countries in the last two wars. For an accurate consideration of this problem it is intensely relevant to recall that certain precedents have revealed a trend toward the extraterritorial application of the American law in respect to foreigners conspiring to defraud the United States. This proposition is vividly illustrated by the case *Ford v. United States*, where the court did not hesitate to hold that certain British subjects could, upon seizure of their vessel, be prosecuted for conspiracy to violate the laws of the United States, regardless of whether or not they were out of the country at the time of the commission of the offense.[47] Despite the irresistible suggestion of this opinion and in view of the strict construction of treason in American law,[48] it may be confidently asserted that the United States is not well disposed to prosecute foreigners for politically hostile acts committed in foreign territory. That the

[44] 343 U.S. 717, 724 (1951).

[45] Other cases of this nature, also dealing with acts committed abroad, conclusively show that the finding of allegiance was the *ratio decidendi*. See Gillars v. United States, 182 F.2d 962 (D.C. 1950); United States v. Best, 171 F.2d 131 (1st Cir. 1948); Burgman v. United States, 188 F.2d 637 (D.C. 1951); and United States v. Chandler, 171 F.2d 921 (1st Cir. 1948).

[46] In reference to the celebrated *Cutting Case*, the Secretary of State said, inter alia, "There is no principle better settled than that the penal laws of a country have no extraterritorial force." J. B. Moore, *op. cit.*, Vol. 2, p. 236.

[47] 273 U.S. 593, 599 (1927).

[48] W. Hurst, "Treason in the United States," *Harvard L. R.*, Vol. 58, pp. 226, 810 (1944–1945).

United States has vigorously resisted the attempt of foreign countries to extend the exercise of their penal jurisdiction would seem to give added support to this conclusion.[49]

THE THEORY OF SELF-DEFENSE

Continental law and practice, profiting by the experience gained from accumulated precedents, have established a somewhat different offense to be exclusively applied to politically hostile acts committed by aliens outside the territory.[50] This offense is generally described as a *crime contre la sûreté de l'Etat*. Though its application may seem in principle clear and settled, concretely, however, considerable flexibility has attended its determination so that no particular element seems clearly discernible. Because the offense is legally justified on self-defense, it often imperatively calls for the most disturbing exercises of jurisdiction. The operative reality of this offense unmistakably reveals that it gives a wider range of prosecution to the state, for the requirement of allegiance, which was found to be controlling in the determination of treasonable offenses in Anglo-American law, does not have to be observed. The only consideration of the courts in the presence of such cases is to ascertain by rather loose and arbitrary standards whether the act in question is one which injures the fundamental interests of the state. This inquiry is the more pointed since it is inevitably accompanied by a large subjective element sharply accentuated by emotional-historical conceptions which explain but do not rationally support conclusions reached. Moreover, the absence in this offense of the solidity of interests necessary to support jurisdiction is reflected in the atmosphere of abstraction and ambiguity in which the issues are presented. In view of all this, it is not at all surprising that decisions based on these premises have yielded results almost bordering on absurdity. French and Belgian decisions illustrate this proposition remarkably well, for their courts have been particularly disturbed by these cases.

[49] The *Cutting Case* is quite in point. For the diplomatic correspondence on this case, see J. B. Moore, *op. cit.*, Vol. 2, pp. 228–242. See also G. H. Hackworth, *op. cit.*, Vol. 2, sec. 135.

[50] Continental law appears to apply the conception of treason only to foreigners while residing within the jurisdiction. See in this connection the following postwar cases: Auditeur-Général Près La Cour Militaire v. Müller and Others, Belgium, Court of Cassation, July 4, 1949, *Annual Digest* 1949, p. 400 (1955); *In re* Bittner, Belgium, Court of Cassation, February 14, 1949, *Ibid.*, p. 95; Public Prosecutor v. Drechsler, Norway, Supreme Court, November 2, 1946, *Annual Digest* 1946, p. 73 (1951); *In re* Penati, Italy, Court of Cassation, November 8, 1946, *Ibid.*, p. 74; and *In re* Mittermaier, Italy, Court of Cassation, May 2, 1946, *Ibid.*, p. 69.

Protective legislation in France has expressly affirmed a right of *légitime défense.*[51] The sweeping operation of its protective legislation can strikingly be illustrated by the often quoted *Code d'Instruction Criminelle,* whose pertinent provision says:

> Aliens who, outside of French territory render themselves guilty, either as authors or accomplices, of a *crime against the security of the State,* or the seals of the State, national currency, public documents, Bank notes authorized by law, are liable to prosecution and sentence under the provisions of the French law, if they are arrested in France or if the Government obtains their extradition.[52]

In similar vein, Article 78 of the French Penal Code provides for the punishment with imprisonment of anyone guilty of correspondence with the subjects of an enemy of the state.[53] These provisions have not remained without practical effect, for they have frequently come before the courts. Their application is well exhibited by the case *In re Urios,*[54] involving a Spanish national and captain of a Spanish merchant ship accused of having, during World War I, in Spain, been guilty of an offense against the external security of the French State by maintaining a correspondence with the enemies of France. Affirming his conviction to twenty years of imprisonment, the Court of Cassation held that "Article 78 of the Penal Code, which punishes with imprisonment correspondence with the enemy such as that with which the accused was charged, was perfectly general in its terms and *allowed no distinction to be drawn between Frenchmen and foreigners.*"[55] Significantly enough, the court found support for its assertion on Article 7 of the *Code d'Instruction Criminelle* previously quoted. A comparable case is *In re Bayot*[56] dealing with a Belgian subject arrested in France on the charge of correspondence with the enemy in Belgium in procuring certain military and other supplies for the German authorities. In sustaining its jurisdiction, the court emphatically said:

[51] D. H. De Vabres, *op. cit.*, p. 87. Such a principle has also been recognized by other writers. See L. A. Podestá Costa, *Derecho Internacional Público,* Vol. 1, p. 127 (3rd ed. 1955); D. Antokoletz, *Tratado de Derecho Internacional Público,* Vol. 2, p. 26 (3rd ed. 1938); and P. E. Corbett, *Law and Society in the Relations of States,* p. 171 (1951).

[52] Article 7. Translation. For the French version see D. H. De Vabres, *op. cit.*, pp. 86–87. Italics supplied.

[53] *Ibid.*, pp. 94–95.

[54] France, Court of Cassation (Criminal Chamber), January 15, 1920, *Annual Digest* 1919–1920, p. 107 (1932).

[55] *Ibid.*, p. 108. Italics supplied.

[56] France, Court of Cassation (Criminal Chamber), February 22, 1923, *Annual Digest* 1923–1924, p. 109 (1933).

Even if the right to punish, which emanates from the sovereign power, does not extend in principle beyond territorial limits, a contrary rule obtains in the case provided by Article 7 of the *Code d'Instruction Criminelle* which, based on the right of *légitime défense*, gives the French courts jurisdiction to take cognizance of crimes aimed at the security of the State committed outside French territory by a foreigner who has been arrested in France. The application of these provisions is not of a temporary nature and does not depend upon the continuance of the state of war with the enemy on whose behalf the offense was committed.[57]

In contrast with the acts involved in the above decisions, the fairly recent case *In re Ernst*[58] shows the application of the provisions of the Penal Code to foreigners residing within the state during enemy occupation. Though no mention is made of allegiance to the state, the court affirmed the conviction of a Swiss national charged with offenses against the safety of the state in aiding and assisting the army of occupation in its supply operations. While this particular decision is legally sustainable since the offense was committed within the territory, it further indicates that the conception of offenses against the safety of the state is available in French law against foreigners regardless of the locus of the crime.

Equally extreme in application are the decisions of the Belgian courts. The relevant legislative provision says:

Any person who participates in the alteration by the enemy of legal institutions or organization, or who, in time of war, undermines the loyalty of citizens towards the King or the State, or who knowingly serves the policy and designs of the enemy shall be liable to be sentenced to death.[59]

It should be added that Article 115, paragraph 2 of the Penal Code, as amended by the Law of May 25, 1945, more specifically provides for the punishment of offenses against the external safety of the state committed by foreigners outside the kingdom.[60] These provisions became of capital importance in the postwar period, when they were applied even to enemy aliens for acts committed abroad. A useful precedent in this connection is *In re Friedman* involving a German national who during the war had been in charge of a detention camp for Belgian nationals in Germany. Applying the provision of the Penal Code above quoted, the court affirmed his conviction on the ground that "the acts of which the appellant is accused constitute crimes

[57] *Ibid.*
[58] France, Court of Cassation (Criminal Division). February 24, 1949, *Annual Digest* 1949, p. 238 (1955).
[59] Penal Code art. 118. Cited in *Annual Digest* 1949, p. 400 (1955).
[60] Cited in *International Law Reports* 1950, p. 136 (1956).

against the external safety of the state... even when they have been committed outside the territory of the Kingdom by an alien."[61] Similarly, in *Nusselein v. Belgian State* the court affirmed the conviction of a Dutch soldier for having given aid and assistance to the enemy in Belgium and elsewhere vigorously asserting the jurisdiction of the Belgian courts to try foreigners for crimes against the safety of the state committed in Belgium or abroad.[62] These decisions are not, of course, without precedents to support them, for in the previous case *Morosini v. Belgian State*[63] the court held that an Italian national could be condemned for aiding the enemy of Belgium and, finally, in *Ministère Public v. D.M.*[64] the court had already said that the provisions of the Penal Code make no difference between friendly and enemy aliens. One could, of course, multiply examples of this kind.[65] But these few cases are perhaps enough to perceive the pattern which seems to run through the application of protective jurisdiction in Continental law. It suffices to add that such an application is not confined to Continental Europe, for the Latin American countries have incorporated the principle of protective jurisdiction in the Bustamante Code, which is the law among some 15 Latin American States.[66] The principle was thus incorporated in Article 305 as follows:

> Those who commit an offense against the internal or external security of a contracting state or against its public credit, whatever the nationality or domicile of the delinquent person, are subject in a foreign country to the penal laws of each contracting state.

Though the available evidence discloses no judicial decision applying the above provision, it can at least be seen that there is a substantial measure of agreement on the matter, since this is a further indication of the manner in which legislative enactments have described offenses

[61] Belgium, Court of Cassation, December 1, 1947, *Annual Digest* 1947, pp. 127, 128 (1951).

[62] Belgium, Court of Cassation, February 27, 1950, *International Law Reports* 1950, p. 136 (1956).

[63] Belgium, Court of Cassation, October 21, 1946, *Annual Digest* 1946, p. 138 (1951).

[64] Belgium, Court Martial, Namur, May 25, 1945, *Annual Digest* 1946, p. 138 (1951). Cf. Von Herd v. Public Prosecutor, Sweden, Supreme Court, February 1, 1946, *Annual Digest* 1946, p. 95 (1951).

[65] See also Art. 7 of the Italian Penal Code, 1930. Cited in M.O. Hudson, *Cases in International Law*, p. 322 (3rd ed. 1951).

[66] For text, see A. Sánchez de Bustamante y Sirvén, *Derecho Internacional Privado*, Vol. 3, p. 414 (2d ed. 1934). Also in the previous chapter it was seen that Art. 8 of the Convention for the Suppression of Counterfeiting Currency adopted the principle of protective jurisdiction. For text, see M. O. Hudson, *International Legislation*, Vol. 4, pp. 2279, 2692 (1931).

against the safety of the state in strikingly similar tones and for roughly similar reasons.

In marked contrast with the above provisions, the new Hungarian Penal Code punishes foreigners for acts committed abroad if they violate "a fundamental interest relating to the democratic political and economic order of the Hungarian People's Republic."[67] It can be readily seen from this provision that protective jurisdiction is available not only to punish political acts which affect the security of the state but also acts considered to be contrary to the Communist social and economic ideology. This assertion acquires special significance when one realizes that Communist legal conceptions consider as transgressions against the state and, hence, as treasonable offenses, acts directed against its economic and social order.[68] It may not therefore be surprising if the Hungarian provision is stretched very far. The offshoot of the matter is that any act may in principle be contrary to the political and economic interests of Communism, thus inevitably falling within the broad provisions of the Code. There can be little doubt that under the Hungarian provision protective jurisdiction is considerably enlarged, thereby giving the state unlimited freedom of prosecution.

In any event, the decisions and legislative provisions examined are of considerable scope and of critical importance. They present themselves as a fundamental break away from the territorial principle of criminal jurisdiction and as an extraterritorial exercise of the competence of the state. The cases here discussed suggest two irresistible observations. First, the elements of the offense against the safety of the state are extremely difficult to detect. While in Anglo-American law the existence of allegiance was seen to be controlling in the determination of treason committed by foreigners abroad, in Continental law no precise element appears to be decisive. It may well be that one's inability to perceive the exact make-up of this crime results as much from its psychological complexity as from the conditions under which it most frequently arises. It is quite conceivable – indeed, perhaps probable – that for the European countries, who have suffered much from wars and invasions, the establishment of such a general crime as the offense against the safety of the state is a matter of deep national necessity. And, secondly, the very nature of this offense inevitably lends itself to inadmissible extensions of state power. For once pro-

[67] For text and discussion of this provision, see S. Gorove, "Hungary: International Aspects of the New Penal Code," *Am. J. Comp. L.*, Vol. 3, p. 82 (1954).

[68] H. Kelsen, *The Communist Theory of Law*, p. 148 (1955). Also H. J. Berman, "Soviet Law Reform – Dateline Moscow 1957," *Yale L. J.*, Vol. 66, p. 1191 (1957).

tective jurisdiction is accepted, it is exceedingly difficult to keep it within measurable bounds. The inevitability of this result would seem apparent in view of the fact that the application of criminal jurisdiction reaches out to acts affecting the state in its supreme function, namely, its external defense and its sovereignty. Thus, because of the primacy of security interests clearly evident in Continental law, prescriptions and concepts in this area naturally exhibit their highest degree of flexibility.

INTERNATIONAL LAW AND PROTECTIVE JURISDICTION

Having thus examined the municipal practice in respect to the assumption of jurisdiction over foreigners for political offenses committed abroad, it is now possible to grasp more accurately the position of this practice before the law of nations. While it has been asserted that the exercise of criminal jurisdiction by the state is a matter wholly dependent upon municipal law,[69] the fact cannot be ignored that the exercise of protective jurisdiction transcends the territorial limits of the state and reaches acts which not only fall within the jurisdiction of another state but which may be perfectly lawful according to the latter's own law. Consequently, the jurisdiction of the prosecuting state presents itself *vis-à-vis* the jurisdiction of a foreign government, and as long as this foreign element is vitally involved, jurisdiction ceases to be a purely domestic matter beyond the reach of international law.[70] It should, therefore, be clear that though the exercise of protective jurisdiction is general in municipal legal systems, and it is the only available method to punish offenses of private persons, so far is this from being internationally valid that there is a well established principle of positive international law, repeatedly stressed by writers and tribunals, that no jurisdiction whatsoever can be assumed in foreign territory unless it is traceable to a specific rule of international customary or treaty law or to the express consent of the state involved.[71] The problem thus resolves itself into one of the competence of the state under international law. From this it would seem to follow that

[69] F. von Liszt, *Derecho Internacional Público*, p. 317 (Spanish transl. of the 12th German ed. by D. Miral, 1929).

[70] Professor Charles Rousseau says in this connection that the exercise of personal competence is limited by the territorial competence of the foreign state. See C. Rousseau *Droit International Public*, p. 240 (1953).

[71] Note 5, *supra*.

the logically conceivable limits on the competence of the state are also the actual limits imposed by positive international law, and the municipal law analogy becomes totally unacceptable. Such assertions as are found in discussing the domestic legal practice can scarcely rank as propositions of positive international law,[72] nor can their soundness meet a rigorous legal testing.

The foregoing observations suggest caution in inferring from the practice of nations any general rule of international law sanctioning the assumption of jurisdiction over foreigners for political acts committed in foreign territory.[73] There are, however, three arguments which have been relied upon by those who contend for the retention of protective jurisdiction. In the first place, it has already been seen that, particularly in Continental law, the exercise of protective jurisdiction has been defended on an alleged right of self-defense.[74] It has already been seen that there is respectable support for the assertion that self-defense is a right of the state under international law.[75] But a critical examination of this concept as a basis of jurisdiction shows it to be either too vague to give us determinate results or else productive of repellent consequences when practically applied.[76] More particularly, the use of self-defense to support the jurisdiction of the state can be attacked on three grounds. First, being essentially a political doctrine, self-defense is singularly exempted from any legal regulation and, consequently, its application to specific cases is likely to make for highly unjust decisions. This result cannot be reasonably doubted since the exercise of protective jurisdiction has been seen to operate in an area peculiarly exposed to the vicissitudes of political demands. Concurrently with these disturbing forces is the fluid and shifting nature of the ordinary political exigencies, which render manifestly impossible any attempt to evaluate objectively concrete situ-

[72] Professor Percy E. Corbett, however, asserts that this jurisdiction is permitted by international law. See P. E. Corbett, *op. cit.*, pp. 171–173.

[73] The League of Nations Codification Committee in 1926 came to the conclusion that the practice of the states was too diverse to warrant a formulation of a rule on the subject. See C. G. Fenwick, *International Law*, p. 272 n. 107 (3rd ed. 1948).

[74] See note 51, *supra*.

[75] D. Anzilotti, *Cours de Droit International*, Vol. 1, pp. 506–507 (French transl. from 3rd Italian ed. by G. Gidel 1929); J. Stone, *Legal Controls of International Conflict*, pp. 243–245 (1954).

[76] See in this connection the case cited by Professor Philip C. Jessup in which, during the Hitler regime, a German court approved the prosecution in Germany of a Jewish alien who had extramarital intercourse with a German girl in Czechoslovakia. The court based its decision on the German law regarding the "purity of the German blood." P. C. Jessup, *op. cit.*, p. 50. For a comparable case, see W. W. Bishop, Jr., *International Law: Cases and Materials*, pp. 363–364 (1953).

ations.[77] Second, as soon as the question of self-defense in this broader sense is approached, there is introduced into the issue the idea of preventive action making it a somewhat curious paradox to talk of self-defense in the presence of a wrongful *fait accompli*.[78] By its very nature self-defense implies advanced action against a threat to the security of the state; yet, jurisdiction based on such a concept contemplates action long after the offense has been committed and, sometimes, after a war has come to an end. There are concealed, therefore, in this use of self-defense highly debatable assumptions. And, finally, since the exercise of self-defense is determined by the unilateral judgment of the prosecuting government, it is generally assumed that what international law does not expressly require or prohibit is entirely left to the discretion of the state and that, thus, any conduct based on such discretion becomes legally sound.[79] That this logic is fallacious can hardly be denied, for it overlooks the common legal theory that in international matters the discretion of the state is most certainly granted by international law and, consequently, a discretion so conferred must be exercised in conformity with the principle of good faith. The latter implies the twofold recognition of due regard to the interests of other states and obedience to the spirit of the law.

In the second place, there are some who, while not expressly saying that protective jurisdiction follows from any basic principle of the law of nations, have maintained that it is nothing more than the expression of the theory of sovereignty according to which every state has the unquestionable right to determine the scope and operation of its penal law.[80] While this proposition is not questioned in respect to the application of a state's penal law within its territorial domain, once this limit has been transcended the matter becomes one of international concern, precisely because the jurisdiction of the state wherein the offense was committed immediately enters into play. There is, therefore, in principle a conflict of jurisdiction, and it will not be seriously suggested that the solution of this conflict lies within the unilateral determination of the prosecuting state, which has extraterritorially enlarged its own competence. Indeed, to rest the power of jurisdiction

[77] H. Lauterpacht, *The Function of Law in the International Community*, pp. 177–182 (1933).

[78] B. Cheng, *General Principles of Law As Applied by International Courts and Tribunals*, p. 97 (1953).

[79] J. Stone, *op. cit.*, p. 160.

[80] For these views, see Research in International Law under the Auspices of the Harvard Law School, "Jurisdiction With Respect to Crime," *Am. J. Int. L. Supp.*, Vol. 29, pp. 554–555 (1935).

on what is admittedly an extraterritorial application of the state's law is too shifting a basis to determine judicial power and too entangled in expediency to serve as a dependable criterion. Certainly, the essential nature of the problem cannot be hidden by an attempt to separate the jurisdiction of the courts from the competence of the state in matters of international concern.[81] These are manifestations of indivisible governmental power.

If the foregoing observations be correct, it must be concluded that notions of sovereignty cannot serve as a legal justification for the enlargement of the criminal competence of the state. This argument can be more forcibly submitted in view of the well established fact that international law fixes the limits of the state's competence by prohibiting its exercise within the internal jurisdiction of another state.[82] This would seem to apply to treason as well as to offenses against the safety of the state, for the cases here examined suggest that even though different label tags may be used and different justifying formulas may be developed, the essential problems of punishing aliens for acts committed abroad are not markedly diverse. Whether the case in question involves treason or an offense against the safety of the state, whether it is determined by the more restrictive concept of allegiance or by the broader concept of self-defense, it nevertheless remains true that the state is exercising its jurisdiction in an extraterritorial fashion and in respect to acts which may be perfectly lawful under the law of the state wherein they were committed.[83] Surely, it is of the very essence of a crime that the act involved be in violation of an already established law to which the accused is subject and, consequently, it is legally objectionable to make every individual subject to the laws of every state at all times and at all places.[84] What is needed is international cooperation to punish these offenses in the jurisdiction of the states where they are committed. Thus, to say that the exercise of protective jurisdiction can be made conclusive where international, and even

[81] In this connection, Chief Justice Marshall said: "The jurisdiction of courts is a branch of that which is possessed by the nation as an independent power." The Schooner Exchange v. MacFaddon, 7Cr. 116, 136 (U.S. 1812). See also E. D. Dickinson, "Jurisdiction Following Seizure or Arrest in Violation of International Law," *Am. J. Int. L.*, Vol. 28, p. 231 (1934); and M. R. García-Mora, "Criminal Jurisdiction of a State over Fugitives Brought from a Foreign Country by Force or Fraud: A Comparative Study," *Ind. L. J.*, Vol. 32, p. 427 (1957).

[82] Professor Georges Scelle defines competence as an "objective power determined by a legal system superior to the subjects of law." See G. Scelle, *Précis de Droit des Gens: Principes et Systématique*, Vol. 1, p. 80 (1932).

[83] V. V. Pella, "Towards an International Criminal Court," *Am. J. Int. L.*, Vol. 44, pp. 37, 46 (1950).

[84] J. L. Brierly, "The Lotus Case," *L. Q. Rev.*, Vol. 44, pp. 154, 161 (1928).

individual, rights are vitally involved amounts to placing those rights at the mercy of unilateral state action, thereby seriously impairing the stability, certainty and security inherent in the very conception of law. That prospect, with the ever-increasing power of the state, is not one to be safely ignored.

Finally, the most persuasive and logically consistent argument in support of protective jurisdiction is that according to which the state has a right under international law to the free enjoyment of its institutions and, as a corollary of this right, to be secured against those who from foreign territory frustrate the possibility of internal peace.[85] But at the same time there is implicit in this very same argument the correlative duty of other states to prevent treasonable and other harmful activities from being carried on under the protection of their territorial sovereignty. It is precisely because the states have failed to discharge adequately this duty that protective jurisdiction appeared as a necessary alternative, thereby filling a gap in the international legal order. Admittedly, this argument lends powerful support to the exercise of protective jurisdiction. And it is probably for this reason that the law of nations has remained silent on the matter. However, with the contemporary shift in emphasis from the state to the individual, the time has undoubtedly come for its abandonment, for compelling considerations of humanity militate against its continuous adherence. It may be thus argued that treason and offenses against the safety of the state as applied to foreigners do not present themselves sufficiently objectively to warrant trial by tribunals of the government against whom the offenses were committed. It is quite conceivable that the exercise of jurisdiction may do violence to traditional safeguards of impartial justice with the greatest danger to the individual. Though the broad, generalized claims urged touch the deepest interest of a society, namely, its right to self-preservation, the political undertones present in these crimes may give rise to a heat of public passion making any orderly and just trial a remote possibility, to say the least. It can therefore be seen that there is against the exercise of protective jurisdiction a well-founded apprehension that public prejudice may invariably influence this type of prosecution. That this may be so is almost certain, for it has been seen that the essential elements of these offenses require that prosecutions be sometimes based on wartime events when public sentiments and passion have undoubtedly

[85] H. Lauterpacht, "Revolutionary Activities by Private Persons Against Foreign States," *Am. J. Int. L.*, Vol. 22, p. 105 (1928).

reached their peak.[86] It is quite probable, therefore, that under present-day demands for the protection of the individual,[87] the exercise of protective jurisdiction may have outlived its usefulness. These arguments substantially undermine the efficacy of the traditional rules and reflect the need for the establishment of new rules more in accord with the requirements of contemporary life.

In view of all this and of the prevailing diverse climate of opinion among international lawyers, a satisfactory solution to the problem would seem to suggest the exercise of jurisdiction by the territorial state over those engaging in treasonable and other harmful activities, for it is the territorial state that has a right to jurisdiction unmistakably guaranteed by international law. But for the lawful exercise of jurisdiction, the territorial state would have to enact legislation clearly punishing hostile activities directed against foreign states. Thus, the strength of this position lies in the recognition of solidarity among the members of the world community, which imperatively demands the suppression within each nation's territory of activities endangering the peace and security of the states.[88] This argument commends itself most cogently in practice, for it is indissolubly linked with the respect which nations owe to each other at all times.[89] However, since the available evidence indicates that there is meager municipal legislation punishing private wrongful acts directed against foreign states, a substantial measure of protection can be obtained if it is frankly recognized, through an international convention, that states have the obligation to punish those who engage in hostile activities within their internal jurisdiction. These offenses seriously endanger the peace and security of mankind.[90] The force of this suggestion

[86] It has been said that these considerations influenced greatly the provision of the Constitution of the United States regarding treason. U.S. Const. art. III, sec. 3. See, W. Hurst, "Treason in the United States," *Harvard L. Rev.*, Vol. 58, pp. 226, 810 (1944–1945).

[87] See Article 10 of the Universal Declaration of Human Rights, adopted by the United Nations General Assembly on December 10, 1948, where the right to a free and impartial trial is guaranteed. For text, see *Am. J. Int. L. Supp.*, Vol. 43, p. 127 (1949). It may be added that Article 26 of the American Declaration of the Rights and Duties of Man, adopted at Bogota in 1948, contains a similar guarantee. For text, *Ibid.*, p. 133.

[88] See in this connection *United States v. Arjona*, 120 U.S. 479 (1887), where some of these ideas are given practical expression.

[89] This has been considered by some publicists as the basis of international law. See Lord Jowitt, "The Value of International Law in Establishing Cooperation Among Nations," *Int. L. Q.*, Vol. 1, p. 295 (1947). Cf. H. Accioly, *Manual de Direito Internacional Público*, p. 56 (1948).

[90] Thus, the Draft Code of Offense Against the Peace and Security of Mankind prepared by the International Law Commission of the United Nations in its third session in 1951 so regards them. For text, see Doc. A/CN.4/48, July 30, 1951: *Am. J. Int. L. Supp.*, Vol. 45, pp. 103, 128 (1951).

reveals itself with more urgency and vitality in view of certain basic changes in the make-up and character of the international society which have greatly increased the opportunity for the resort to hostile activities against foreign states. Quite pertinent in this regard is the increased role of modern communications which has broadened the opportunity for the commission of these crimes and the appearance of tyrannical regimes that aim at the destruction of societies built on different foundations.[91] But in order to safeguard traditional standards of justice, it is similarly essential to establish in this convention precisely the acts which are included in the exercise of jurisdiction by the territorial state, prescribing their lines of demarcation with as much particularity as it can reasonably muster. Jurisdiction on these bases will then be uniformly applied, thereby reducing to a minimum the large subjective element which accompanies the assumption of jurisdiction on protective grounds. In proportion as jurisdiction for treasonable acts committed by foreigners abroad becomes the function of the territorial state, the interaction of political forces on which the law in this area was seen to depend is bound to disappear accordingly. The stability to be derived from such an approach would certainly do much toward regulating an otherwise fluid and disorderly situation.

CONCLUSION

The body of evidence presented in this chapter would seem to lead to the conclusion that substantial restrictions on the exercise of protective jurisdiction are highly desirable and that such restrictions can be more effectively imposed by an international convention of sufficient authority and the highest impartiality. The cause both of the individual and of international law would seem to demand this course of action. From the standpoint of the individual, it is hoped that sufficiently valid reasons have been given to support the contention that treason and offenses against the safety of the state committed by private persons in other jurisdictions are too subjective and emotional in nature to allow trial by the tribunals of the injured state. From the standpoint of international law, it is undeniable that in exercising jurisdiction over these offenses the prosecuting state is giving extraterritorial effect to its penal law, thus transgressing the limits of its

[91] H. Lauterpacht, "Revolutionary Activities by Private Persons Against Foreign States," *Am. J. Int. L.*, Vol. 22, pp. 105, 108 (1928).

competence. On the other hand, by imposing upon the territorial state the duty to punish those who within its jurisdiction commit harmful acts against other nations, an international convention would fundamentally transform the exercise of jurisdiction over these offenses into a matter of international concern. But before the states themselves can be safely regarded as the agency which under all conditions will protect the fundamental interests of other states, there is a compelling need to develop a high degree of political integration of the international community. The fact, indeed, may have to be faced that future legal action in this area demands an overhaul of the basic principles upon which the international community has thus far rested. Only then can the abuses of jurisdiction exercised on protective grounds be adequately controlled.

CHAPTER X

INTERNATIONAL CRIMINAL JURISDICTION AS AN ALTERNATIVE

It has been seen that the exercise of protective jurisdiction as a means of punishing private persons for their actions against foreign states leaves much to be desired from the standpoint of justice. This is so not only for the practical difficulty of reaching an impartial judgment in matters deeply involving political interests of governments,[1] but also because the exercise of protective jurisdiction entirely depends upon such an uncertain factor as the ability of the state to get its hands on the offender either through the regular process of extradition or, even more uncertain, through the remote possibility that the offender may sometime fall within its jurisdiction. The inevitable result of this situation is really to allow offenders to go unpunished in the commission of offenses which vitally affect the peace and security of mankind. It is largely for these reasons that an international criminal court, with jurisdiction to prosecute individuals, has been forcibly suggested since the end of World War II.[2] Most discussions of this court center on its jurisdiction over individuals acting for the state. However, it is believed that its competence over private persons for the commission of international crimes is deserving of similar consideration.

TOWARDS AN INTERNATIONAL CRIMINAL COURT

As a reaction to the cruelties which human beings have proved capable of committing under the stress of war, the firm conviction has arisen that human atrocities have nothing to do with the waging of a war and that, therefore, they must be stamped out in the conduct of hostilities. The most immediate step in this direction found

[1] This was so recognized by the Committee on International Criminal Jurisdiction created by the United Nations General Assembly in its resolution of December 12, 1950. See Report of the Committee on International Criminal Jurisdiction, U.N. General Assembly, Official Records, Seventh Session, Supplement No. 11, (A/2136), p. 4 (1952).

[2] Q. Wright, "Proposal for an International Criminal Court," *Am. J. Int. L.*, Vol. 46, pp. 60, 63 (1952).

concrete expression in the efforts to set up an international tribunal for the trial of those charged with crimes against humanity. Though many proposals have been submitted since the end of World War I,[3] there are four which merit a special mention.

The first important development in the creation of an international criminal court took place in 1920, when the Advisory Committee of Jurists that drafted the Statute of the Permanent Court of International Justice recommended the establishment of a High Court of International Justice with jurisdiction "to try crimes constituting a breach of international public order or against the universal law of nations," and with "power to define the nature of the crime, to fix the penalty and to decide the appropriate means of carrying out the sentence."[4] Though clearly reflecting mankind's sentiment, this recommendation was decisively rejected by the Third Committee of the Assembly of the League of Nations, on the ground that "If crimes of this kind in future be brought within the scope of international penal law, a criminal department might be set up in the Court of International Justice. In any case, consideration of this problem is, at the moment, premature."[5]

Secondly, the most significant official attempt in a similar direction was the conclusion on November 16, 1937, of the Convention for the Creation of an International Criminal Court to try persons accused of terrorism.[6] The court thus proposed was designed to implement the Convention for the Prevention and Punishment of Terrorism of the same date.[7] The Convention creating the court is of singular significance for three reasons. First, it contemplated exclusively the criminal responsibility of private persons engaged in terrorism, establishing this offense as an international crime.[8] Secondly, since the Convention did not deal with crimes incidental to war, it made it unmistakably clear that its underlying philosophy was the recognition of the principle of "universality of repression" of offenses which affect the peace and security of mankind.[9] And, finally, in signing the Convention, states for the first time not only agreed fundamentally on the desirability of

[3] For a full consideration of proposals, see United Nations Secretariat, *Historical Survey of the Question of International Criminal Jurisdiction* (1949).

[4] This is discussed in R. J. Alfaro, "Report on The Question of International Criminal Jurisdiction," U.N. International Law Commission, A/CN.4/15, March 3, 1950, p. 9.

[5] *Ibid.*, p. 9.

[6] For text, see M. O. Hudson, *International Legislation*, Vol. 7, p. 878 (1941).

[7] For text, *Ibid.*, p. 862. This Convention is discussed in Chapter VI, *supra.*

[8] Convention for the Creation of an International Criminal Court, Art. 1.

[9] R. J. Alfaro, *op. cit.*, p. 13.

establishing a permanent international criminal court, but also on the feasibility of rendering international judgments on matters which were formerly amenable to the jurisdiction of national courts.[10] It must regrettably be added that this Convention never came into force, and its provisions were finally discarded under the pressure of events leading up to the outbreak of World War II.[11] But since this Convention has marked a decisive phase in the development of an international criminal jurisdiction, its significance as a useful precedent for future international action can scarcely be doubted.

The third important landmark in the evolution of an international criminal jurisdiction is represented by the establishment of the International Military Tribunal at Nürnberg under the London Agreement of August 8, 1945,[12] for the trial of Nazi war criminals for crimes against peace, war crimes and crimes against humanity, as described in the Charter of the Tribunal.[13] The objections raised against the Nürnberg trial are familiar history to international lawyers and, therefore, there is no need to discuss them here. However, from the standpoint of an international criminal jurisdiction, the Nürnberg trial represents a striking illustration of its feasibility and clearly adverts to the elimination of substantive difficulties in the establishment of an international criminal court.[14] As subsequent proposals have been patterned after the Nürnberg judgment, the substantive questions regarding the criminality of individuals under international law, such as the *ex post facto* character of the charges and the dubious composition of the tribunal, which were precisely the objections raised against the Nürnberg trial, will largely be eliminated.[15]

Finally, the need for an international criminal jurisdiction appeared with renewed urgency and vitality shortly after the termination of World War II. Faithfully responding to the sentiments of those who clamor for the establishment of an impartial international criminal tribunal, the General Assembly of the United Nations adopted a resolution on December 9, 1948, in which it frankly recognized that "in the

[10] V. V. Pella, "Towards an International Criminal Court," *Am. J. Int. L.*, Vol. 44, pp. 37, 39 (1950).

[11] *Ibid.*, p. 38.

[12] For text, see *Trial of the Major War Criminals Before the International Military Tribunal*, Vol. I, pp. x, xi (1946–1947).

[13] Charter of the International Military Tribunal, article 6, paragraphs (a), (b) and (c). The International Military Tribunal for the Far East for the Trial of Japanese War Criminals, established in 1946 should also be noted here.

[14] See L. A. Podestá Costa, *Derecho Internacional Público*, Vol. 2, pp. 321–323 (3d ed. 1955).

[15] J. Stone, *Legal Controls of International Conflict*, p. 377 (1954).

course of development of the international community, there will be an increasing need for an international judicial organ for the trial of certain crimes under international law."[16] In the same resolution, the General Assembly invited the International Law Commission "to study the desirability and possibility of establishing an international judicial organ for the trial of persons charged with genocide or other crimes over which jurisdiction will be conferred upon that organ by international conventions."[17] After a full exploration of the matter, the Commission confidently concluded that the establishment of an international criminal court was both desirable and feasible.[18] The Commission's conclusions were subsequently endorsed by the General Assembly at its fifth session in 1950, at which time a resolution was adopted setting up a committee of seventeen member states "for the purpose of preparing one or more preliminary draft conventions and proposals relating to the establishment and the statute of an international criminal court."[19] The committee met at Geneva on August 1, 1951, and, after laborious deliberations, adopted a Draft Statute for an International Criminal Court,[20] which was subsequently considered by the Seventh General Assembly in 1952.[21] The proposed Statute represents the most sustained appeal thus far made for an international criminal court with jurisdiction over individuals. It is also the most novel proposal of this kind, though it represents a somewhat unsuccessful attempt to treat the international criminal responsibility of individuals within the context of vital political interests of the states. As these matters must be treated in relation to existing doctrine and practice discussed in this book, the Draft Statute certainly merits a more extended discussion in the present chapter.

[16] Resolution 260 B (III) of December 8, 1948. For text, see U.N. General Assembly, Official Records, Third Session, Part I, Resolutions, p. 177 (1948).

[17] *Ibid.*

[18] Report of the International Law Commission Covering Its Second Session, 5 June–29 July, 1950. For text, see U.N. General Assembly, Official Records, Fifth Session, Supplement No. 12 (A/1316), pp. 15–16 (1950).

[19] Resolution 489 (V) of December 12, 1950. For text, see Report of the Committee on International Criminal Jurisdiction, U.N. General Assembly, Official Records, Seventh Session, Supplement No. 11, (A/2136), p. 1 (1952).

[20] For the text of the Draft Statute, see *Ibid.*, Annex I, pp. 21–25.

[21] See U.N. General Assembly, Official Records, Seventh Session, Sixth Committee, 321 st. to 328th Meeting (1952).

THE DRAFT STATUTE AND OFFENSES OF PRIVATE PERSONS

The Court, according to Article I of the Draft Statute, would try "persons accused of crimes under international law, as may be provided in conventions or special agreements among states party to the present Statute." International consensus regards this article as placing under an international criminal jurisdiction the offenses which individuals may commit affecting the peace and security of mankind.[22] Surely, a criminal tribunal of international dimensions should be expected to deal with crimes, by whomsoever committed, which are destructive of the international legal order. It is therefore believed that the offenses defined in the Draft Code of Offenses against the Peace and Security of Mankind[23] would be included within the competence of the proposed International Criminal Court. It should be recalled that the following offenses committed by private persons and by the authorities of the state, are defined in the Draft Code: acts of aggression, invasion by armed bands, fomenting civil strife in other countries, encouragement of terrorist activities, violation of treaty obligations dealing with restrictions on armaments, intervention in the internal affairs of another state, genocide, annexation of foreign territory, acts in violation of the laws and customs of war as well as conspiracy, incitement, complicity and attempts to commit the foregoing acts.[24] In presenting the Draft Code, the International Law Commission of the United Nations left no room for doubt that these are crimes under international law, for Article 1 of the Draft says that "Offenses against the peace and security of mankind, as defined in this code, are crimes under international law, for which the responsible individuals shall be punished." It may significantly be added that the International Law Commission clearly envisaged the trial and prosecution of these crimes by an international criminal court, but pending its establishment, allowed measures to be taken by national courts.[25] It may be relevant to point out in this connection that since Article 2 of the Draft Statute for an International Criminal Court provides that "The Court shall apply international law, including international criminal law, and where appropri-

[22] Q. Wright, *op. cit.*, p. 63.

[23] For text, see Report of the International Law Commission Covering the Work of its Third Session, 16 May–27 July, 1951, U.N. General Assembly, Official Records, Sixth Session, Supplement No. 9 (A/1858), pp. 10–14 (1951).

[24] Article 2 of the Draft Code.

[25] Report of the International Law Commission Covering the Work of its Third Session, 16 May–27 July, 1951, U.N. General Assembly, Official Records, Sixth Session, Supplement No. 9 (A/1858), p. 11 (1951).

ate, national law," certainly the Draft Code proposed by the International Law Commission and the Convention for the Prevention and Punishment of Genocide,[26] would be included in the law to be applied by the Court.

The essentially political nature of the foregoing crimes would seem to impose a limitation upon the proposed International Criminal Court both in terms of its competence and in terms of the willingness of a state to agree to the prosecution of these offenses.[27] As to the first, though there are other crimes not political in nature that also have international repercussions, thus affecting the peace and security of the world community, the 1951 Committee on International Criminal Jurisdiction clearly meant to keep them out of the jurisdiction of the International Criminal Court. In reaching this conclusion the Committee proceeded upon the distinction between crimes under international law and "crimes under national law as are of international concern."[28] Included in the latter category are counterfeiting of currencies, traffic in persons and narcotics, damaging of submarine cables, attacks upon foreign heads of state or government, and upon members of the United Nations missions. The contrast thus presented between "crimes under international law" and "crimes under national law as are of international concern" became embodied in the Draft Statute, though perhaps not so very obvious at first glance. It is to be noted that, initially, the Committee included "crimes under national law as are of international concern" within the jurisdiction of the Court on the ground that these crimes affect the interests of several states and in their punishment "national courts might not always be impartial or adequate."[29] However, foreseeing difficulties in reaching agreements among the states, the Commission finally decided not to mention that category of crimes in the Draft Statute, thus following the recommendation of the International Law Commission regarding the Draft Code of Offenses against the Peace and Security of Mankind to the effect that "the meaning of this term should be limited to offenses which contain a political element and which endanger or disturb the maintenance of

[26] For the text of this Convention, see *Am. J. Int. L. Supp.*, Vol. 45, p. 7 (1951). This Convention has been ratified by a substantial number of states and entered into force on January 12, 1951.

[27] G. A. Finch, "Draft Statute for an International Criminal Court," *Am. J. Int. L.*, Vol. 46, pp. 89, 93 (1952).

[28] See Report of the Committee on International Criminal Jurisdiction, U.N. General Assembly, Official Records, Seventh Session, Supplement No. 11 (A/2136), p. 4 (1952).

[29] *Ibid.*, p. 4.

international peace and security."[30] The subsequent history of Article 1 of the Draft Statute immediately reveals further limitations upon the jurisdiction of the Court, for under a Revised Draft Statute adopted in 1953 by a new Committee on International Criminal Jurisdiction appointed by the Seventh General Assembly, the amended article confines the jurisdiction of the Court to the trial of "natural persons accused of crimes *generally* recognized under international law."[31] It was quickly made clear that the adoption of the qualifying word "generally" was to exclude from the Court's jurisdiction any crime on which there was no general agreement among states. As the Israeli representative clearly stated when proposing the amendment, "generally recognized under international law... implied that international criminal law could not be invoked against a state which did not recognize that particular part of international law."[32] It would seem, therefore, that the protection of the world community and the legal sanctions for the violations of its norms are worked out in the present Draft Statute under the most careful qualifications. Despite this limitation, there can be no reasonable doubt that, with the exception of counterfeiting, the offenses of private persons against foreign states discussed throughout this book may be included in the jurisdiction of the proposed International Criminal Court, even under the amended version of Article 1 of the Draft Statute.[33]

The second fundamental difficulty stemming from the purely political nature of the offenses included in the Court's jurisdiction lies precisely in the possible unwillingness of the states to confer jurisdiction over these offenses. It has been aptly pointed out that these offenses may be committed on behalf of a particular government and, even if they are not, their commission may stem from a firm conviction that motives of national security, human considerations or patriotism are vitally at stake.[34] As these are generally the reasons why a state grants asylum to persons who have been unsuccessful in their attempt

[30] See Report of the International Law Commission, Covering the Work of its Third Session, 16 May–27 July, 1951, U.N. General Assembly, Official Records, Sixth Session, Supplement No. 9 (A/1858), p. 11 (1951).

[31] Italics supplied. For a discussion of the Amendments adopted and the views of representatives, see Yuen-Li Liang, "Notes on Legal Questions Concerning the United Nations," *Am. J. Int. L.*, Vol. 47, pp. 638 (1953).

[32] Quoted in Yuen-Li Liang, *op. cit.*, p. 646.

[33] Cf. J. Paoli, "Contribution à L'Etude des Crimes de Guerre et des Crimes contre l'Humanité en Droit Pénal International," *Rev. Gén. de Droit Int. Public*, Vol. 39 pp. 146–147 (France, 1941–1945).

[34] G. A. Finch, *op. cit.*, pp. 89, 93.

to overthrow an existent government,[35] and since it has been seen that some of these offenses are not punished by national law, it is exceedingly hard to see how the states will commit themselves in advance to support an international criminal jurisdiction over such charges. It is precisely in recognition of this consideration that the Draft Statute itself has given the states discretion to grant or to withhold jurisdiction as they see fit. Thus, Article 26 says that "Jurisdiction may be conferred upon the Court by states parties to the present Statute, by convention or, with respect to a particular case, by special agreement or by unilateral declaration." It is particularly significant that under amendments proposed by the 1953 Committee on International Criminal Jurisdiction, Article 26 has become even more restricted. In its revised form, it says:

(1) Jurisdiction of the Court is not to be presumed.
(2) A state may confer jurisdiction upon the Court by Convention, by special agreement or by unilateral declaration.
(3) Conferment of jurisdiction signifies the right to seize the Court, and the duty to accept its jurisdiction subject to such provisions as the state or states have specified.
(4) Unless otherwise provided for in the instrument conferring jurisdiction upon the Court, the laws of a state determining national criminal jurisdiction shall not be affected by that conferment.[36]

This provision was the result of an uneasy compromise between the conflicting interests of the world community and the sovereignty of states. What is vastly more important is that the manner in which the compromise was reached threw the balance in favor of sovereignty, thus subordinating the Court to the will of the states.[37] Ample support for this conclusion can be found in the deliberations of the Committee that amended the Draft Statute. It seems most likely that the Committee intended to establish the Court's competence under the following conditions. First, the Court would have only such jurisdiction as governments confer upon it, thereby eliminating the possibility that jurisdiction could be derived from the Statute itself.[38] Second, in conferring jurisdiction, states would still be at liberty to impose whatever

[35] M. R. García-Mora, *International Law and Asylum as a Human Right*, ch. 6 (1956).
[36] For text, see Yuen-Li Liang, *op. cit.*, pp. 647–648.
[37] P. M. Carjeu, "Quelques Aspects du Nouveau Projet de Statut des Nations Unies pour une Jurisdiction Criminelle Internationale," *Rev. Gén. de Droit Int. Public*, Vol. 50, pp. 401, 410 (France, 1956).
[38] This had been presupposed by the 1951 Committee on International Criminal Jurisdiction. See Report of the Committee on International Criminal Jurisdiction, U.N, General Assembly, Official Records, Seventh Session, Supplement No. 11 (A/2136). p. 8 (1952).

conditions they wish. And, third, conferment of jurisdiction would not abrogate the concurrent exercise of national jurisdiction over the same offense.[39] Contrary to the latter proposition, it may be suggested that since the International Criminal Court presumably will deal with crimes under international law, its competence should certainly displace that of national courts.[40]

When the foregoing observations are examined, it immediately becomes clear, as the 1951 Committee on International Criminal Jurisdiction recognized, that the effect of compelling states to accept the jurisdiction of the Court by acceptance of the Statute, may well discourage them from accepting the Statute in the first place.[41] This was probably the major reason for the drastic curtailment of the Court's jurisdiction under the articles discussed. Yet this conviction can only be sustained on the now obsolete conceptions that national law is superior to international law and that the only way to entice the states to accept the International Criminal Court is to offer them avenues of escape by which they can avoid their international obligations. It should be kept in mind that it is an international tribunal of the greatest hope and authority which is being proposed, and that by its very nature should find its roots in vital interests of the world community, such as the maintenance of peace and the prevention of war. Since such hopes and aspirations of mankind are desperately at stake, it is fairly difficult to see why so much primacy should be given, even at the present time, to the isolated, and often conflicting, interests of states. It is highly relevant to recall that the failure of previous projects of this kind is an instructive illustration of thinking that suffers from the illusion that the interests of the states are relatively more important.[42] It may be added that even in terms of historical consistency the proposed International Criminal Court does not follow immediate precedents, for, as Professor Quincy Wright has well observed, the Draft Statute contains certain elements of retrogression, since by permitting governments to refuse to extend the jurisdiction of the Court, it "does away with the principle, accepted in the Nürnberg Charter, that international criminal law is superior to national legislation."[43]

[39] Yuen-Li Liang, *op. cit.*, pp. 647–648.
[40] Q. Wright, *op. cit.*, p. 69.
[41] See Report of the Committee on International Criminal Jurisdiction, U.N. General Assembly, Official Records, Seventh Session, Supplement No. 11 (A/2136), pp. 8–9 (1952).
[42] K. W. Thompson, *Political Realism and the Crisis of World Politics: An American Approach to Foreign Policy*, p. 145 (1960).
[43] Q. Wright, *op. cit.*, p. 68.

There are other provisions of the Draft Statute which are similarly restrictive of the competence of the Court. In dealing with its jurisdiction as to persons, Article 25 confines the Court's competence to the trial of "natural persons only," thus excluding states and corporations, though making it clear that natural persons may include "persons who have acted as Head of State or agent of government."[44] The subsequent amendment of Article 25 is perhaps more explicit, for it says that "The Court shall be competent to judge natural persons, whether they are constitutionally responsible rulers, public officials or private individuals."[45] For present purposes, it is highly significant to stress that the jurisdiction of the Court is clearly extended to the trial of private persons for offenses against the peace and security of mankind. By so doing, the Draft Statute has certainly filled a gap in the international legal order, and the door has been left open for the replacement of the so-called protective jurisdiction by an international criminal jurisdiction of more authority and impartiality.

Yet this hope is by no means certain, for other provisions of the Draft Statute greatly limit the jurisdiction of the Court in many ways. Thus, Article 27, which was left intact by the 1953 Committee on International Criminal Jurisdiction, says:

> No person shall be tried before the Court unless jurisdiction has been conferred upon the Court by the state or states of which he is a national and by the state or states in which the crime is alleged to have been committed.

The full impact of this provision can be most clearly seen in relation to the reasons adduced for its adoption by the 1951 Committee on International Criminal Jurisdiction. From its Report, two compelling considerations of national policy can be discerned. The first is the belief in the necessity "to proceed with caution in order to ensure that a large number of states would adhere to the statute of the Court."[46] Underlying this consideration is the belief that Article 27 in its present form affords a double protection to the individual in that it permits the state to withhold jurisdiction for international crimes which are not crimes under national law, and also in situations where guaranties

[44] The Commission on International Criminal Jurisdiction felt that by extending the jurisdiction of the Court to states, the Court might be involved in decisions of a political character. See Report of the Commission on International Criminal Jurisdiction, U.N. General Assembly, Official Records, Seventh Session, Supplement No. 11 (A/2136), pp. 10–11 (1952).

[45] Yuen-Li Liang, *op. cit.*, p. 647.

[46] Report of the Committee on International Criminal Jurisdiction, U.N. General Assembly, Official Records, Seventh Session, Supplement No. 11 (A/2136), pp. 8–9 (1952).

of a fair trial according to national standards are absent.[47] Under the present arrangement, a government accepting the Statute may at the same time retain discretion to adhere to the jurisdiction of the Court in specific cases. It is perhaps for this reason that an able commentator has emphatically asserted that Article 27 in reality gives the Court "discretionary jurisdiction."[48]

The second reason for the adoption of Article 27 is more closely related to state policy. In this connection, the Committee's Report alludes to the necessity of "protecting the state itself, in so far as the trial of a high ranking political leader of a country involves a review of the internal or foreign policy of that country."[49] It can readily be seen, therefore, that under Article 27 of the Draft Statute, it is quite possible – indeed, perhaps, probable – for a state to exempt from trial its public officials, and even its nationals accused of international crimes, thus rendering the jurisdiction of the Court a practical nullity.[50] It certainly requires no feat of the imagination to perceive that under the present Statute the proposed International Criminal Court might be reduced to a pious hope without much practical value.

A reading of other provisions of the Draft Statute raises further doubts. The considerations of national policy which have been seen to permeate many provisions of the Statute are instructively illustrated again by a perusal of Article 30, paragraph (1). This provision reads as follows:

> The jurisdiction of the Court may be challenged not only by the parties to any proceeding, but also by any state referred to in Article 27, which may intervene for this purpose.

"The parties to the proceeding" here mentioned are clearly individuals, and no one can really object to their right to challenge the jurisdiction of the Court. The 1951 Committee strongly felt that since a fair trial is guaranteed by Article 38 of the Draft Statute, the right to challenge the jurisdiction of the Court must certainly be implicit in that provision.[51] It seems quite obvious, however, that in adopting this stipulation, the Draft Statute was merely incorporating already existing principles of national law. But this is not all that there is to Article 30, for the right to challenge the jurisdiction of the Court is also given to both the state of which the individual is a national and

[47] G. A. Finch, *op. cit.*, p. 97.
[48] P. M. Carjeu, *op. cit.*, p. 410.
[49] Report of the Committee on International Criminal Jurisdiction, *op. cit.*, p. 9.
[50] Q. Wright, *op. cit.*, p. 68.
[51] Report of the Committee on International Criminal Jurisdiction, *op. cit.*, p. 9.

the one in which the crime was committed. Though it may seem strange to give this right to states which are not technically parties to the trial, the 1951 Committee justified its position by invoking conceptions which engage vital political interests. The Committee said:

> The trial of a high-ranking political leader of a state was a matter which transcended the individual interests of the accused, since it might involve, implicitly or explicitly, that the court would examine and pass judgment upon the internal or foreign policy of that state. The state would therefore have an independent right, over and above that of the accused, to challenge the jurisdiction of the court, and should not be compelled to leave that question to be taken up by the accused.[52]

It may well be that in granting to the state the right to challenge the jurisdiction of the Court, the Committee was simply motivated by a desire to maintain consistency in the Draft Statute, for other provisions already discussed permit a government to block the jurisdiction of the Court, if considerations of national policy demand it. But in adopting such provisions the Committee apparently was not aware of the insuperable difficulties which they raise, for if a state can challenge the Court's jurisdiction in respect to the trial of a political leader, it may similarly do so in respect to one involving a private citizen. Even if a government has accepted the jurisdiction of the Court, there is still considerable doubt under Article 30, paragraph (1) that it will act accordingly, specially if it considers the exercise of jurisdiction in a specific case as being detrimental to its own interests. The full impact of this situation can mostly clearly be seen when remembering the many instances given throughout this book where the state has used private persons as concealed means of aggression. They have been seen to include such offenses as invasion by armed bands, encouragement of revolutionary activities, the sending of volunteers and the toleration of hostile military expeditions against friendly countries, to mention only a few. A trial on these charges may conceivably be challenged by the state involved for the very same reasons for which it may challenge the jurisdiction of the Court in respect to a high-ranking political official, thus ending unilaterally the organized judicial action of the world community. Admittedly, there may be in principle no sufficiently valid reason to be disturbed over these possibilities, more specially when the Court itself is empowered to consider the validity of such challenges. What must be emphasized is simply that the right to challenge jurisdiction is likely to become an instrument by which governments can engage in tactics which may effectively hamper

[52] *Ibid.*, p. 10.

the administration of justice in the international society. The Belgian representative to the Sixth Committee of the General Assembly admirably perceived this possibility when the Draft Statute was under discussion. As his words directly bear upon the matter, it may be beneficial to quote them, *in extenso*, here. He said:

> The existence of the court's powers, their limits and the conditions governing their exercise might well depend on the convenience of the plaintiff state. Moreover, regardless of the seriousness of his crime, a person's trial could be objected to by the state of which he was a national or by the state on whose territory the crime had been committed. As a direct result of its statute, the court would be incapable of administering justice uniformly and equally to all who were brought before it; its dispensation of justice would be *ad hoc*, haphazard and sporadic. Acts committed under identical conditions might or might not be punishable, depending on the preference of each government, or they might be punishable differently.[53]

It may be quite relevant to add that the subordination of justice to political expediency in this context may ultimately defeat two basic postulates of the world community, namely, first, that the realization of justice is an overall goal of the international legal order[54]; and, secondly, that an international criminal court may impart justice to individuals and states. Clearly, therefore, the reference to considerations of a political nature may undermine the authority of the proposed Court seriously impairing its prestige.[55]

Finally, of singular significance is Article 28 of the 1953 Revised Draft Statute which says that "A state may withdraw its conferment of jurisdiction. Such withdrawal shall take effect one year after the delivery of notice to that effect to the Secretary-General."[56] This provision takes on striking importance when viewed in relation to the manner in which the International Criminal Court may be established. The 1953 Committee suggested that a Court may be established in one of four ways, namely, by amendment of the United Nations Charter, by multilateral convention, by resolution of the General Assembly, and by resolution of the General Assembly to be followed by conventions.[57] It seems that whatever method is adopted involves the incorporation

[53] U.N. General Assembly, Official Records, Seventh Session, Sixth Committee, 328th Meeting, p. 136 (1952).

[54] J. Stone, *op. cit.*, p. 53.

[55] P. M. Carjeu, *op. cit.*, p. 412.

[56] Actually, the 1953 Committee deleted the original Article 28 of the Draft Statute which said that "No jurisdiction may be conferred upon the Court without the approval of the General Assembly of the United Nations." Instead, the present Article 28 was included. See Yuen-Li Liang, *op. cit.*, pp. 649–650.

[57] *Ibid.*, pp. 639–645.

of the Court into the United Nations system. On these bases, the position of the International Criminal Court would be similar to that of the International Court of Justice, and like the latter's Statute, its Statute would be susceptible of denunciation by the states along with the United Nations Charter.[58] In addition, as an organ of the United Nations, the Court's Statute would conceivably partake of the limitations imposed upon the United Nations by the Charter itself. The limitation implicit in Article 2, paragraph 7 of the Charter is particularly important in this connection, for it essentially prohibits the United Nations "to intervene in matters which are essentially within the domestic jurisdiction of any state..." As this limitation is implicitly existing in reference to the International Court of Justice,[59] it is exceedingly difficult to see how the proposed International Criminal Court, established as an organ of the United Nations, can escape its application. It was perhaps with these considerations in mind that a small group of representatives to the Sixth Committee of the General Assembly, where the Draft Statute was discussed, maintained that an International Criminal Court should not be established at this time because it would be inconsistent with the principles of sovereignty of states and non-intervention, and that it would be contrary to the principles of the United Nations Charter and the Charter of the Nürnberg Tribunal.[60]

THE FUTURE OF AN INTERNATIONAL CRIMINAL JURISDICTION

The preceding observations have made it crystal clear that the Draft Statute for an International Criminal Court runs the risk of establishing a tribunal handicapped by the greatest limitations. Certainly, if the jurisdiction of the Court is entirely dependent upon the will of the states, there is little reason for expecting that it would be a means of deterring the commission of international crimes.[61] This has been the hope of the proponents of the Court.[62] It has been seen that no state is ever likely to be willing to allow an international tribunal to try either its national officials or its private citizens for the commission of

[58] Cf. C. Rousseau, *Droit International Public*, pp. 525–527 (1953).
[59] J. Stone, *op. cit.*, pp. 142–143.
[60] See the remarks of the Canadian Delegate, U.N. General Assembly, Official Records, Seventh Session, Sixth Committee, 328th Meeting, p. 135 (1952).
[61] Cf. P. E. Corbett, *Law and Society in the Relations of States*, p. 237 (1951).
[62] A. K. Kuhn, "The Pella Memoranda Relating to International Crimes and Criminal Jurisdiction," *Am. J. Int. L.*, Vol. 46, p. 129 (1952).

acts which are to its national advantage. Such misgivings are unfortunately confirmed by the marked concern of the proposed Statute to protect the state in its political interests. Governments themselves have echoed concern for the possibility that an International Criminal Court might invade matters which formerly fell within their jurisdiction. Thus, in speaking of the Draft Statute, the Polish representative to the Sixth Committee of the General Assembly said:

> Clearly, therefore, learned authorities as well as practice bore out the assertion that criminal jurisdiction was part of the sovereign rights of states. Any attempt to set up an international criminal court would be equivalent to depriving states of one of their fundamental rights and to transferring that right to another level, which was neither desirable nor compatible with contemporary international law.[63]

Yet a warning has been repeatedly given that if an International Criminal Court is ever to attain any success, it should be endowed with independent jurisdiction to try all individuals accused of international crimes.[64] The participation of the states should consist in assisting the Court in obtaining jurisdiction over the accused individual by means of extradition as well as in securing the necessary proof. These constitute the irreducible minimum without which an International Criminal Court is doomed to failure.

Moreover, the cold and calculated instigation of the horrors of war by individuals, even as agents of their government, is most forcefully condemned by men of good faith everywhere and has been seen to be punished by many municipal legal systems. Since past international experience in this connection has cast the greatest doubts upon tribunals unilaterally established by victorious powers after the termination of a war, the future punishment of persons responsible for such hostile actions will only be accepted by mankind in the objective atmosphere of an International Criminal Court, itself composed of judges not directly identified with the interests of the states.[65] From this standpoint, justice can be done entirely free from any doubt.[66] No one will deny that the punishment of individuals by the aggrieved state rarely meets the demands of justice. In addition, the advance enumeration of the offenses for which individuals are criminally responsible is a *conditio sine qua non* of an international criminal juris-

[63] See U.N. General Assembly, Official Records, Seventh Session, Sixth Committee, 327th Meeting, p. 130 (1952).

[64] Q. Wright, *op. cit.*, p. 70.

[65] M. Miele, *Principi di Diritto Internazionale*, p. 276 (1953).

[66] J. Stone, *op. cit.*, p. 370.

diction that seeks to administer justice in the world community on a technically sound legal basis. Perhaps even more important is a reasonable consensus among the members of the world community upon the offenses to be punished.[67] Thus, the adoption of the Draft Code of Offenses Against the Peace and Security of Mankind is a significant step in this direction, even if in its present form this Code falls short of reasonable expectations. This requirement seems entirely proper in principle and policy, if actions of private persons endangering the peace and security of mankind are to be adequately punished.

Unfortunately, however, these are not the only assumptions which will insure the success of an International Criminal Court. For it should be kept in mind that this Court is intended to operate in the world community, where crosscurrents of political interests of national governments are ever present. Concurrent with this is the nature of the offenses which would fall within the jurisdiction of the Court, for as these are generally offenses which affect states in their independence and sovereignty, the primacy of security interests thus exhibited are likely to make the Court a sounding-board for the continuation of the propaganda warfare in which governments are presently engaged.[68] On this level, the international import of the Court is seriously confronted by the countervailing interests of the states. This would put in doubt the judicial contribution which the tribunal might make towards the growth of an international criminal law.

Finally, it should be recalled that proposals have been made to integrate the Court within the system of the United Nations. Since the effectiveness of this organization largely depends upon a precarious balance of political forces, there is the corresponding danger that an International Criminal Court under such a system would be exposed to a similar fate.[69] Professor Quincy Wright has brought out this matter with breath-taking clarity. He says:

> If nine-tenths of the members of a society sincerely support a system of criminal law and procedure it is not difficult to organize that system so that it will be generally observed. Such a system will strengthen the society and its law. Past offenses will be punished and potential law breakers will be deterred. If, however, half of the members of a society believe that the other half is actually or potentially criminal, conditions are unfavorable for the functioning of a system of criminal law, and the society is likely to disintegrate.[70]

[67] Q. Wright, *op. cit.*, p. 65.
[68] J. Stone, *op. cit.*, p. 378.
[69] V. V. Pella, *op. cit.*, p. 43.
[70] Q. Wright, *op. cit.*, p. 65.

It can scarcely be denied that under such conditions the expectation that an International Criminal Court might be established to try objectively those accused of international crimes may not materialize, thereby striking a serious blow to the hopes and aspirations of mankind. It should immediately be pointed out, however, that these problems do not seriously minimize the importance of establishing an International Criminal Court endowed with sufficient jurisdiction to try individuals for crimes against all law and humanity. The purpose of this discussion is rather to emphasize the complexities inherent in such a task. The urgency of the matter is indeed apparent if a more effective international law is sincerely desired. For there is no doubt that the establishment of an International Criminal Court to try individuals accused of international crimes would immediately abolish the glaring shortcomings inherent in the exercise of protective jurisdiction. The existence of these shortcomings is obviously due to the imperfection of the present international legal order, so that its complete elimination will require the achievement of a high degree of political integration of the states in the form of a community of nations. An International Criminal Court with adequate jurisdiction may help to attain precisely that.

CONCLUSION

The preceding exposition has made it quite obvious that the proposed international criminal jurisdiction is fraught with restrictions imposed upon it by political exigencies. The primacy of state interests in the world community casts profound doubts upon the possibility of replacing the exercise of protective jurisdiction discussed in the previous chapter with an international criminal court to try individuals for the commission of international crimes. As the proposed Court's jurisdiction is entirely dependent upon the will of the states, it is highly doubtful whether its establishment would correct the shortcomings present in the exercise of protective jurisdiction as regards offenses against foreign states. It is therefore concluded that if an international criminal court is to fulfill its mission of protecting the world community against offenses of individuals directed at its peace and security, a more extensive and independent jurisdiction must be given. In the absence of such a development, the exercise of protective jurisdiction is likely to be implanted as the only reasonable course of action for the trial of individuals committing international crimes.

CHAPTER XI

SUMMARY AND CONCLUSIONS

The program suggested in this book rests upon the twin conceptions that the state is internationally responsible for hostile actions of individuals committed within its jurisdiction, and that the private person involved is similarly liable under international law. A twofold control of unlawful actions of private persons is therefore suggested, namely, one through the responsibility of the state; and, the other, through the direct responsibility of the individual. Both of these conceptions ultimately prevent hostile actions of individuals both from going unpunished and from remaining outside of the province of the law. For the immediate purpose of this book, the most important result of these conceptions is the expectation of an international community in which certain private actions affecting the good relations between nations may be effectively controlled, thus helping to realize mankind's yearning for peace and security.

In the light of the evidence examined, it can persuasively be argued that governments show no slackening in their efforts to escape responsibility for private actions committed within their jurisdiction. They have tenaciously followed the age-old principle that a government is liable for acts of private persons, only if it has neglected to take reasonable measures for the prevention and punishment of the offense. Deep frustration results from the application of this principle in a situation where a state suffers a wrong from the action of private individuals, and must depend for redress upon the will of the government in whose jurisdiction the offense originated. The position of the aggrieved community is further complicated by the fact that no government is really willing to punish individuals when in so doing its political interests might be jeopardized. This observation is even more compelling in situations where a state avails itself of the activities of private persons to promote its international objectives.

On closer scrutiny, however, it may well be that the true explanation for this discouraging situation lies deeper than the desire to justify an otherwise unlawful political conduct. It may thus be said that the doctrine of non-liability of the state for a person's private actions is essentially an insistence upon the traditional, and threadbare, state-individual dichotomy which has dominated much of international legal thinking. Starting with the highly untenable assumption that international law is exclusively concerned with states, it quite logically follows that the sphere of the state is wholly separate from that of the individual, and that certain activities in which the state cannot engage, can be carried on by the individual with impunity.[1] The end result of this position is to treat the state independently of the individuals who compose it; a notion which has been mostly responsible for the government's virtual freedom from liability for private hostile actions affecting foreign nations. The literature of international law has largely proceeded from this base and, with a few marked exceptions, has ignored, and even obscured, the revolutionary changes which the breakdown of nineteenth century *laissez faire* conceptions has brought upon the law.[2]

It is a venerable if trite observation that law must be adjusted to the circumstances of the time. While in municipal societies this process of adjustment is peacefully effected through legislation, in the international society, on the other hand, it must take place through the voluntary agreement of sovereign states.[3] It is a sad commentary upon the good faith of governments that agreement is not easily reached, even on the most elementary matters engaging vital interests of the world community. The inexorable result of this situation is that the law of the world community lags far behind the conscience of mankind. Thus, while in respect to the so-called volunteers the existing law – which allows single persons to cross the frontier to join belligerent or insurgent forces without engaging the responsibility of the state – was laid down more than fifty years ago, there is a general conviction, expressed in municipal legislation and bilateral agreements, that permitting the recruitment and departure of volunteers should be made an international delinquency. Similar observations may be safely made in respect to revolutionary activities and hostile propaganda directed against foreign governments. Since international law has not clearly imposed upon states the duty to prevent and punish these offenses,[4] it is not at all surprising that a body of domestic legislation and a

[1] J. Stone, *Legal Controls of International Conflict*, pp. 383–384 (1954).
[2] For a general plea in this connection, see H. J. Morgenthau, "The Dilemmas of Freedom," *Am. Pol. Sci. Rev.*, Vol. 51, p. 714 (1957).
[3] P. E. Corbett, *Law in Diplomacy*, p. 276 (1959).
[4] Cf. C. Rousseau, *Droit International Public*, p. 374 (1953).

small number of conventions on these subjects are far ahead of the requirements of international law. It is only in respect to counterfeiting foreign currency that an unmistakable duty of prevention was found to exist under conventional international law. It seems sufficiently clear, therefore, that, unlike international law, the law of some municipal societies has more faithfully responded to the demands of the world community. The international community is thus confronted with the glaring paradox that what a state may prohibit the individual, international law does not demand upon the state, and much less upon private individuals.[5] This argument cannot be met by saying that, inasmuch as individuals are the real offenders, punishment by their own state would seem to satisfy the demands of the world community, for it should be kept in mind that as long as governments feel no legal compulsion to punish hostile actions of private persons, they can always fall back on the absence of this duty to justify their unlawful conduct. Most governments operate upon the assumption that what international law does not expressly require or prohibit is entirely left to the discretion of the states and, thus, any conduct based on such discretion becomes necessarily sound.[6] It is perhaps with this kind of consideration in mind that an earnest student of international law has observed that "International law must never lag so far behind the moral conscience of mankind as to afford a refuge for governments which choose to ignore the conscience of the world."[7] It may be confidently expected, however, that the successful regulation of private actions by national societies will pave the way for international action in similar areas, and that the common prosecution and punishment of the same offenses by states may be sure steps leading to a universal legal order.

It may nevertheless be suggested that the existing situation is not as free from legal regulation as it has been made out to be, for in the absence of a clear duty of the territorial state to prevent the commission of the acts in question, international law grants the wronged community the liberty to punish the offending individuals who fall into its jurisdiction. It was seen in this connection that persons threatening a state's political institutions and internal peace from foreign territory are amenable to the jurisdiction of the aggrieved government on the

[5] This has reference to the fact that according to international law, states do not have responsibility unless fault is found to exist.

[6] J. Stone, *Legal Controls of International Conflict*, p. 160 (1954).

[7] M. Moskewitz, *Human Rights and World Order: The Struggle for Human Rights in the United Nations*, p. 161 (1958).

basis of the so-called principle of protective jurisdiction.[8] Though under the present international legal order this method of approach may appear highly desirable, it is believed that its continuation is likely to hinder deplorably the development of a world community of shared values and solidarity. However firmly one believes in the desirability of prosecuting and punishing those who plot against the institutions of a country from a foreign land, one must nevertheless entertain the gravest doubts whether the threatened nation should undertake to bring this about by the extraterritorial exercise of jurisdiction over the offender. On such a basis, it is really incongruous to think of protective jurisdiction as being functionally related to world community processes. It should be recalled in this connection that the offenses in question are committed within the jurisdiction of another state, and that it is the latter's obligation to contribute to the creation of a peaceful world order by the prevention and punishment of offenses which are likely to affect the peace and security of mankind.[9] It has been stressed throughout this book that peace is the first value of the world community that every government must promote and cultivate. Certainly, the exercise of jurisdiction for unlawful acts that have occurred in another country's territory is likely to be a source of friction between nations, for the element of extraterritoriality which accompanies it is highly incompatible with the respect that nations owe each other at all times.

The great shift in the postwar era from an international law exclusively concerned with states to one equally concerned with individuals strongly suggests the possibility of holding individuals criminally liable for international crimes.[10] This has clearly emerged as a desirable alternative to the exercise of protective jurisdiction. Liability would then be imputed to private persons for acts which similarly engage the responsibility of the state. This tantalizing proposal is founded upon the firm conviction that for the adequate suppression of unlawful activities of private persons against foreign governments some kind of personal liability must unequivocally follow. But the imposition of criminal responsibility upon private persons is intimately

[8] D. H. De Vabres, *Les Principes Modernes du Droit Pénal International*, p. 87 (1928).

[9] Though not dealing with the punishment of offenses of private persons, Dr. Wallace McClure approaches the problem of world peace from the standpoint of the contribution that states can and must make. Specifically, he discusses most courageously the contributions that the United States can make to world order. See W. McClure, *World Legal Order: Possible Contributions by the People of the United States* (1960).

[10] J. Stone, *Aggression and World Order: A Critique of United Nations Theories of Aggression*, ch. 8 (1958).

linked with the complex problem of establishing an international criminal court with sufficient jurisdiction to try those accused of such crimes, as well as with the formulation of an acceptable code which would clearly define the acts for which criminal liability would arise.[11] Unfortunately, however, agreement among states on these two questions is not forthcoming, and the available evidence does not hold much hope for its being forthcoming, even in the distant future.

Undoubtedly, the reasons why cooperation among states for the establishment of an international criminal jurisdiction to try individuals is not readily obtainable lie deep in the deficiencies of the international legal order still vitally concerned with the rights of sovereignty. It is indicative of the unsatisfactory nature of international law that so much emphasis should be placed, even in modern times, upon the liberty of the states to act as they see fit, instead of upon the values of the world community.[12] In this light, the absence of even the weakest consensus on the establishment of an international criminal jurisdiction is undoubtedly a reflection of the inability of the international legal order to protect the world community from aggressions proceeding from private persons. This argument cannot be answered by asserting that individuals can be punished either by the state in whose jurisdiction the offense is committed or by the threatened community, for the evidence irrevocably shows that reliance upon the state as a law enforcing agency in these matters is not always certain. Hence, the fact that private persons may be punished by either of these two states is at present too uncertain and shadowy to shape the course of justice. It must of necessity yield to the over-mastering need, so vital in contemporary life, of preserving the values of world peace and security against the inroads of unlawful private action. Moreover, before the state can be regarded as the agency which under all conditions will protect the world community, there is a compelling need to develop a high degree of political integration and solidarity among

[11] This is essential if legal objections are to be met. See P. M. Carjeu, "Quelques Aspects du Nouveau Projet de Statut des Nations Unies pour une Jurisdiction Criminelle Internationale," *Rev. Gén. de Droit Int. Public.* Vol. 50, pp. 401, 405 (France, 1956). Also Q. Wright, "Proposals for an International Criminal Court," *Am. J. Int. L.*, Vol. 46, pp. 60, 65 (1952).

[12] It is pertinent to quote what Professor Edwin D. Dickinson says: "Within the widest of limitations the nation is assertedly free, as matter of legal right, to live its own life in its own way. Its rights are presented characteristically in a bold and embracing system." E. D. Dickinson, *Law and Peace*, p. 38 (1951). Reflecting similar sentiments, Professor Percy E. Corbett says that the great obstacle to an effective law for states "is the tenacity with which governments and peoples cling to the notion of majestic independence lodged in the state." P. E. Corbett, *op. cit.*, p. 278.

its members. Only then can nations be expected to discharge their responsibilities in the preservation of international peace and security.

The prospects for the establishment of a workable international criminal court to try individuals have been seen to depend almost entirely upon concessions made to political interests of governments. This certainly is the sad story permeating the discussions that took place in the two committees appointed by the United Nations General Assembly to draft a statute for the court. More significantly, the present view regarding an international criminal court seems to be based on two irreconcilable assumptions. On the one hand, an international criminal jurisdiction is generally regarded as the most desirable course to follow for the punishment of individuals accused of international crimes. On the other, since the jurisdiction of this court is made entirely dependent upon the unfettered discretion of the state, the trial and punishment of certain persons vitally connected with the policy of their government are likely to fail. The unfortunate result of this second assumption is to expose the international criminal court to the vicissitudes of political demands, for any obligation of a state to adhere to the jurisdiction of the court is contingent ultimately on its own choice. Here, again, it is necessary, if any progress is to be made, that practical considerations should not too far outrun the needs of justice. A tribunal set up by the voluntary action of the states, exercising jurisdiction only with the consent of the territorial sovereign affected, subject to the voluntary withdrawal of jurisdiction, even if already granted, can scarcely rank as an organ of the world community dispensing justice with impartiality. Moreover, the total absence of any obligation to submit its nationals or residents to the court's jurisdiction is highly significant, for it still reflects the liberty of each state to be a judge in its own case. In the treatment of this matter it was seen that it is conceivable for a state to paralyze the judicial action of the international society in situations where the trial of a highly important leader is likely to expose its political motives. Similar observations may be made regarding the trial of private persons involved in the execution of governmental policy. Frankly, therefore, the statute which has been proposed for the international criminal court in no way helps its prospects; nor does it further the cause of international justice. In such circumstances, the ultimate question arises whether, with the power of independent jurisdiction virtually excluded, an international criminal court should at all be created. Obviously, those who see in the creation of an international criminal jurisdiction a powerful deterrent to the commission of international crimes by individuals, will draw little comfort from the proposals presented thus far. They will offer, perhaps, even less comfort to those who consider an international criminal court as a first step, shortly to be followed by other peace-enforcing instruments, to control the commission of crimes before they develop into "a holocaust for mankind."[13]

As a final conclusion it may be stressed that peace and security are not only endangered by the military threat confronting the world today. Mankind is faced with all kinds of perils which manifest themselves in an infinite variety of ways. Characteristic of the present situation is the so-called concealed technique of aggression, which includes the use of private persons for the execution of a deliberate state policy.[14] It is in this sense that the position of individuals becomes of critical importance in international life, and it is for this reason that the actions of private persons against foreign nations bear an intimate relation to the peace and survival of mankind. It is therefore submitted that the control of hostile actions of private persons is a most basic ingredient of international order. As international law does not hold the state responsible for these actions, the international responsibility of private persons envisaged in these pages would seem to go a long way towards closing a loophole in the international legal order. This conclusion would seem to be inescapable, if world peace and security are ever to be attained on firmer grounds.

[13] Borrowed from J. Stone, *Aggression and World Order: A Critique of United Nations Theories of Aggression*, p. 183 (1958).

[14] Q. Wright, "Intervention, 1956," *Am. J. Int. L.*, Vol. 51, pp. 257, 266 (1957).

INDEX

GPSR Compliance

The European Union's (EU) General Product Safety Regulation (GPSR) is a set of rules that requires consumer products to be safe and our obligations to ensure this.

If you have any concerns about our products, you can contact us on ProductSafety@springernature.com

In case Publisher is established outside the EU, the EU authorized representative is:

Springer Nature Customer Service Center GmbH
Europaplatz 3
69115 Heidelberg, Germany

Batch number: 10824476

Printed by Printforce, the Netherlands